Neil Kirke

Johnny Walke

Mark Jordan

Joe Lampard

Dipak Gohil

Peter Rowe

Jase & Gaz Whelan

Darren@DarrenNorwich

Steve Roberts

Conker Editions Ltd
22 Cosby Road
Littlethorpe
Leicester
LE19 2HF
Email: books@conkereditions.co.uk
Website: www.conkereditions.co.uk
First published by Conker Editions Ltd 2022

A CIP catalogue record for this book is available from the British Library.
13-digit ISBN: 978-1-7397705-2-5
Design and typesetting by Gary Silke.
Printed in the UK by Mixam.

Get Shirty

The Rise & Fall of Admiral Sportswear

Andy Wells

INTRODUCTION
Sunny Afternoon

Wembley Stadium, August 2016

North London is smothered under a warm blanket of haze. What little breeze there is offers brief respite among the thousands of bodies pouring down the tube station steps behind me. A week before the start of the new Premier League football season, with heat radiating from every inch of its concrete pores, I'm walking up the litter-strewn concourse that is Wembley Way. Passing by Bobby Moore's statue, guarding the entrance to English football's spiritual home, before peeling left towards what was once called the Tunnel End at the Empire Stadium – a place I first visited 40 years earlier when my dad brought me here to watch England play a World Cup qualifier under the brightest floodlights, on the greenest pitch imaginable. Today, I'm here to watch Leicester City, the club I grew up supporting, take on Manchester United for the Community Shield. Like every other City supporter around me, I'm still basking in the glow of our team's astonishing 2016 title win.

With just five minutes left until kick-off, most of the other 85,000 spectators are already inside. Not that you could tell from outside as it's strangely quiet, apart from the rattle of empty beer cans being kicked about by the wind, and the occasional shout among the last few stragglers weaving towards the turnstiles. My escalator ride to the upper tier offers views over the city where I've been living since the early '90s, and the noise levels are also rising as I ascend into the stadium. On entering the huge bowl I'm immediately submerged into a cobalt sea of man-made fibres. It seems everybody at this end of the stadium is wearing a replica football shirt – male and female fans, young and old alike. Directly opposite, wrapped around the other goal, it's exactly the same only in red.

I make my way down the steps towards where my dad, niece and two friends are already in their seats, bedecked in a variety of replica shirts spanning the eras of their match-going lives. Dad, who watched his first game at Filbert Street in 1954, is wearing a copy of City's home shirt from the late '60s. Minimalist by today's standards, it's a simple blue affair with a contrasting white crew-neck collar and white cuffs – no sponsor's name or manufacturer's logo to be seen. The friend sat next to dad is clad in a similarly stylish pin-striped design that City wore in the mid '80s. This time, a sportswear brand's trademark appears above the name of a local brewery that became the club's first shirt sponsor. Next up, my niece is proudly sporting City's 2015/16 shirt which they wore on their way to becoming Premier League champions. Here, the beverages being promoted belong to an international duty-free business, and there are three of the kit supplier's feline logos leaping around. Appropriately enough, the jersey also features gold trim.

Besides winning the title, Leicester City chalked up another first in 2016: the club sold out of replica shirts for the first time, with more being purchased abroad than in the UK. And now, with Champions' League football on the menu, the club's latest kit deal is set to become its most lucrative yet. The new season's design appears to be the polyester of choice among the majority of fans around us. It's a busier offering, incorporating sublimated two-tone stripes and gold piping, in tandem with the sponsor's name and manufacturer's logos. Not forgetting the all-important merchandising touch of a Premier League winner's patch on the sleeve.

Bob Wells and Becca Cross: choose your own golden era.

City's improbable achievement of last season has seen sales of the new jersey rocket, and the club will eventually go on to sell over 350,000 shirts. It's enough to catapult Leicester City into 12th spot in the global replica sales charts, rubbing shoulders with the biggest clubs on the planet. Counterfeiters are cashing in too, and not all of the tops on display today have been bought from official stockists – perhaps unsurprisingly, when fakes are readily available to buy online for as little as a third of the retail price. Despite the patchy quality of such black-market garments there are clearly enough fans here, including a friend I'm with, who feel £90 is too much to pay for the genuine article. Especially for an item that's inevitably going to be superseded in less than a year's time.

City lose 2-1 to United – not that either set of supporters seems overly bothered by the result. My tube ride home is packed with easily identifiable football supporters, nearly every one dressed in a replica shirt from recent seasons, including a surprising amount of second- and third-choice strips, while a few Reds have opted to wear older original or reissued tops as a reminder of the club's glory years under Fergie. Their accents are as diverse as their outfits and it's striking just how far and wide United's fanbase is drawn from, which explains in part why the Old Trafford club topped the replica sales charts in 2016, selling almost three million shirts worldwide.

Fast-forward to 2022 and, global pandemic withstanding, the market has grown to be worth an estimated £265 million a year in the space of half a decade. The landscape has shifted once again, with Spanish giants Barcelona and Real Madrid reportedly having annual £100 million-plus deals in place with Nike and Adidas respectively. Meanwhile, Manchester United's £75 million-a-year Adidas sponsorship maintains their status as the Premier League's highest earners.

Wigston, Leicester, 1966

To understand how we got to this point, we have to return to Wembley 50 years earlier and talk about another unfashionable team from Leicester – a small hosiery firm with a groundbreaking idea, that used England's 1966 World

Cup-winning triumph as a launchpad to kick-start a multi-billion-pound business. Before too long, Admiral Sportswear would create the world's first official replica football kits, and revolutionise sport and fashion forever. Operating from a backstreet factory, the family-run firm's label became one of the world's most recognisable brands, almost overnight. Its management team realised that young supporters would pay a premium to own kits identical to those worn by their heroes on Saturday afternoons – the genesis of a garment that children wore to play sports in, which quickly evolved into an established item of adult leisurewear.

Paul Oakley is the designer responsible for creating one of the world's most iconic football jerseys ever: England's early-1980s shirt with the broad bands of colour across its shoulders. He began working for the Wigston firm just as it was "starting the ball rolling," and making its first forays into the replica-kit world. "Obviously, when we were doing it, we never thought in our wildest dreams it'd ever get to those kind of figures. And sponsorship deals were going to be astronomical, we had no idea. But the core concept of branding items lay with Admiral, that's where it all started."

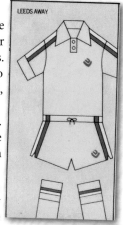

Peter Shilton concurs, and was one of the label's early adopters. "It was impossible, when I got involved with Admiral, to visualise how the football shirt would have evolved to this day, from putting a few stripes on a shirt."

In a marketplace dominated by generic off-the-peg uniformity, the firm started supplying clubs with unique and individually designed playing strips, "making football kits particularly more interesting," adds Paul Oakley.

As obvious as it sounds now, the concept of paying clubs a fee to reproduce replicas was not only considered pioneering, but also financially risky. Yet the firm's business model not only proved hugely successful, as the first children's jerseys sold in their tens of thousands, but also transformed the dynamics between clubs and their kit suppliers. This alchemy also changed the way younger, and later older, fans related to their teams, as described by a Thames Television documentary voiceover at the time:

"Supplying kit to some of the world's top teams provided the froth and glamour but these were only sales promotions. With the England side and other top teams in instantly recognisable Admiral strips, every kid in the country was a potential customer for the replica kits, which could be bought in every high-street sports shop. Every football-crazy schoolboy could persuade Mum or Dad to buy him a kit to make him look like his football heroes on TV. In the England strip, every boy could dream."

In the early '70s, the 'Wembley' of my own six-year-old mind's eye was a balding patch of grass with a single set of goalposts on a small estate of 'Army quarters' in Wigston. In the next field was a construction site and the skeletal frame of what would mushroom into Glen Parva Young Offenders' Prison – a place Mum and Dad ensured me I would end up if I didn't behave and do as I was told. A couple of miles away was another local landmark, not that I was even aware of its existence at the time; but within a few short years the whole country would know its name: Admiral Sports.

It's very easy to romanticise 1970s football, and part of the appeal is the revival of childhood memories from seemingly simpler times. When accessible players lived on suburban streets, and clubs were run and sponsored by small business owners and local car dealerships. A time of standing on packed terraces wearing a snorkel parka, as a steady stream of toilet rolls rained down into muddy goalmouths, whilst watching maverick forwards take on brutal defenders. It

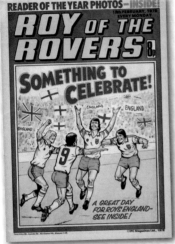

was all so idyllic – just so long as you overlook the endemic hooliganism and racism, and disregard the ramshackle surroundings, of course.

Even so, in the rose-tinted memories of many supporters of a certain age, myself included, the name Admiral Sports still conjures up a golden age of soccer. That *Wizard of Oz* moment when our monochrome worlds suddenly appeared in glorious Technicolor, and the beautiful game received a strikingly feminine makeover. According to football authors Hammond & Silke, it was as if Admiral's bold and outrageous 'new kits looked like how David Bowie and Marc Bolan sounded'.

Despite the wistful idealism, there is something genuinely special about what the sportswear company created and achieved during its '70s heyday, culminating in a 'David vs Goliath' battle that saw the plucky British underdog slugging it out against all-powerful multinational corporations. In many respects, the story of Admiral Sports is a metaphor for the flux of top-flight football as a whole.

"This isn't a xenophobic comment, but there's something special about English clubs' kits being manufactured and supplied by English suppliers," says football kit historian John Devlin. "But it has changed, it's now become global and much bigger companies are involved, much bigger sums of money."

Perhaps it was always inevitable that we would end up here, once soccer developed its swagger and a brave new world of commercial opportunities suddenly opened up. The '70s was, after all, a decade populated by larger-than-life showmen capable of drawing huge television audiences, whether it be Elvis Presley on the Las Vegas stage, Muhammad Ali in the ring or Evel Knievel on a stunt bike. Football simply followed suit and offered a platform to a new generation of outspoken managers, revelling in their own machismo, cigar smoke and opinions.

Despite the inflated egos of those on the sidelines, the domestic game still flourished on a level playing field, and there are further parallels to be drawn here. Provincial clubs like Derby County, Ipswich Town and Stoke City regularly challenged for honours, mirroring the Wigston firm's own meteoric climb to the top. To carry the analogies further, if the sportswear company was likened to a player from that era, Admiral was Stan Bowles, Tony Currie and Frank Worthington, all rolled into one. Dressed in a crimplene jumpsuit.

As with any story, there's often more than one beginning, and a family-run hosiery firm called Cook & Hurst had been in existence since Edwardian times. Early on, they established a reputation for making sturdy woollen underwear for the Armed Forces, but the business only really took off in the 1950s, when a headstrong 23-year-old called Bert Patrick took over the reins. He transformed the company over the following two decades, whereby the young entrepreneur's factory was no longer reliant on making hosiery, having successfully launched its own sportswear brand. Helping Bert to drive his company forward in its blockbusting heyday was his managing director John Griffin. Often described as 'chalk and cheese', the two men's personalities and skillsets complemented each other perfectly.

According to designer Lindsay Jelley (nee Tucker), "I would refer to them as 'Mr Patrick' and 'Mr Griffin', and I still would to this day, because that's what they were to me. They were the bosses. They were very charismatic characters, but very different. I remember Mr Patrick, he was more the marketing and salesperson and the overall boss of the company, while Mr Griffin was my boss and would deal with anything coming into the factory or the sample room or that side of it. So they were quite different people, and I would say each fulfilled his role perfectly. I remember them fondly, that they were good bosses and very fair."

The two men were also described as 'ambitious' and 'talented', and both were clearly unashamed and unapologetic opportunists. After all, spotting a gap in the market had got them to where they were: market leaders in a fledgling business.

"I think there was always somebody around with a barrow and a T-shirt, and we did it in a more organised way," says John modestly. "Maybe we accelerated it," he adds, and while its true that other manufacturers were looking at ways of monetising replica strips, Admiral was first to take the plunge.

John's old boss was more emphatic when I asked him about his company's legacy, and Bert was in no doubt that, "We were responsible for starting a multi-billion-pound industry. It wasn't there before, really."

John's correct, of course. Sooner or later somebody else would have latched on

Vroom at the top: Bert Patrick leans casually on his Lamborghini Espada.

to the same idea. But I doubt whether it would have been realised with the same panache, or captured the public's imagination in the same way. Clearly not, judging by the initial efforts of other sportswear firms playing catch-up, and no other brand has such a splendid body of work to look back on. Equally telling, Admiral emerged during a time hardly renowned for sartorial longevity, yet the firm's creations have weathered remarkably well. Possibly because its success can be attributed to the company's greatest asset, which conversely was also its biggest failing: Admiral's modest size.

Bert and John assembled a talented creative team alongside a 'tight-knit' community of machinists, and together they blazed a trail across the fashion world. They created an elaborate collection of outfits that were incredibly desirable to young fans previously fed on a diet of plain, thick cotton jerseys, bought from stockists like the Army & Navy Stores. Admiral's exposure on *The Big Match* and *Match of the Day*, as well as in magazines such as *Shoot!*, saw the brand's revolutionary new kits take off spectacularly – particularly once the firm had concluded a groundbreaking deal with the Football Association to commercialise the England kit for the very first time. Suddenly, Admiral found itself on the world stage.

Photographer Neville Chadwick, responsible for capturing many of the iconic images found in this book, had known Bert since they worked together on a local newspaper as 16-year-olds. He told me that today's eye-popping figures sometimes prompted him to ask his old mate, "'What have you done?' But I don't think Bert knew what he was doing really, to start with. I mean, it was a brilliant idea of Bert's, but whether he could see so far into the future just where it was going. I'm sure nobody could see where it was going."

At the height of its success, Admiral Sportswear sponsored over 100 top clubs and international teams. In doing so, the company signed up the 'Big Three' of

Leeds United, England and Manchester United; was denounced in Parliament for 'ripping off kids' with high prices; went bust, and bounced back again, making its World Cup debut in onerous circumstances. And all this while competing against major global brands at the start of the replica-kits arms race.

In the space of a few short years the company's workforce had gone from making nun's knickers to mixing with '70s football luminaries including managers Brian Clough, Don Revie, Bobby Robson, Bill Shankly and Tommy Docherty, as well as wily boardroom operators such as Manny Cussins, Doug Ellis and Jimmy Hill – not to mention showbiz celebrities Elton John and Eric Morecambe.

Admiral often had a ringside seat at pivotal events, whether Revie's ill-starred stint in charge of England or tiptoeing around the Elland Road corridors during Clough's 44-day reign at Leeds United. Many of these encounters proved highly entertaining, while others ended badly. Nearly all provide a compelling story, some of which have never been told before, at least not in public.

Other anecdotes go some way to filling in the missing blanks surrounding some football-strip urban myths. How did Coventry City end up wearing a chocolate-brown strip? What made Manchester United's red jerseys turn pink in the wash? And why did Liverpool's sponsorship deal with Admiral not come off? And then there are the horror stories about various kit malfunctions, where England's 1982 World Cup kit debacle is explored in greater detail.

Many of these accounts have been provided by ex-employees, including the two men most responsible for Admiral's success – owner Bert Patrick and his managing director John Griffin. By the late '70s, at the height of the company's powers, and with replica sales booming, the two men fell out and cut short their working partnership. Perhaps unsurprisingly, given this story is about the beginnings of football's big money, the pair's bust-up was about finances. Like a

13

Portsmouth FC versus Chelsea
Saturday, August 5, 1978
Kick Off 3 pm
LEAGUE DIV. 4
78~79 SEASON

brilliant songwriting duo following the break-up of a band, neither was as successful on their own. John's talents were swallowed up by the Adidas and Nike behemoths, while Bert failed to recover his mojo as Admiral slipped into decline.

During their '70s heyday, it's difficult to escape the feeling that the two bosses were 'winging it' to a certain extent, and there's no doubt they happened to be in the right place at the right time, or that Admiral benefitted from some outrageous good fortune. The firm also inadvertently contributed to its own downfall, in helping to usher in football's new commercial era – and within a few short years the company was fighting for its very survival.

By the early '80s, its contracts and roster of big clubs had all but disappeared, and despite often being heralded as a beacon of British manufacturing at its best during troubled times, Admiral had 'created a monster they couldn't feed', according to several insiders. By the time Adidas, Le Coq Sportif and Umbro had effectively taken over the replicas market, Admiral finally succumbed to the march of global trade and sadly went bust. Local businessman Peter Hockenhull stepped in and briefly revived the brand's fortunes – including that appearance at the 1982 World Cup finals – but it was to prove a last hurrah. And when the FA awarded its next kit contract to Umbro, the game was finally up.

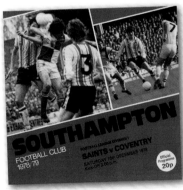

SOUTHAMPTON
FOOTBALL CLUB
1978/79
FOOTBALL LEAGUE DIVISION 1
SAINTS v COVENTRY
SATURDAY 16th DECEMBER 1978
Kick Off 2.00 p.m.
Official Programme 20p

As profitable an industry as sportswear became, Bert was quick to point out that his company "didn't reap the benefits of it in the end." So why is Nike and not Admiral the most successful global sportswear brand today? And how could a manufacturer go bust with a million-pound-plus order book, still described as 'one of Britain's most glamorous firms'?

The easiest answer to both questions is 'foreign competition', and on the surface it appears Admiral suffered the same fate as so many other textiles firms in the East Midlands at that time. Just another casualty of a collapsing industry. But while it's true the company faced the same problems engulfing much of the UK's manufacturing base, it falls short as an adequate explanation. Despite huge popularity, Admiral was never in a strong

A rare surviving Admiral poster, as Blu-Tacked lovingly on thousands of '70s bedroom walls.

enough financial position to make the jump from local British concern to genuine worldwide operation, which proved its undoing. Its downfall was preceded by the firm's creditors becoming nervous. However, the sportswear brand and the Admiral name didn't disappear altogether. Its trademark and marketing rights have been bought and sold many times over, and football strips and leisurewear continue to be made bearing its emblem. But since its early-'80s demise Admiral has struggled to once again become a real force in the kit world.

Apart from spotting an occasional fanzine piece or an old photo, the brand slipped out of my consciousness for 30-odd years, until I spotted somebody in a T-shirt with rows of tiny nautical badges down each sleeve. At first, I thought it was an old replica jersey I didn't quite recognise, before being told it was part of a leisurewear range sold in Sainsbury's supermarkets supermarkets. My antenna twitched immediately, as if finding out the singer from a favourite old band had just released a new album of covers.

It's the power and appetite for nostalgia that probably best explains why I ended up making a documentary and writing a book about Admiral's rise and fall. Both are a love letter to some wonderful-looking football kits and the place where I'd once lived. *Get Shirty: how a small Midlands underwear firm changed football forever* was first broadcast on ITV1 in September 2016. Most previous documentaries I had made tended to disappear into the television ether after an initial flurry of reviews and messages. But *Get Shirty* refused to slip away quietly and the interest continued, especially when the film was repeated or made available to view on the ITV Hub. The documentary had clearly resonated with other people, which in turn piqued my own interest to dig a little deeper, knowing I'd only skimmed the surface of the story. I was also sitting on a wealth of recorded interviews, and I wanted to give full voice to these accounts, as only a fraction of the chats I'd had with ex-employees had made it into the final cut.

There was clearly scope to cover the story more fully in a book, and one that offered an opportunity to write about design, social history and the Holy Trinity of popular culture: football, music and clothes. Yet without realising it from the very outset, delving into the past also became a personal journey into my own childhood, as I unpacked a story intertwined with my own life. One friend described my research as 'therapy', and perhaps he's right. If I could have afforded an Admiral top 40 years ago, *Get Shirty* may never have seen the light of day. This is also a story about the importance of local manufacturing, a tribute to all of the people who worked at Cook & Hurst, and a celebration of what they achieved so brilliantly together – being partly responsible for the mass popularisation of sportswear, fusing into leisurewear.

John Devlin is in no doubt as to what the firm's legacy entails. "I'm in awe of what they did – in looking at something that wasn't there, they created this opportunity, and they weren't afraid to punch above their weight. They really went for the big guns. They had this idea that was revolutionary. And now the biggest clubs in the world, the biggest nations in the world, huge amounts of

Flares 'n' Grifters 'n' Admiral 'tramlines'.
Is this the most '70s photo ever taken in the '70s?

income are given to them by their kit suppliers. Without being patronising, what this little firm in Leicester created has rippled out throughout the whole of football ever since. It can't be underestimated what they have achieved."

Over several years, I've spoken at length to many people who passed through Admiral's doors about their time in Wigston – as well as to their family members and friends, and various business associates who had dealings with the firm. Firstly, about the running and transformation of Cook & Hurst into a major sporting goods company, followed by the rise and fall of Admiral Sports.

The various accounts helped corroborate and fill in missing details, though sometimes the chronology of these events has understandably become muddied over time – including whether it was Bert or John who made that first approach to Don Revie which 'lit the blue touch-paper'. Perhaps that's what happens to our most important recollections after 40-odd years; but it doesn't really matter whether the deal came about via an impromptu meeting in a club car park, or as a result of an appointment secured through contacts and networking.

What we do know for certain is how that first encounter at Leeds United changed sport and fashion forever. It helped to pioneer a multi-billion-pound industry which, ever since, has enabled football fans the world over to Get Shirty.

CHAPTER 1
Get It On

EARLY MORNING ON THE M1 MOTORWAY...

Leicestershire, October 1973

The M1 was Britain's first full-length motorway, built primarily to connect London and the commercial south to the industrial powerhouse cities of the north. Constructed in stages from the 1950s onwards, the 200-mile-long arterial road was completed the following decade, and an extension into the centre of Leeds opened in 1972. Halfway up the new 'special road' bisecting the country sat the city of Leicester, its sprawling post-war estates in the west now within earshot of the rumbling new highway, at the heart of an area renowned for its engineering, textiles and bootmaking. The local Chamber of Commerce's proud boast from the 1920s, 'Leicester clothes the world,' harks back to a time when over 200 hosiery firms operated locally, and the League of Nations described the manufacturing hub as Europe's most prosperous trading city alongside Lille.

The region remained a 'boom town' after World War II, home to over 100 distinct industries, prompting the government to impose a temporary ban on new factories as it sought to regenerate other areas. Despite these controls, Leicester remained a thriving centre of the textiles industries, which in the postwar period accounted for a quarter of British hosiery exports. The city continued to benefit from some of the lowest unemployment figures in the country into the '70s. It prompted the local evening paper to note that, 'You walk through Leicester and sense the spirit of a town that is quietly doing well... there is an air about these people which gives you the impression that they know where they are going' – a sentence that could so easily be applied to Cook & Hurst's young management team.

It was horribly dark and dank on the morning John Griffin joined the M1 at Junction 21, heading north towards Yorkshire and Leeds, 100 miles distant. Driving conditions were atrocious, and lashing rain made visibility poor on a three-lane motorway devoid of overhead lighting or crash barriers. Fortunately, there was also little traffic in October 1973, but John still remembers getting too close to some large trucks and receiving warnings blasted at him through air horns. The 43-year-old had joined Cook & Hurst 15 years earlier. Originally taken on as its new factory manager, he had risen to become the firm's managing director, and very much the owner's right-hand man.

Together with the equally energetic Bert Patrick, John was working hard to try and transform the ailing knitwear firm. A task that involved drumming up vital new business, and the reason for his 8.30am appointment at Kays mail-order business on the outskirts of Leeds. After pulling off the motorway, John recalls meeting up with his firm's northern rep at a Holbeck industrial estate in order

to run through their sales patter and price list. Cook & Hurst was expanding its lines of stock, and had started trading under the name of Admiral Sports to reflect a move into athletics and leisurewear. Armed with rugby and football jersey samples, the two men presented their wares to an uninterested buyer in a meeting that John admits couldn't have gone much worse. The pair found themselves back outside on the pavement within half an hour of their arrival.

"They were very, very demanding," the MD remembers, and for good measure, he was told his garments were too expensive. Much to John's frustration, he can't recall the other rep's name but says both men were left dispirited by the experience. "My friend said to me, 'Look, neither of us have had breakfast, I know a great café down the road.' And it was on Elland Road, opposite Leeds United. We had a big English breakfast, which obviously made us feel good."

By the time the pair had finished their second cups of tea the rain had abated, and the day was about to get even brighter. Wiping away condensation from the window of the steamy café, John "noticed that Leeds United were training on the pitch across from the stadium, so we watched for a while, until they finished." Leaning in, John recounts the conversation that was about to transform Cook & Hurst's fortunes, and turn Admiral Sports into a household name.

"As Don Revie was coming out through the gate, my colleague said, 'Mr Revie, I'd like you to meet my boss, he's from your old town.' And Revie stopped, shook hands, and asked us what we were doing up here. So I gave him a brief version of how we'd been kicked out. He was interested, he invited us into his office for some tea. So I explained to him how we were making football jerseys now, and we'd got our own brand name and were making progress. And he said, 'Well, what could you do for us?' So I said, 'It depends, what could we do for the home jersey?' And he said, 'Very, very little. Nothing, I want it to be all white,' he said. 'I use Real Madrid as an incentive for them, but,' he said, 'you can do what you like with the change strip and with the tracksuit.'"

After taking a moment to calculate costings in his head, John came back to Revie with a deliberately low offer. "I thought it'd have to be more than five. Remember, this was really green days, and I was surprised when he was so acceptable to seven." John was proposing a radical new arrangement whereby Admiral would pay Leeds United for the privilege of producing and supplying its playing strips. Up until then, professional and amateur clubs alike had simply bought generic off-the-peg strips from sports retailers. In return, Admiral would manufacture identical replica kits in children's sizes that they would then sell to the club's young fans, covering their sponsorship and manufacturing costs, as well as hopefully turning a profit.

"It was a completely new idea," football kit historian John Devlin told me. "Prior to that, shirts were just anonymous. Branding did exist but it wasn't clearly visible, you'd see it occasionally on tracksuits as teams were coming out to play. But really, the whole idea, it just turned the football world on its head."

Negotiations with Revie moved quickly, remembers John. "So I said, 'Look, if I say £7,000 a year, plus five per cent on sales over what we make, to reach our basic payment to you.' 'Well,' he said, 'That's the best offer we've had.'"

Having agreed terms with the manager of one of Europe's most successful football clubs, John now had to convince Bert and his board of directors that

it was also a good deal for Cook & Hurst. "As I'm driving back just to Leicester, I'm thinking, 'how the hell can I make this £7,000 work?' You know, that sort of thinking. 'How the hell? What have I done? How can I make it work?'"

Bert remembers this initial contact with Revie differently, telling me he'd already met with the Leeds boss prior to John's chance encounter. "I saw the opportunity first of all with Don Revie at Leeds, because he was introducing lots of things in order to popularise the club." According to the Admiral boss, he already had "an in" with Leeds through the Duncan family, as Revie's wife Elise was the daughter of former Leicester City player Tommy Duncan, and the niece of the club's former manager, Johnny. Through these connections, an intermediary helped set up an appointment for Bert at Elland Road.

"I went to see Don Revie, it really was a question of what would he – how far would he go? And he said, 'I'm not going to let you touch my home shirt, but you can do anything you like with the away strip: design us an away strip,' which we did. 'Design me a tracksuit,' which we did. And they just took off overnight. In terms of sales they were a huge success." The two parties eventually agreed a five-year deal that would see Admiral Sports pay Leeds United £10,000 per annum, or a ten per cent royalty on kit sales if greater.

Later that month Leeds United took to the field for the first time in an Admiral-branded playing strip. As fate decreed, this took place just a few miles from Cook

& Hurst's factory, at Leicester City's Filbert Street stadium. The all-important manufacturer's logo appeared on the chest and shorts of an outfit that looked almost identical to the previous Umbro strip, with the crew neck replaced by a V-neck wing collar. The players' white track tops were markedly changed though, with yellow collars and waistbands, and blue and yellow striped armbands. More significantly, each jacket was emblazoned with 'Admiral' in large letters across the chest – and a photo of the team waving to the crowd in its new sponsored kit featured on the club's official Christmas card that winter.

Three days before the festive break, the champions elect beat Norwich City 1-0 at Elland Road, with Bert and John looking on from the directors' box. Afterwards, the floodlights were still burning bright as the two men said their goodbyes and swapped seasonal wishes with Revie and his board. The mood inside the Jaguar on the unlit journey south was anything but dark: the sense of triumph and excitement was palpable. The pair had managed to get sets of their replica children's strips into the shops in time for Christmas, just before the government imposed nationwide power cuts and a 'three-day week' on manufacturers. And the new 'official' kits would go on to sell in tens of thousands – not just in Leeds but throughout the country, thanks to the Yorkshire club's profile and success.

It was, according to both men, the moment that 'lit the blue touch-paper'. But, while they obviously recognised that their 'concept' worked, it's doubtful either guessed just how big a success it would become. Or how it would transform their own lives and those of their hundred-odd employees back in Wigston.

By the 1950s, most professional football clubs in Britain tended to be kitted out by one of two long-standing manufacturers from Cheshire: Bukta and Umbro.

Through a fairly rigid supply chain, both sportswear firms provided retailers and distributors, who in turn took along catalogues to clubs and acted as third-party brokers. Other smaller manufacturers did exist, including Hope Brothers, who made England strips for a while, but in the main, "if you saw a kit in the 1950s or '60s, nine times out of ten it would either be Umbro or Bukta," according to John Devlin. As most clubs purchased a blank set of jerseys, it would be left to the 'kit man' or 'laundry lady' to sew on numbers and badges. That said, some clubs didn't affix club crests on to jerseys until the early '70s, when manufacturer's names still remained hidden on an inside label or the hem of a jersey.

The heavy cotton tops players were wearing up to this point were not universally popular. When I visited Norman Hunter at his home up in the hills overlooking Elland Road, the first thing he mentioned about the shirts he initially wore is how heavy they became once wet or caked in mud. He added that most professional players during the '60s wore the same set of jersey, shorts and socks for an entire season. After each match, a kit man would pick these strips up off the dressing-room floor and have them washed for the following fixture. On reflection, Hunter remembered a new set of strips sometimes turning up mid season, but that was probably due to the high number of games Leeds United were playing each week. Rather than being thrown away, old match strips were often worn at training sessions the following season. Unsurprisingly perhaps, it wasn't unusual for old and new kits to get mixed up, as they often looked identical. Which in itself wasn't a problem, or often even noticeable, given how little styles changed from one year to the next. But it did lead to some anomalies.

If you look closely enough at photos or archive clips from that era, it's often possible to spot a rogue collar here, or a different sock top there. However, that was all about to change with the advent of branded strips and keen-eyed sponsors to consider. When Admiral hit its stride, Bert would get his employees to pore over photos in the day's sports pages, to make sure the teams they supplied were wearing the correct kits.

Bukta and Umbro also supplied schools and amateur teams with playing kits, identical to those worn at professional clubs and available in sets of 12. The first recognised 'replica' kit targeted at individuals was the groundbreaking 'Umbroset for Boys', launched in 1959. There is also anecdotal evidence of a precursor: jerseys in the colours of England, Scotland and Wales, that came accompanied by a separate 'unofficial' cloth badge – a rose, thistle or dragon – which allowed Umbro to circumnavigate the home-nation FAs' own crests. The manufacturer's club 'Umbroset' was available in children's sizes and came neatly packaged in cellophane-fronted boxes, each set containing a mini version of the same unadorned jersey, shorts and socks, as worn by the country's top teams. Not that the strips had any other connection to the professional clubs, inasmuch as they didn't receive any fees or royalties from Umbro. And why should they have? After all, a plain red shirt with a white collar and cuffs could as readily be worn by a young Liverpool or Nottingham Forest supporter as by a Manchester United fan – even if they were initially advertised as being 'styled by' Old Trafford boss Matt Busby, and later endorsed by star striker Denis Law.

By the early 1970s, an 'Umbroset for Boys' was firmly bleeping away on my 'can I have' radar, but when my incessant pleading eventually triumphed and my parents agreed to buy me a 'proper' football kit, it was a victory tinged with trepidation: my dad would be taking me clothes shopping. I came to dread these expeditions, as they inevitably ended in disappointment, followed by ridicule and embarrassment. The routine went something like this: enter shop and identify item to buy, Dad baulks at cost and chooses a cheaper alternative, then picks a size far too large that I can 'grow into', cue howls of laughter from my mum and sister when I return to model my new oversized clobber. I think Mum eventually put a stop to proceedings when we returned from one trip with a cagoule so large that it accompanied me into adulthood, and even then it was still too big.

It's fair to say I was nervously excited as Dad drove into town on the morning of the big day. Bob's team, and therefore my team, was Leicester City, who wore royal blue shirts, white shorts and white hose. Exactly the same as Birmingham City, Chesterfield, Everton, Ipswich Town, Millwall and Oldham Athletic, give or take a different collar style and sock-top here and there. Not that any of this mattered, of course, as an 'Umbroset' was open to interpretation, and far more important was the fact that one of these boxes would soon be in my possession. Sadly, reality announced itself with the ominous clang of the Army & Navy Stores' overhead doorbell, and there were no cellophane-fronted football strip parcels on offer at my dad's outfitters of choice. But all was not lost just yet, and across the counter I was presented with a plain long-sleeve cotton royal-blue jersey, with a white crew-neck collar and elasticated cuffs. I knew instinctively to forget about the missing packaging and to conclude this transaction as quickly as possible. I was still tantalisingly close to leaving with a jersey of the right colour, that also looked like it might fit me now instead of in ten years' time. A pair of white shorts and socks were added to the bag, and *voilà*, I was the proud owner of a full Leicester City strip. A look completed by Dad buying a cloth badge from the club's souvenir shop that Mum would later sew onto my highly prized jersey.

The style of top I'm referring to will be recognisable to anybody who has ever seen *Kes*, Ken Loach's film adaptation of Barry Hines' novel, *A Kestrel for a Knave*.

The one where Brian Glover's man-child PE teacher, Mr Sugden, imagines himself as Bobby Charlton as he proceeds to win and convert a dubious penalty during a games lesson.

From now on, I'd be doing exactly the same, running around in my 'proper' shirt pretending to be playing in thrilling FA Cup ties, and scoring last-minute winners. I couldn't have been happier, now I had a real football kit that I would wear until I outgrew it. Because one of life's certainties was that your team's shirt stayed pretty much the same, season after season. There was no such thing as 'last year's kit' in the early '70s.

The East Midlands' manufacturing legacy dates back to Saxon times, when the traditional sheep-rearing area was known for producing fleeces. When the demand for knitted woollen clothing took off in the 16th century, the region established itself within the textiles industry as the manufacturing process became mechanised. Leicester's worsted yarn products became a more affordable alternative to the cotton and silk hosiery produced in Nottingham and Derby respectively.

The city flourished during the industrial revolution. By the 19th century, most framework knitters had transferred, albeit reluctantly, from domestic production into workshops which in turn were superseded by larger brick factories, including the site at St Margaret's Works, built by Edwin Corah to house 2,000 workers at the height of the manufacturer's success.

Driving into Leicester from the north of the city nowadays invariably involves idling at traffic lights along Burleys Way, where one's gaze is drawn towards the old Corah's complex, some of which is now being converted into 'inner-city living' apartments. There are many such old garment and textiles factories dotted around the city, very much part of the fabric of the place I remember from adolescence. Most days it wasn't uncommon to see rails of clothes being wheeled through loading bays, or groups of hosiery workers on cigarette breaks huddled around open fire doors.

The day I meet Bert Patrick for the first time is another trip down Memory Lane. I drive across the centre of town, which was my daily commute in the 1980s, past the design studio where I worked off London Road, and then south

Wigston firm's products brighten the soccer world

"UP AND DOWN the country the big names in league football are realising that looking good makes you feel good, and that when you feel good you feel confident." These are the words of Mr. Bert Patrick, the 38-year-old managing director of Cook and Hurst, of Long Street, Wigston, manufacturers of jerseys and tracksuits for many of the country's leading football teams.

The firm, which is rapidly expanding and claims to be one of the biggest suppliers of leisure wear in the Midlands, if not in the country, in addition to manufacturing football jerseys at Wigston also has premises at Market Harborough specialising in the latest type of nylon track suits, which are being marketed all over the world.

The company originally produced underwear but they abandoned this in favour of sportswear is produced has undergone some changes. Nylon is now being used extensively and is of far

Packer Mr. Arthur Hancock and warehouse order clerk Mrs. Barbara Ball photographed at work in the packing department of Cook and Hurst Ltd.

greater appeal because of the little attention it requires. Only recently the firm successfully kitted out the Lions Rugby team for their New Zealand Tour.

Said Mr. Patrick: "The advent of colour television has been a big factor in the introduction of a far wider range of colours in sports wear. It was surprising too to find how many young football fans

made a hobby of collecting the jerseys of their favourite teams. Here was a real need, to produce something which was authentic and which would fill a definite need. Cook and Hurst manufacture a special range of souvenir jerseys.

Here then the company has a vast market which is earmarked for obvious expansion. They are already making inroads in this respect by exhibiting at a special exhibition for the manufacturers of sports and leisure wear in Chicago in February.

The company is anxious to export, particularly to America, a country which

said Mr. Patrick, can no longer politically afford to stay out of the World Cup series. In America the soccer scene has been receiving a long hard look and now the game is being introduced in schools, though as yet in the world of adult sport it is no competition for baseball and American football. But with a new generation being weaned on 'English soccer,' Mr. Patrick sees the time when it will be an important rival to these sports.

along the A6 towards the Wigston suburbs where I lived as a child. Bert's home is located on the edge of a picture-postcard village of the English idyllic type dotted across Leicestershire and Rutland. Described as 'the man who changed the face of British football', Bert appears fit and remarkably youthful for somebody who's just turned 80. He's immediately recognisable as the young entrepreneur who appeared in news archive I've seen, sporting blond floppy hair and wide-lapelled suits. His attire today is more casual, but his demeanour is equally relaxed, and he appears as confident as he did in Admiral's blockbusting heyday. That was a time when 'Mr Admiral's' sociability and networking skills proved key to his company's success – and it's easy to understand how.

Over the course of the next few hours I discover that Bert worked as a reporter for the long-defunct *Leicester Evening Mail* before moving over to broadcast journalism at the city's local BBC radio station. He ended up in the textiles industry by default, thanks to his wife Elizabeth Flude, whose family owned local manufacturing firms, including the successful Dorothy Vernon tights business.

Through these connections, Bert joined an established but struggling hosiery firm called Cook & Hurst in the mid 1950s. Founded around the turn of the century by two textile workers, Christopher Cook and Harold Hurst, the business initially employed a dozen local workers, occupying two courts of cottages in Bell Street before an expansion into Long Street in 1903. By then the village of Wigston, located five miles to the south of Leicester, was already melding into the urban sprawl of the city, and was fast becoming a hive of small textiles factories. Over the course of the next 50 years Cook & Hurst grew to become a byword for dependable, utilitarian wool clothing. A reputation enhanced during both world wars in which it supplied both the British and American military with long-johns and vests. It was firmly established as what historian Colin Hyde calls a "stoic brand of British underwear." Or makers of un-fancy pants, if you like.

However, by the time Bert joined its ranks in 1956, the underwear orders that had sustained the business for over half a century had started to wane dramatically. Despite this drop-off and an array of other problems, Bert bought the company for £34,000 a couple of years later, installing himself as chairman at the ripe old age of 24, prompting the *Leicester Advertiser* to describe him as, 'the young and energetic managing director'. And for good reason. Working alongside founder Christopher Cook's two sons, directors Leslie and Jack, Bert set about overhauling the firm by hiring new key personnel, including the man who would help him transform his company from top to bottom: John Griffin.

After several lengthy phone calls over a number of years, I finally met up with John in Los Angeles, his home since the late '70s. From our very first conversation, and even more so meeting him in person, it was obvious that he was smart, knew his own mind and didn't suffer fools gladly. Forty years on from being involved in the deals that shaped Admiral Sports' name, John retained an interest in getting down to business straight away, outlining the start of his career, at Corah's Textiles. At the time one of the biggest knitwear manufacturers in Europe, it boasted an annual £20 million contract with Marks & Spencer that ensured it was one of Leicester's major employers. The firm's global reputation for quality also opened doors for any employee with one of its prestigious training programmes on their CV. By the mid 1950s, John had been schooled in eight of the company's 14 factories.

The Griffins moved from Cork in Ireland to find work in England during the 1940s when John was ten years old. With less than a year to adapt to a new curriculum, Master Griffin failed his eleven-plus exam and attended Moat Secondary Modern. But the disappointment of not getting into Grammar School only made John more driven and determined to succeed in the workplace, according to a former school friend.

He joined Corah's production engineering office, and described his role within the Work Study Department as "stimulating" and "competitive." Life among the firm's "high-flyers" motivated John to raise his ambitions further. Yet he also recognised that his chances of progression within Corah's was slim, and after five years of working on ways to improve factory efficiency made the decision to realise his own potential.

Finding another position elsewhere wouldn't be difficult, after all. The *Leicester Evening Mail's* Jobs & Careers section was awash with vacancies. But securing an opening that offered John the chance to showcase his skills and climb the

Sign of the times: Admiral's Long Street HQ in Wigston.

management ladder would prove trickier. He scanned the jobs pages for months before spotting an advert for a factory manager at a hosiery firm called Cook & Hurst. His application was received favourably and John was invited for an interview; but this in itself presented a problem. How could he disappear during a work day without his absence being noted?

Corah's was based to the north of the city centre, whereas Cook & Hurst was five miles to the south in Wigston, which was too long a return journey by bus without asking for time off. Also, if he turned up for work in his best suit, his bosses would realise he was looking for a job elsewhere.

John's initial instinct was to turn the interview down. But, displaying the type of ingenuity that would become his trademark, he persuaded a vehicle-owning workmate to drive him to Wigston and back. On the morning of his appointment he hid his suit in the boot of his friend's car, who duly drove him across town at noon whilst John changed on the back seat. He says he "got on okay" with owner Bert Patrick, and recognised the post was a real opportunity. After his interview, both passenger and driver returned to Corah's hoping their disappearance hadn't been noticed – only to repeat the same trick two weeks later after John was called back for a second interview. Fortunately for the shredded nerves of both men, John was offered the job the following day.

The first few weeks of his role as Cook & Hurst's factory manager was something of a culture shock, admits John. At Corah's he had been surrounded by modern machinery and was taught about the latest mass-production techniques, whereas walking into Long Street was like stepping back into the 1920s. Still using belt-driven machine lines, Wigston's operatives were more or less hand-crafting the same items of underwear he'd been making before, but taking twice as long.

One of his first acts was to abolish his workers' flat hourly wage in favour of 'piece rates'. Each machinist's pay was incentivised from now on, and would be based on the number of units or 'pieces' made per day, irrespective of the time a person clocked in and out. John told a sceptical workforce that more pairs of knickers ensured a bigger Friday pay packet. To prove his point, he picked a group of his quickest machinists to perform a time-and-motion study, in which the 'girls' duly beat their hourly rate by producing enough garments to guarantee a pay rise. This raised efficiency and sped up the manufacturing process overnight, but

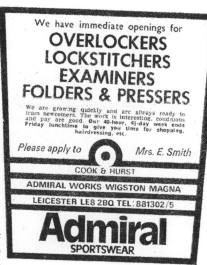

there was some push back from the factory floor. Especially after the move into sportswear, when machinists started working with shinier and thinner materials that tended to slip and slide about more. But once machinists got to grips with each new design, I was told, "it was good money, in the end."

The Long Street factory was also in desperate need of modernising, which was more involved than simply replacing pre-war equipment. The company employed around 60 people, and needed to expand both its workforce and premises to become more productive – and so more competitive. A two-storey extension was added to the existing factory, and the ground-floor warehouse was converted into a knitting room, housing brand-new, modern machinery. Most of the original knitting plant was scrapped, and Bert declared the £50,000 overhaul "a terrific leap forward" for the business. So much so that the company expanded again, and the original factory was demolished within a few years, making way for a new building with a larger cutting room and warehouse, a basement to house stock, as well as offices and a canteen on the top floor.

Keeping apace with growing orders now relied on getting enough workers through the gates each morning. 'Booming Britain' was in full employment, which meant that places like Wigston experienced labour shortages, and employers struggled to fill vacancies. "Cook & Hurst had a reputation at that time of being very, very mean, and it was very difficult to get labour," remembers John. "But, word of mouth with half a dozen ladies, and we started to gather some good people and good machinists."

Another factory was opened, this time 12 miles south in Market Harborough on the Rockingham Road Industrial Estate. John's wife Pat was installed to run the new operation, which would become the firm's knitting plant, where different fabrics would be manufactured and cut before the garments were made up in

Wigston. Moving to Market Harborough would make it easier to attract workers, it was reasoned, as there was less competition from firms looking to hire. Not that the new site didn't have to make an effort to woo potential employees, with 'coffee mornings' being held to encourage local recruitment.

The next time I arranged to meet Bert, with a notebook crammed with questions, was on Long Street itself. "The textile industry was very busy, this whole area here was buzzing in the '60s and '70s, with shoes, knitted textiles, light engineering," he tells me outside his old factory. Such activity meant Cook & Hurst was continually short of skilled labour, but then local industries did provide job opportunities and training for school leavers.

"When I walk by, I can remember where everything was in that factory, still after all these years." Mandy Hutchins was a machine operator at Admiral, and her story is typical of many other local women who worked there. You could literally "walk straight into a job" from school, which is what Mandy did as soon as she turned 16. She arrived unannounced at the factory door one day and, after a brief chat, was taken on and told to come back the following week. Mandy says she literally finished school on a Friday and started work the following Monday. The transition was "a big shock." She says she found the "huge factory scary"

at first, until finding her feet. Mandy's first task was learning how to thread a machine, and she recalls being paid £23 per week during six weeks of initial training before she was set to work as an overlocker, which involved producing finished seams along the joins and edges of garments.

Working for Admiral was also designer Lindsay Jelley's first job, who joined straight from Loughborough Art College, and spent the following few years at the Wigston factory. "I was very sad to go back there recently, and it's all boarded up and it looks a very different. A shell of a place to how I remembered it, it's quite sad. But that's true of a lot of places in Leicester now, that were real hives of industry. That industry has gone."

The firm's old Long Street building was up for sale when I first visited the site, derelict ever since a computer company moved out in the '90s. Situated on a busy road leading into Wigston, the facade of the red-brick building occupies half a block, butting directly up to the pavement. Looking rather unloved and forlorn, its windows are either boarded up or broken, and weeds sprout up from the masonry around its fractured guttering and rooftop, indicating years of neglect. Only once you're inside does the full extent of its abandonment become clear. It's eerily quiet, walking around the large, dank shell. In between the puddles and rotten wooden boards are gaps in the floor mirrored by holes in the roof above. The low-level murmur of cooing turns into the sound of frantic flapping as I turn a corner into an open space that has become a crowded pigeon loft. Yet despite the malaise it's not hard to imagine row upon row of busy machinists and the whirl of knitting spindles filling the air, once you close your eyes.

Down a flight of stairs is the reception area, and even though I've never been here before the space feels strangely familiar, instantly recognisable from news archive I've seen. I identify the area used as a backdrop for interviews, and the wall where Admiral's latest products were once displayed. Most of the flimsy partition walls have all but collapsed and it all seems far smaller than how it once appeared to the outside world. I slowly venture downstairs via a rickety set of steps to the basement, which is dark apart from the areas where there are gaps in the ceiling above, projecting shafts of daylight on to the floor ahead of me. I locate what I assume is the imprint of the sauna, where Bert once entertained his customers with chilled white wine, and negotiated contracts with club managers and chairmen.

Granted, it hardly equates to the discovery of long-lost Roman baths; but it did feel poignant wandering around the silent husk of a site that had clearly meant so much to the people who once worked there. Before leaving, I spot a few brightly coloured cotton reels on the floor. A reminder that by the time Lindsay and Mandy had joined the company's workforce, Cook & Hurst was no longer in the business of making underwear, but was instead making a name for itself in the football world as Admiral Sports.

In his portrait of post-war British life, *On the Cusp: Days of '62*, David Kynaston describes a country edging towards huge change. "The 'real' '60s began on 5th October 1962. On that remarkable Friday, the Beatles hit the world with their first single, 'Love Me Do', and the first James Bond film, *Dr No*, had its world premiere in London: two icons of the future heralding a social and cultural revolution." Cook & Hurst was experiencing a renaissance of its own, with John having been promoted to 'works and production director' following the successful overhaul of its Long Street factory and second site opening. Having made their operation more efficient, the two men next turned their attentions to the firm's order book.

"We had to really abandon doing some of the outlandish garments for these periphery customers, like nuns and so forth." John recalls. Ah yes, the ecclesiastical undies. It wasn't just the antiquated machinery and work practices that had so shocked John on his arrival. Forty years on he still squirms uncomfortably, thinking back to certain items on the company's niche roster. "For nun's we made very large knickers, with a special flap in the front and back, and tie cords. I was too embarrassed to look at them being made. But a very difficult garment to make. Gradually, I think they had to accept more common styles. They were very, very expensive, and we still weren't making enough profit on them."

It wasn't just Cook & Hurst that was 'moving with the times' by the early 1960s. Britons had "never had it so good," according to Prime Minister Harold Macmillan, referring to the social changes that had brought about greater free time and more expendable income. The mood of confidence was reflected across the clothing industry where "cotton and nylon terry-towelling" leisure wear was *de rigueur*, according to Bert. He told the *Oadby & Wigston Advertiser*, that "men are becoming more fashion conscious these days – the Englishman isn't so staid in  his dress but is looking for colour and style. People are going abroad for their holidays and want to wear bright colours – tangerine, lime green and yellows – which completely cut across the plain greys and formal colours we are used to wearing. The man wants to get out of his suit when he gets home and wear something he can relax in. This is what we think is the future."

Even in these early days Bert displayed a knack for creating free publicity, and clearly knew how to generate a headline. He told the same paper that, "Carnaby Street is a big shop window for tourists. We see our merchandise there sometimes." The clothing Bert's referring to was a range of striped dresses similar to rugby jerseys that became fashionable for a time. Polish-born designer Barbara Hulanicki asked him to make "the jerseys a little bit longer and more feminine to turn them into dresses," which were then sold in Biba stores across Europe. One of the firm's yellow and red 'minis' appears in *Two for the Road*, worn by Audrey Hepburn, who starred opposite Albert Finney in the French Riviera-set movie.

This new direction resulted in Cook & Hurst producing more garments and at greater speeds than ever before, whilst making the company more adaptable and less reliant on its diminishing line of underwear orders. A different way of working was also introduced, whereby each machinist manufactured a single section of a garment, rather than making up an entire item of leisurewear from scratch. John told me it was a simple measure that speeded up productivity by doing away with the need to stop work every few minutes to change threads.

"I knew we could make life easier for everybody with more straightforward garments, and just with a little bit of design or interest factor, and the owners then allowed me to buy a big camber machine which produced at a great weight, sort of tennis fabric. And we managed to get some orders from Fred Perry."

The double-knit fabric used for lightweight briefs and vests could also be used to produce football jerseys. And, John says, "it wasn't that difficult. In fact, it felt quite good, really progressive, and we were able to run the machines more." Cheshire-based manufacturers Bukta and Umbro also began putting business Long Street's way, chiefly to help the two suppliers fulfil their own orders, making football and rugby tops for pro and amateur teams.

The move into sportswear didn't come entirely out of the blue, either: Cook & Hurst had been producing swimwear and athletics outfits since Edwardian times. The firm's 1935 product catalogue included 'bathing costumes for men, women and children, as well as a special line of Cream Interlock Sports Wear', according to historian Colin Hyde. The company also had a long-standing contract to supply the Royal Navy with rugby jerseys, and in the 1960s a trade magazine called *Sports and Camping Goods Dealer* noted that 'new Spanish-style football clothing' was being produced by the firm.

Reported in the *Leicester Advertiser* as being designed by Bert himself, the 'Toreador' was made from heavy 'combed cotton interlock', and was described as a warm long-sleeved jersey. Also mentioned was a quilted goalkeeper's top and accompanying lightweight warm-up trousers. By the time the country was readying itself to host the 1966 World Cup finals, Cook & Hurst had launched a new sports jersey called, but what else, 'World Cup'. The goalkeeper's top featured 'built-in elastication at the neck and cuffs to give complete freedom of movement and to maintain garment shape throughout its life'. One employee described the new blouson as not dissimilar to a rugby jersey, and I was told it was considered far more stylish than other goalie tops available at that time.

Leicester City's Gordon Banks had worn a similar jersey during the previous season's domestic campaign, which had included a visit to Wigston for a special fitting – chiefly to ensure the sleeves were one and half inches longer than usual, in order to make sure 'Yorkie' was as unrestricted as possible whenever he made saves or collected crosses.

Even in these early days Cook & Hurst was trying to push boundaries, with Banks being provided with an additional pale blue shirt, that he was subsequently stopped from wearing by Football League administrators. He did of course swap his green club top for the famous yellow England jersey he wore throughout the World Cup tournament, which was also produced by Cook & Hurst – while England's outfield strips had been provided by Umbro, along with the kits worn by 14 of the other 15 finalists. It was a supply line that Bert and John would not only soon covet but actively seek to muscle in on.

Cook & Hurst's decision to move more into sportswear was about to pay off spectacularly, in a way that neither Bert nor John could ever have foreseen or imagined in their wildest dreams. Following England's glorious World Cup triumph, 1966 is the year the story of Admiral begins in earnest, with the popularity of football and the demand for playing strips taking off like one of Bobby Charlton's thunderbolts. The Wigston firm was still sub-contracting work from established sportswear brands such as Bukta and Umbro, but the profit margins were too small to make it worthwhile, says John. "We decided then, what the hell, let's go direct," and cut out the traditional supply chain of stockists and suppliers, by supplying sports shops and school outfitters straight from the factory. "We started getting orders for local football clubs which were quite profitable, it was good experience." Adopting a catchphrase from *Never Mind the Quality, Feel the Width*, a popular '60s TV sitcom set in the 'rag-trade', John told me that from now on they decided to "miss out the middleman."

The following year, the *Oadby & Wigston Advertiser* reported Bert as saying, "We have completely stopped making underwear... and realising the enormous potential of sports and leisure wear, such as football and rugger jerseys, we have completely gone over to it." Prophetically, Bert said, "This is a young team we have now – we are building for the future, and feel we are really going places. Now the firm is pausing, ready for the next surge forward."

I doubt even Bert could quite believe how well his statement of intent would pan out over the next few years. At the forefront of this future success, of course, was the launch of a unique range of soccer outfits with their own brand name: Admiral Sports.

CHAPTER 2
Marching On Together

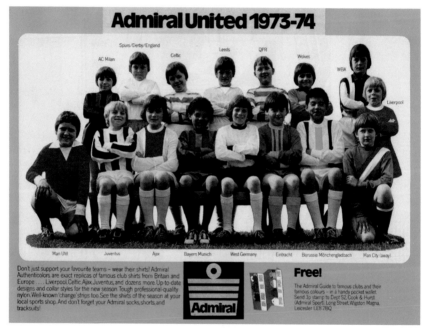

Admiral United 1973-74

Spurs/Derby/England · AC Milan · Celtic · Leeds · QPR · Wolves · WBA · Liverpool

Man Utd · Juventus · Ajax · Bayern Munich · West Germany · Eintracht · Borussia Mönchengladbach · Man City (away)

Don't just support your favourite teams – wear their shirts! Admiral Authenticolors are exact replicas of famous club shirts from Britain and Europe . . . Liverpool, Celtic, Ajax, Juventus, and dozens more. Up-to-date designs and collar styles for the new season. Tough professional-quality nylon. Well-known 'change' strips too. See the shirts of the season at your local sports shop. And don't forget your Admiral socks, shorts, and tracksuits!

Admiral

Free!
The Admiral Guide to famous clubs and their famous colours - in a handy pocket wallet. Send 3p stamp to Dept S2, Cook & Hurst (Admiral Sport), Long Street, Wigston Magna, Leicester LE8 2BQ

The prosperity and 'feel-good factor' of 1960s Britain was carried forward into the following decade. The country's garment industries were thriving, and there were independent retailers and made-to-measure tailors on most high streets, while the clothes sold in chain stores such as Littlewoods were mostly made in the UK, many carrying the labels of East Midlands firms. Cook & Hurst was also in rude health, with Bert Patrick's ambitions for the company he took over 15 years earlier seemingly realised. He'd managed to turn the manufacturer's fortunes around, and his business was no longer reliant on underwear orders to turn a profit, having segued deftly, with impeccable timing, into the burgeoning football strips market off the back of England's 1966 World Cup triumph. It was a wave also being surfed by other Leicestershire companies, including the manufacturers of the popular Action Man figures, Coalville's Palitoy, whose 'dolls for boys' could now be kitted out in an array of football outfits whenever they fancied a day off from jungle warfare or polar expeditions.

Cook & Hurst's own range of playing strips was equally impressive, having built up a reputation for making quality athletics-wear by helping more established sportswear firms fulfil their own orders. According to the *Leicester Advertiser*, 'Wigston is rapidly becoming the centre for the manufacturer of sports kit, and many of the leading professional clubs in the country turn out in shirts with a Wigston trademark.'

The *Oadby & Wigston Advertiser* reported Bert's boast that, "Cook & Hurst are now the biggest manufacturers of soccer clothing in the entire country. He said the firm carries over 250 ranges in soccer jerseys alone, together with tracksuits, shorts, socks and rugby jerseys. It supplies many of the leading League football clubs." Bert was also acutely aware of how beholden he was to the whims of other manufacturers, and sought to strike out on his own. "Initially we made [kits] for some of the sports firms like Umbro and Bukta, and then I decided that we could paddle our canoe and start making these jerseys ourselves."

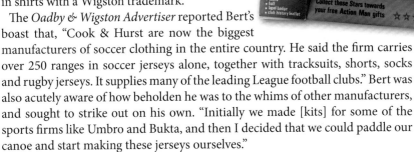

The launch of Cook & Hurst's own sportswear line would require a new brand name, it was agreed, and the creation of a distinct and separate identity to that of the firm's founding fathers. Fortunately, the company's bosses didn't have to look too far and found exactly what they were looking for by digging around in its own offices. According to John, "In the annals of the firm's records is the name 'Admiral'. And it was very interesting because it was used by Cook & Hurst in the First World War. The Navy had made them exclusive producers of certain garments, and it was registered in various places. So, you know, that was a lucky thing, actually. We could've made a name, but it would've taken us months, arguing, so we decided we'd go with that one, it was already registered."

But adopting Admiral's original motif as well was considered a stretch too far: a traditional doughty sailor in a cocked hat. The seafaring figure that had once helped sell woolly long-johns was immediately dismissed out of hand for being too staid. Ironically, I also saw another version of the old logo on a brochure that couldn't have been more apt, this time featuring an image of a headstrong young naval officer gazing out towards uncharted horizons.

Instead, it's believed the company commissioned Mitchell G. Advertising to freshen up Admiral's brand identity. "It was quite powerful," John remembers

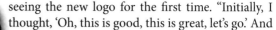

seeing the new logo for the first time. "Initially, I thought, 'Oh, this is good, this is great, let's go.' And again it was pioneering for something new."

The Admiral emblem had been transformed into a punchy, recognisable mark: the naval insignia for the rank of Admiral, with the brand name appearing underneath. Not dissimilar to a cross-section drawing of a cherry Bakewell cupcake.

Historian Colin Hyde says, "The company employed two sales reps; one covered the north of England and one covered the south of England. They each travelled the country for four days a week, usually by train. They were accompanied by a wicker skip which contained the merchandise. The skips were usually handled by the railway porters and placed in the guards van and then taken directly to the hotel where buyers would view the goods which were either displayed in kiosks or showrooms."

The first sets of Cook & Hurst's Admiral-labelled kits were aimed primarily towards domestic amateur clubs and schools as well as North America's burgeoning college soccer market. These were, for the most part, recognisable yet unbadged nylon team strips marketed under an 'Authenticolours' banner: 'detail-perfect soccer shirts in the authentic colours and styles of most famous league clubs'. Alongside these staples was a range of less familiar outfits proffering a nod towards popular culture, with an array of jerseys carrying vertical stripes and asymmetric blocks, more readily associated with late-'60s mod fashions. It was a dynamic, streamlined range of strips previously only ever seen in the pages of *Scorcher & Score* and similar cartoon strips, most often worn by the opposition sides that allowed the artists' imaginations to run riot. It was perhaps a first reflection that high-street trends were about to burst into the consciousness of Admiral's marketing.

Sportswear was evolving rapidly, and the Wigston firm stole yet another march on rivals Umbro, whose Tangeru cotton jerseys were susceptible to shrinkage, by cultivating a reputation for working with innovative man-made fabrics. *Sports Equipment News* reported that the company's use of 'Blue 'C' nylon' allowed items to 'be machine washed without fear of colours running or shape distortion, it also dried quicker and resisted mildew'. According to John, one of Admiral's key selling points was the durability of their new, lighter-weight materials.

"We'd actually developed a fabric from a nylon manufactured by a company called Monsanto, who guaranteed it for a year. School [sportswear] and cotton jerseys received a tremendous hammering, and they couldn't be machine washed. Or they could be, and it wasn't very good, so that started to get accepted by housewives and mothers."

The company was also attracting the attention of some high-profile international teams, resulting in a contract to supply the British Lions rugby team with sets of lightweight red jerseys for their 1971 tour of New Zealand. Made from a fabric called Acrilan the shirts were lauded as a 'breakthrough' inasmuch as they 'repelled mud and water yet would not restrict the player from sweating'. The following year Admiral made headlines at the 1972 Munich Olympics. Or a few lines in the *Oadby & Wigston Advertiser*, at least, when following a colour clash 'at only 24 hours' notice, the Wigston hosiery firm of Cook & Hurst, Long Street produced 16 white nylon cellular jerseys, with collars and V inserts, for the British women's Olympic hockey team in Munich.' History would repeat itself ten years later, when Admiral was called upon to pull off a similar trick at the World Cup finals in Spain, albeit in far more chaotic circumstances.

Not that any of the watching millions would ever know about Admiral's presence at The Games. As was the norm, manufacturers' labels had largely tended to remain tucked away on the inside of their garments, up until that point. But sports sponsorship was changing, and it was becoming increasingly common for high-profile footballers and nominally amateur athletes to receive cash for wearing boots and spikes adorned with a trademark.

Running shoes were also being handed out for free to athletes, and overt branding wasn't restricted to footwear, according to Barbara Smit's *Pitch Invasion: Adidas, Puma and the Making of Modern Sport*. "Until then, Olympic athletes had worn nondescript and often shabby singlets... but Adidas signed endorsement deals with several national athletics federations and supplied them with thousands of shirts that were branded with the trefoil. The company's clothing was even more visible outside the track, where athletes freely walked around in three-striped tracksuits supplied by Adidas."

It's surely no coincidence that 1972 was also the first time the world watched a major global sporting event in colour.

Man may have landed on the moon in 1969, but equally seismic as far as Cook & Hurst was concerned was the BBC and ITV starting to broadcast their football coverage in colour. "Television really helped us enormously," says John, who admits, "Admiral wouldn't have happened without colour TV."

Bert told me how he'd excitedly announced the breaking news of advances in audiovisual entertainment, by proclaiming it "would make us" to anybody within earshot. And how "one lady turned round and said, 'It's alright for you,

Mr Patrick, you can afford a colour television, we'll never be able to afford it.'"

Fortunately, such misgivings proved unfounded. It is true that most people were still watching the UK's trio of television channels in black and white at the start of the 1970s; but that was about to change. Over the next few years the demand for colour sets exploded. Sometimes quite literally if my own family's experience is anything to go by, as our first forays into the world of small-screen rented Technicolor was often punctuated by visits from Granada's repair man. The catalyst for most of these call-outs was my sister and I shouting, "It's smoking again," or Dad banging on top of the set to stabilise the picture.

Despite the potential threat of sitting in front of a UXB, I would watch telly for hours, ignoring repeated warnings of contracting 'square eyes,' because hours spent avoiding school homework or thinking up excuses to dodge my household chores could never be described as wasted.

The worst item on the familial timesheet was the weekly Sunday afternoon 'drive' to visit relatives – particularly as these awkward social interactions invariably clashed with ATV's *Star Soccer*. I rarely came willingly or quietly on such occasions, until my parents and I came to an agreement: I would comply on condition of arriving in time to watch the start of the football highlights unencumbered. Such trips had to be timed to ensure all stilted pleasantries were out of the way before Hugh Johns' honeyed tones announced the start of a featured match played in the Midlands the day before. BBC's *Match of the Day* also highlighted the action from two or three games but was broadcast on Saturday nights at 10pm. If I stayed still long enough during *Kojak*'s end credits I would occasionally get to see the opening game before my dad realised I was still up, and sent me packing off to bed.

Colour television coverage and more live broadcasts were also having an effect on football strip suppliers. Umbro's diamond logo had been appearing on the outside of its jerseys since the 1950s, but in the form of a subtle, embossed stamp above the hemline that largely went unnoticed, invariably tucked inside a pair of shorts. The likes of Fred Perry with Anderlecht and Le Coq Sportif supplying other Belgian and French sides were much bolder, their trademarks appearing on the front of jerseys by the middle of the following decade. Perry's laurel wreath logo had also regularly featured on the shirts of pro tennis players since the postwar years. Similarly, football boot manufacturers Dunlop and Gola, and new arrivals Adidas and Puma, displayed their trademarks throughout the '60s.

Towards the end of the decade Umbro followed suit, and its own label was tentatively displayed on its football clothing, taking advantage of what amounted to free advertising. Initially, it was at tournaments and big occasions where broadcast exposure was guaranteed, most notably at the beginning of the 1969 FA Cup final, when Leicester City emerged from the Wembley tunnel in specially made white track tops featuring a small diamond opposite the club's badge. The following year, a navy, white and red rhombus popped up on England's tracksuits for the ill-starred World Cup defence at Mexico '70. The diamond then started to appear on goalkeepers' jerseys the following season, including Gordon Banks' yellow England top and Ray Clemence's 1971 FA Cup final shirt. Within a couple of years, Umbro's logo also turned up on the jerseys of outfield players at showpiece events, with both Leeds United and Sunderland wearing visibly branded tracksuits and shirts during the 1973 FA Cup final. Likewise the Liverpool side that lifted the UEFA cup at Borussia Mönchengladbach later that month. The Wilmslow company then ensured the trend continued into the following season's domestic campaign with Derby County and Sheffield United leading the charge.

The country's top teams were also taking more of a sartorial interest in how their players appeared. In August 1972, Bert told the *Oadby & Wigston Advertiser* that, "at least a quarter of the 92 clubs in the Football League decided this season to change colours or styles. This resulted in many new orders for the firm."

This appetite for change was seized upon within the walls of Long Street, where its designers set about playing with colours and shapes. Early adopters of the Wigston avant-garde included West Bromwich Albion embracing broad stripes, and Leicester City, now clad head to toe in all white, in a move that saw keeper Peter Shilton attired in a royal-blue jersey. Thus City became the first club to receive a fee from Admiral for wearing their kit, despite the absence of any overt nautical logos on the team's new strips.

But Bert still sensed there was a yet bigger and more exciting business opportunity to be explored beyond switching collar styles or swapping the colours of shorts. He wanted to give clubs a unique identity by creating an individual strip for each team. "Realising that colour television was coming in, that was a huge factor because I felt that being able to see different teams in their colours rather than black and white, particularly if I could persuade the clubs to change their designs – which were just, in those days, plain red, plain white, plain blue. So I thought, well, we could design special away kits, we could design special home kits, and the first club we went to was Leeds United."

The modernising spirit of the age was epitomised by Don Revie. The Elland Road boss appeared to be streets ahead of most other managers both tactically and in how he organised his team's affairs away from the pitch. Following his appointment in 1961 he transformed a rag-tag band of Second Division strugglers into one of Europe's most successful club sides. As an indicator of just how little he cared for convention, one of his first acts upon taking charge was to ditch United's traditional blue and gold colours. In their place he introduced a single-colour, 'continental-style' all-white strip, born of a desire to emulate one of the game's elites. Norman Hunter told me, "I think he had one aim and that was to make Leeds United great, and he succeeded in that. I'll never forget him saying, 'We're going to be the next Real Madrid, we're going to play in all white.'" When Revie's own side started competing in European matches regularly he introduced another change of strip, this time wearing all blue, and then all red if ever there was a colour clash. Finally, by the early '70s, he settled on an all-yellow kit, which became synonymous with his last great Leeds side.

Despite its success, Revie's team was reviled by many outside of the West Riding. Some sportswriters and supporters of other clubs thought United were overly physical. Too well schooled in the dark arts of winning at all costs, employing the sort of gamesmanship that most supporters simply take for granted nowadays, notes Hunter, who retains nothing but the utmost respect for his old boss. "He was ahead of his time, wasn't he? Nobody did what we did. Nobody went and kept the ball in the corner for two minutes to go, and we did that. So, we were very professional, and in that given time it was something that the public didn't quite appreciate and didn't like, but he was very forward-thinking."

Peter Shilton accepts his former England manager was innovative, with the following caveat: "Some things we didn't like, it's sort of what we called 'cheating things', like Billy Bremner would stand on the goalkeeper's foot when he was going for a corner or something like that. But it was all the start of tactics and being professional."

Hunter told me that outside criticism was used to motivate Leeds' players, and unfavourable newspaper headlines were often pinned to the dressing-room wall. He revealed how Revie hated the club's 'dirty Leeds' tag, and felt his team deserved more respect for their endeavours. One of the ways he sought to win over the doubters was in the way his team presented itself to the public. The traditional club crest featuring an owl was jettisoned in favour of a groovy-looking 'smiley' badge made up of the letters 'L' and 'U'. Hammond & Silke describe its introduction as a "masterpiece of doublethink irony," such was United's reputation for bad behaviour, going on to describe other "showbiz" innovations, including pre-match synchronised waving to the crowd, "as gimmicky [and] at worst false goodwill."

The man behind 1972's 'Super Leeds' rebrand was Paul Trevillion, otherwise known as 'The Beaver', and the illustrator responsible for the 'Roy of the Rovers' and 'You Are the Ref' cartoon strips. He was brought on board to help soften Leeds' image, and clearly some of the Beaver's suggestions worked better than others. In *The Glory Game*, Hunter Davies describes the first outing of the team in "gleaming white tracksuit tops with their names printed large on the back" as "causing a sensation." There was also a suggestion to add crosses on to the fronts of Leeds' white shirts so "they'd look like Crusader knights going into battle," but Revie wisely vetoed this idea.

The most successful piece of PR involved giving away team sock tags as souvenirs. The idea being that, at the end of each game, the players would untie these numbered bands and throw them into the crowd. Hunter remembers another new routine or stunt backfiring spectacularly. "One of them was that we went away from home, and we signed a few footballs and we'd kick it into the crowd. Well, with Leeds' reputation, we kicked it in the crowd and it came straight back at us with everything."

As mentioned previously, replica football outfits did already exist around this time: unbadged 'Umbrosets' were available from sports shops in a generic range of popular colours. It was sometimes even possible to find a smaller trader flogging plain football shirts adorned with a team crest, usually off a souvenir stall or via a small-ad in the back pages of *Goal* or *Shoot!* magazine. This concept was seized upon by Trevillion, who is also credited with floating the idea of 'official' replica kits to Umbro in the early 1970s, though his sales pitch fell on deaf ears. The

Wilmslow hierarchy was left unconvinced by the notion, apparently telling the Beaver: "Kids don't have the money to buy reproduction strips."

Despite this assumed lack of appetite Umbro did 'test the market' in 1972, launching a range of children's 'club' tracksuits available in a 'dazzling range of colours', according to the advertising blurb. Costing from £4.80 upwards, the nylon two-pieces featured an authentic team badge opposite Umbro's own logo, and the 'training suits' were 'just like the biggest names in soccer wear'. Except they weren't. What's interesting about these tracksuits is that although they looked like the real McCoy, they weren't identical to the teamwear being worn on matchdays. Rather a very nice and desirable range of template tracksuits that most football-mad kids would love to get their hands on. They were also unlicensed, in that Umbro didn't pay a fee or any royalties for using the clubs' name and badge – not that Umbro was doing anything wrong.

More likely, permission would have been granted in exchange for a free set of playing strips, such was the infancy of the market, according to former Umbro sales director Bobby Brown. At that time, hawkers selling 'unofficial' souvenirs were all part and parcel of the matchday landscape, while an array of scarves, bobble hats, pennants and cloth patches was available by mail order to anybody with a postal order and enough stamps to cover carriage.

Besides, most clubs didn't seem overly bothered with official souvenirs, their own ramshackle kiosks and portakabins being geared towards selling programmes rather than potentially more lucrative merchandise. Seemingly, they were happy to co-exist alongside independent sellers – until it became obvious there was a lot more money to be made from football fandom.

Younger fans were starting to look and dress very differently to their dads and older siblings, let alone previous match-going generations. Utilitarian-looking skinheads and suedes gave way to long-haired fans who wore star-spangled jumpers and stripy tank tops with waist-high Oxford bags and 'Boot Boy' Doc Martens. Clothing became more colourful too, with scarves around wrists and denim jackets smothered in pin badges and cloth patches becoming the norm. There was even a brief fashion for decorating white butcher's coats in marker pen slogans, such was the home-made nature of much of the pageantry.

Taken in Manchester, Iain S.P. Reid's wonderful collection of photos perfectly

encapsulates this period. As Iain said, they show "the way in which the football supporters used to dress and treat the whole match as if it were a carnival." Supporters had traditionally 'made an effort' with their outfits for Wembley cup finals, and now some supporters were choosing to dress that way every week.

The winds of change didn't go unnoticed in Wigston, and "football was gathering pace," according to John Griffin. "More personalities were coming into it, and suddenly this market started to appear." The country's top clubs were also starting to realise that selling souvenirs to young fans could prove lucrative, with Leeds among those setting up popular mail-order services. John says adding replica shirts, like those worn by players, to the growing list of club merchandise "was the natural thing to do, the market was there. It was really pushed in our face with Leeds, so we had to take advantage of it once we'd woken up."

In a feature film or a play, John or Bert's character would have had a 'lightbulb' moment in the middle of the night. Or perhaps a seamstress working secretly during the evenings would hold aloft a replica football shirt for the first time, and announce the creation of a sportswear phenomenon. In reality, the actual 'eureka moment' owed more to evolution than revolution.

The idea was first mooted by a sales rep feeding back on a customer's query, believes John. "He was going around school outfitters, et cetera, and I was playing around with fabric, and he said, 'Can you make a football shirt?' And I said, 'Yeah.' And it happened like that." The 'it' referred to is the creation of the world's first official replica jersey, even if John is too modest to admit it himself.

Despite Admiral's best efforts, Bukta and Umbro still supplied the majority of Britain's professional clubs with playing strips. The Wigston bosses had been looking for ways to break up this duopoly and perhaps now they'd found one. But Bert was initially cautious, telling me, "I class myself as a visionary and an entrepreneur, and those two things together sometimes can be too early. I brought products out and they failed miserably because they were too early." But on this occasion there were two solid foundations on which to build. "The advent of colour television, then of course the 1968 Design Copyright Act, which gave us protection when we'd signed up with football clubs. And from there, we used those vehicles to go forward."

Rather than a generic football kit, of the type it was already supplying to schools

and retailers, Admiral was about to offer something new: a distinctive and unique set of playing strips for each team. On top of which, the supplier would pay clubs for the privilege of doing so. In exchange, the new teamwear and accessories would carry Admiral's logo and brand name, with the company recouping its sponsorship money by selling replica versions of these 'designer' shirts and tracksuits to young fans. From now on, no one would be left in any doubt as to whether or not they were wearing an authentic club strip.

According to kit historian John Devlin, "the whole idea just turned the football world on its head." Bert "realised that he could completely corner this market and create a new business model which had never been seen before, in tying clubs up to these exclusive deals."

Coming up with a good idea is one thing, but it's quite another to get others to buy into it – particularly in the conservative, smoky boardrooms inhabited by football club directors. Whether by luck or design, Bert and John managed to align themselves to a kindred spirit in Don Revie. Not only was the Yorkshireman "hungry for new ideas," his club "was big and successful enough to sell thousands of shirts," football writer Richard Benson told *Esquire* magazine.

As well as redesigning and copyrighting the home strip, Admiral also supplied new tracksuits and an away kit: "Leeds would wear it to most away games, thus establishing two official kits." But in truth, the firm's first offerings were not that dissimilar to what had gone before, apart from a new collar style and the logos added to the jersey and shorts.

The club's yellow away strip received the same minimal makeover at first, giving the production team in Wigston time to come up with something radically different to launch the following year. The new home strips were made from lightweight Monsanto fabric similar to that used for the British Lions and the GB Women's hockey teams' kits.

When John took a prototype version of the new Leeds strip to show to Revie, "He was very, very pleased with them, wanted them as soon as possible, which we were able to do."

His players were equally receptive, and Norman Hunter "noticed straight away how much lighter the Admiral shirts were." The defender says there were other sartorial advantages as well. "I do think it made you think you looked smarter, with the proper tracksuit on. It was good for everybody to be dressed the same."

The Leeds squad also benefitted financially, as Revie insisted on all fees from the deal being paid into the players' pool. This included additional bonuses should his side win further honours in their sponsor's kit, which was a deal not to be entered into lightly given how successful the club had become under Revie, amassing eight trophies to date and finishing runners-up on six other occasions. United were already on course to win the First Division title again, and were among the favourites to lift that season's FA Cup.

Smiling at the memory, Bert told me he managed to sidestep this not insignificant threat to Admiral finances by having a wager on Leeds himself. "It occurred to us that we could lay off with the bookies at the beginning of the season, the odds of them winning things, which was a cost-effective way of being able to pay the clubs if they were successful."

When I relay this story to Hunter he nods approvingly, clearly appreciative of Bert and John's own desire to succeed. "You've got to admire the guys who hit the top of the tree and thought, 'right, we're going in, we'll go and get Leeds United.' And it was very successful, wasn't it? But they did pick the best club in the country at the time, and it just went on from them."

CHAPTER 3
𝕭lockbuster

Elland Road, Leeds, October 1973

"I knew that once I'd got Don Revie to accept change, that we were on the way, and it all just happened." Bert Patrick's instincts proved prophetic when, towards the end of 1973, the Admiral hierarchy struck a deal with Leeds United that would change football forever. Prior to Bert and John's negotiations with Revie, United and most other clubs had paid a sports retailer or agent to supply its playing strips, which were nearly all manufactured by Bukta or Umbro, and to a lesser extent Litesome, Matchwinner or Spall. Now, sat in front of the Leeds boss, were two upstarts from an underwear company in Leicester, offering to pay him for the privilege of making his team's kit. A unique proposition that would guarantee Leeds United at least £10,000 a year in sponsorship. In return, the two factory bosses proposed making and selling an 'official' line of children's teamwear reproductions, that would be in the shops by Christmas.

On and off the pitch Leeds appeared far more savvy than most other clubs, and boasted a commercial department capable of wringing every last penny out of its success. Not that there was much of a fanfare announcing the arrival of United's new replica strips which, in any case, would have probably been drowned out by Slade's 'Merry Xmas Everybody', Now Admiral's merchandise would have to slug it out for attention among a dizzying array of club souvenirs, including anoraks, ties, T-shirts, eiderdowns, reading lamps, pyjamas, hankies, soft toys, books, pens, key rings, sew-on patches, jewellery, candles, car stickers, rosettes, swimming trunks, autographed photos, bobble hats, scarves, duffle bags, towels, his-and-hers jumpers and pairs of ladies panties, to name but a few – all vying for attention on the shelves of a tiny, cramped gift shop on the edge of an Elland Road car park.

Similarly, buried within the pages of the club's lucrative mail-order catalogue, was a simple line drawing of the new Admiral-branded outfits and an accompanying price list. White 'nylon honeycomb stitch' jerseys with 'no badge' were available in both child and youth sizes costing between £1.55 and £2.10. This was around the same price as a new LP, and comparable to what other manufacturers were charging for generic football shirts at that time. Admiral tracksuits 'as worn by the players' were available in sizes up to a 36" chest and retailed at between £6.97 and £8.96, which was about half a week's wages for one of Long Street's young machinists. It was a fair reflection of the work involved to produce what were essentially hand-made jackets, but also perhaps a sign of things to come.

"They were a big club and they launched us in a very short time," acknowledges John, who told me Admiral's 'official' Leeds strips proved hugely popular almost immediately. "The big surprise was the garments sold nationwide, considering the popularity of Leeds. They were rated to be too physical on the pitch, et cetera, but that was a fact. They were, arguably, the biggest club at that time." He added that the deal couldn't have gone much better even though "I was a bit nervous" about the initial sponsorship outlay. But "I almost think we blew that away on the first day."

The Wigston firm's arrangement with Leeds wasn't universally popular. Football kit historian John Devlin says the contract was viewed as "a very cynical marketing ploy, that by getting into bed with this company they were effectively cornering this way of supporting your side." The groundbreaking contract also confirmed what many of Revie's detractors thought all along: it was a brash, money-grabbing move. The United boss had been saddled with an unwanted moniker even before the Admiral deal: 'Don Readies'. The spectre of match fixing and bribery hung over the club throughout his tenure despite none of these allegations ever being proven. Club captain Billy Bremner successfully defended himself in court against similar accusations and, in hindsight, Revie was reported as saying he wished he'd done the same to clear his own name.

Critics immediately assumed Admiral's tie-in with Elland Road was in some way corrupt or suspect. John Griffin says he "was asked time and time again by media, 'how much did we pay him?' And we paid him nothing. Anything that they could get was for his players, and he was straight down the middle. The press didn't believe that. Again, he was unpopular with the London press; but no, he was very straight and... yeah, he was a nice man."

Bert concurs, and responds similarly when I ask him about the nature of the Leeds deal. "I've been asked that question many times, but in all the time I knew Don Revie when he was Leeds manager, England manager, being in his company many times, travelled abroad with him with the England team, never once did he mention money. The only thing he did say to me right at the beginning, 'Billy Bremner sweats blood, I want this money for the team.'"

Ever protective of his on-field 'family', Revie made sure all monies were paid into a players' pool rather than the club's own coffers – a clause that chairman Manny Cussins soon reversed when the kit contract came up for renewal a few years later, by which time the 'Don of Elland Road' was no longer in charge at Leeds.

"We went along like this for about nine months or so. Quite well, you know. No real problems with Revie or the team, it was good," says John. Buoyed by the success of its first sets of strips, Admiral set out to make its mark in the spring of 1974, as Leeds closed in on their second title, by launching a bold new eye-catching away kit. Or so they'd hoped, explains John, who was busily overseeing the production of the new-look replicas. With Revie's blessing, a previously blank all-yellow outfit was given a dash of extra colour and style with the introduction of blue and white stripes along the sleeves, shorts and sock tops, and a once-plain crew neck had been replaced by a smart, button-up polo-shirt collar. "Then I was out one day and a girl called me, and she said, 'You must ring Don Revie as soon as you can.' I got him at home and he said, 'I don't want you to mention this to anybody, but I'm going to be the next England manager.'" For now though, the Yorkshireman was still in post at Elland Road to oversee his side being crowned champions, and Admiral's souped-up new away strip duly made its bow towards the end of the run-in.

The FA's choice to succeed Alf Ramsey as national coach was as much a shock to sportswriters as it was to the Yorkshireman's adopted city. When word of Revie's impending appointment spread, chairman Manny Cussins addressed a hastily assembled press pack outside Elland Road's main entrance, to confirm that his manager would be leaving with the board's blessings. But after 13 hugely successful years in charge, Leeds supporters weren't the only ones fretting over Revie's departure.

"He left Leeds United and that worried us, because who were we going to get?" John's reaction was born from commercial self-interest, but it's a question that fixated football followers up and down the country. It was clear that whoever took over would need a strong enough character to match those found within a formidable but ageing squad that was going to need rebuilding. The eventual answer was as shocking as it was puzzling: Revie's old nemesis, Brian Clough. The brash and confident young coach had won the First Division title with unfashionable Derby County, but he was also one of Leeds' fiercest public critics. Often voicing his disapproval of "the dirtiest, most cynical team in the League," he even suggested Revie's team should be punished with automatic relegation.

John admits he felt a certain amount of trepidation at the appointment, given the amount of personal baggage Clough would be bringing with him. "We were a bit worried, actually. How the hell are we to deal with him?" Shifting in his seat, he raises his eyebrows as he recalls meeting Leeds' new boss for the first time. "So, after a couple of weeks I went to see him, and I waited in his office. He came in after training and he said, 'Hello, you.' And I said, 'Oh, you're much fitter than I thought you'd be.' And he said, 'If that's not a compliment, I'll punch you on the nose.' So I said, 'It's a compliment.' We had a bit of a general chat which went okay, lots of interruptions by him shouting down the corridor to his staff, getting people in for extra training, et cetera."

Clough is famously reported to have told his new charges, "The first thing you can do for me is throw your medals in the bin because you've never won anything fairly; you've done it by cheating." The new boss also made no secret of his desire to overhaul the culture of the club from top to bottom, which often led to a certain amount of tiptoeing on John's part around the subject of playing strips. "So, we chatted in general and then he said, 'Everything's okay as far as I'm concerned with the plain kit.'" Yet despite Cloughie's assurances, the Admiral bosses remained on tenterhooks, and "for 44 days we were anxious that he'd try and give Leeds United a different identity than Revie had done."

The Clough era got off to an ominous start at Wembley, with Leeds losing out to Liverpool in the Charity Shield following a bruising encounter remembered for the dismissals of Billy Bremner and Kevin Keegan after the pair traded blows and threw away their shirts. United's title defence didn't fare much better, and with Leeds fourth bottom by the middle of September, Clough was sacked by the club's board.

Incredibly, the outgoing manager appeared on Yorkshire Television's *Calendar* show later that evening to discuss his dismissal, sat alongside the man he'd replaced in the Elland Road dugout. During an extraordinary piece of theatre, host Austin Mitchell acted as ringmaster as Revie and Clough, his confidence seemingly undimmed, endeavoured to outscore one another with verbal barbs.

The first few weeks of the 1974/75 season weren't disastrous as far as Bert and John were concerned. Leeds' new yellow away kit was on display at Stoke City's Victoria Ground on the opening day, in front of ATV's *Star Soccer* cameras. An Admiral double bill, as the Potters had also signed up in the close season. That summer, sales of United's revamped yellow replicas had exceeded all expectation. Bert remembers figures in the region of, "thousands of dozens of shirts, shorts, socks, tracksuits. Not so many tracksuits, of course, because they were more expensive being a suit, but we did sell a lot of tracksuits. Parents were buying them, for the children."

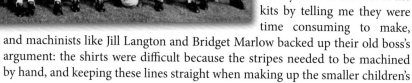

The price of new yellow jerseys included a 50 per cent mark-up on their white counterparts, while tracksuit tops were available in adult sizes for the first time, but came with a whopping great £13.90 price tag attached. Bert always defended the thorny issue of the cost of the kits by telling me they were time consuming to make, and machinists like Jill Langton and Bridget Marlow backed up their old boss's argument: the shirts were difficult because the stripes needed to be machined by hand, and keeping these lines straight when making up the smaller children's sizes was particularly tricky. They added that this work became even more fiddly when the business later took off and the kit designs grew ever more elaborate.

Handling one of these original Admiral jerseys now, it's easy to see why they were tricky to make, as they look and feel very different to the lighter, silkier reproductions manufactured today. Unlike contemporary fabrics, which come ready printed, it's possible to see and feel the joins and panels on a replica that's over 40 years old. Indeed, the shirt I have in front of me is more akin to a garment you'd buy off a craft stall rather than a mass-produced item of sportswear.

John Griffin remains rightly proud of Leeds' famous yellow away kit, and it's still his his favourite Admiral strip of all time. "It looked fabulous under lighting," he says. "It wasn't too fussy, but the colour and the fabric punched out."

Perhaps unsurprisingly, Bert looks upon the home strip equally fondly, "Because that was the first, that was the start, that was the dream kit for me." It certainly proved that the concept Admiral and Bert had come up with could work. "The vision was, eventually, I'd be

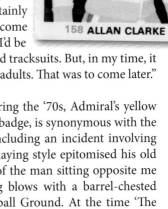

158 ALLAN CLARKE

able to persuade the adults to wear these shirts and tracksuits. But, in my time, it was the children that were wearing them, not the adults. That was to come later."

For many fans who fell in love with football during the '70s, Admiral's yellow Leeds away kit, with its sleeve stripes and smiley badge, is synonymous with the memory of televised moments from that era. Including an incident involving United's Norman Hunter whose 'bite yer legs' playing style epitomised his old team's spirit and tenacity. It's hard not to think of the man sitting opposite me without conjuring up an image of him trading blows with a barrel-chested Franny Lee on the mudheap that was the Baseball Ground. At the time 'The Derby Battle' sent soccer 'hurtling faster still towards its complete moral decay', according to the *Daily Express*, such was its notoriety.

I think I've managed to reference the incident breezily enough into our conversation – until I notice Hunter's eyes narrow, and he fixes me with the stare of a man who's been asked about this particular altercation more times than he cares to answer. Fortunately, Hunter has the good grace and patience to indulge yet another person one more time. "There's certain things in your playing career that you regret doing, and that was one. That was against a very, very nice guy who conned me for a penalty, and I reacted in a silly way, really. But the amazing thing about it is, even now at the age I'm at, I go throughout the country and one thing or another, and all I've to do is mention Derby or Francis Lee, and

Kit-astrophe alert: when Leeds United's smiley badges were sewn on upside-down.

everybody remembers it was in the yellow kit, wasn't it?"

When Leeds first began wearing all yellow, Norman says it attracted too many "adverse comments" from opponents, and wearing bright colours wasn't really the "done thing." "I didn't like it at first," he tells me. "I've got to be honest. But then after a bit I started to enjoy wearing it, [and] it became part of Don Revie's make-up, because he was rather a superstitious individual and he quite liked us wearing that kit because I don't think we lost that many games in the yellow kit. Every opportunity he got, if he got a chance to change, and it didn't clash with anything – which it wasn't going to – then we'd go to the yellow kit."

Leeds had effectively established themselves as a team that wore two different strips: all white at home and all yellow away, irrespective of colour clashes. It was a trend that Admiral was able to exploit by marketing both sets of strips, with the yellow shirt "outselling the white one," such was its appeal, remembers Hunter. As I prepare to leave the former England international's home, he's still shaking his head and smiling ruefully. "'Norman bites yer legs', and my punch-up with Francis Lee, those were the two things – and messing the goal up against Poland – those were the three things that people remember about me." Ah yes, the Poland game. We'll be coming to that in the next chapter, Norman.

Directly across the road from Admiral's old Long Street factory is Neville Chadwick's photography studio. When the genial octogenarian emerges from an upstairs office, he's instantly recognisable as the 'snapper' who regularly patrolled Filbert Street's touchline before the Premier League era. A period in which his own business orbited the world of Admiral by acting as its official photographer on a weekly, if not daily basis. After a brief reminisce, Nev leads me along a shiny corridor with rows of metal roller cabinets operated by gearwheels at the end of each rack. Quite fittingly, the archive is just the type you find in library vaults housing precious historical documents and records.

"There's probably a million pictures filed away here," he tells me, wheeling back a cabinet to reveal a fraction of what 50 years' worth of prints and transparencies looks like. "We did have a staff of eleven working here, with six photographers working every day, so it soon adds up. So, well over a million pictures, but we've never counted them." When I emerge from my sense of wonder, I ask him about numbers relating to his old client from across the road. "What, for Admiral alone? You're talking the hundred thousands."

Nev had always been a sports photographer, starting out at the local *Evening Mail*, which is where he met Bert who was a junior reporter. The two friends teamed up again when the *Mail* closed and Bert took over Cook & Hurst, which is how he came to chronicle Admiral's meteoric rise, he tells me by way of explaining the treasure trove in front of us.

"They've got their own filing-cabinet section," Nev indicates towards the far end of a row and begins pulling out drawers crammed with suspension files. His fingers flick across the tops of the green folders, partially pulling out random prints, offering brief glimpses of tantalisingly familiar images that once appeared in the *Shoot!* magazines of my childhood. "Every time Admiral teams were playing each other, we photographed them for action pictures." Nev holds a contact sheet up to the light before announcing, "These are of the Leeds teams, all the Leeds teams."

The first colour print he shows me is a team group taken on one of his first trips to Elland Road. The image is instantly recognisable, as are the names of the players beaming back at the camera in their bright yellow strips.

As one of the club's official sponsors, Admiral was given exclusive access to photograph the players inside the stadium during the pre-season press day. "All the players neat and smart and all looking at the camera, nobody fooling about at all," explained Nev. Meanwhile, a second photocall was arranged for the national press later in the day outside by the training pitch – during which sessions the players were strangely, perhaps suspiciously less compliant. "You've got two of them having a little chat together. And there was always somebody looking away. And why? Well, obviously, they didn't want that picture to be the greatest picture. They wanted our team group to be the best because that one was going to be sold..." And so add a little more Admiral money into the players' pool set up by Revie to reward his players.

The next image Nev pulls from his extraordinary archive is a black-and-white print he declares is the very first photograph he ever took for Cook & Hurst in 1973: Leicester City's Peter Shilton striding purposefully towards camera. He looks every inch like Colonel Steve Austin from *The Six Million Dollar Man* TV series, in a tracksuit top with 'Admiral' writ large across the chest. The keeper had agreed a promotional tie-in the year before his record transfer-fee move to Stoke City, which despite the hefty £325,000 valuation, still fell somewhat well short of Lee Major's all-action hero's price tag.

Bert told me he'd previously shied away from sponsoring individual players, despite being offered the services of high-profile stars such as George Best, mainly because sportsmen and women were susceptible to injury or loss of form. Also, some were notorious in football circles for having very little appetite for endorsement duties once their sponsor's cheque had cleared, but local lad Peter Shilton was full of enthusiasm according to Bert, who signed him up to become the firm's first "brand ambassador" – a partnership that earned the keeper an extra £1,000 a year, and also led to the well-known gambler owning a racehorse called Admiral Jersey, even if the gelding did turn out to be "hopeless."

Filbert Street, Leicester, August 1974

Leicester City's playing strips were supplied by Admiral at this time, albeit without the 'designer' touches – though the manufacturer's branding was becoming more overt, and changes were clearly afoot. During press day on the eve of the new First Division season in August 1974, Shilton's green goalkeeping jersey was noticeably adorned with a single nautical logo opposite the club's crest, and the firm would push its branding even further once the campaign started.

Admiral

Peter Shilton originals tracksuits
for boys and youths. As worn by the England goalkeeper himself. 100% stretch nylon. Hard-wearing, easy to wash, non shrink, 12 month 'fair wear' guarantee. Contrast pants with linking stripes. Roll necks. Peter Shilton crest. Small boys, boys and youths. (See tracksuit measurement chart.)

Goalkeepers jerseys
personally designed by England's Number One keeper. 100% cellular nylon. Snug fit turtle neck. Non-restricting sleeves. Peter Shilton badge on chest. Colour choice now includes Peter's famous all-white version. Small boys, boys, youths, small men's, men's, large.

Complete Gift Pack
contains white PS jersey with matching white shorts and socks plus black knitted gloves. Full size range.

Goalkeepers' jerseys at that time were universally green, or yellow for international matches, and that was pretty much it. As strange as it sounds now, the thought of adding a couple of stripes to the underarm seams or choosing an unconventional palette was considered 'revolutionary'.

"I was fiddling about with the *Football League Handbook*, and it said at the back the approved colours for goalkeepers jerseys: they could wear green, blue, red and white." Jon Holmes was the keeper's agent, and knew exactly what to do to increase his rising star's exposure. "I said to Shilts, 'Y'know what? You can wear a white jersey next year.' And that was a good gimmick, because nobody wore white jerseys. So, we went for the all-white kit."

Working together with Bert and John, agent and client launched a personalised range of colourful new outfits, marketed with the England shotstopper's name and image. "It was very exciting," remembers Shilton, because it "was quite forward thinking. Obviously, this management team wanted to build a big business, and they wanted me to be part of it." He admits he jumped at the chance of working with the Wigston bosses, not least because their ideas chimed with his own interests. "Being a local company, it was special. I could go up and visit them. I could chat and share ideas of mine on a regular basis."

"Peter came in," John confirms, "and we agreed we'd make him a shirt in white, which he was keen on."

The result was a white roll-neck top adorned with its very own badge featuring the initials 'PS' underneath Admiral's own naval emblem. It was an audacious move on the manufacturer's part to generate some noise in the press – which it did, of course, along with a frisson of excitement in playgrounds across the land. In what was to become a recurring theme, Admiral benefited from a huge slice of good fortune when Shilts debuted his new look under the Filbert Street floodlights against Manchester United, with the BBC's *Sportsnight* cameras in attendance to help create even more of a stir.

With more than a whiff of 'space-age' glamour, and aided and abetted by the likes of *Shoot!* magazine, the jerseys proved eminently desirable.

Follow the City!

Team up with Admiral soccer strip.
Latest-style jerseys, socks, shorts, and tracksuits. Plus the spectacular new **Peter Shilton** goalkeepers jerseys.
Cook & Hurst (Admiral Sport) Long Street, Wigston Magna, Leicester LE8 2BQ. Telephone Leicester 881302

Admiral

I, like many avid young readers, duly entered a competition to win one of the '12 Peter Shilton jerseys' up for grabs. Needless to say, I wasn't one of the lucky recipients, and the only time I got my hands on one of the white 'PS' replica jerseys was 40 years later, having borrowed a now-yellowing child-sized top to take along for Shilton to comment on when I interviewed England's record appearance holder:

"We decided to have a goalkeeping pack – shirt, shorts and socks – which was unheard of, the first goalkeeping pack that was ever brought out. I had a couple of ideas before that; but the Football League at the time were very adamant that there was nothing going to be added to kit. They banned the stripes under the arms. They banned the buttons added to the neck so it could be worn on a hot day as an open neck. They banned the zip added so you could use it as a roll-neck in really wet and windy days in the winter. They said they were too dangerous, when in fact in those days we used to play in all conditions."

The goalkeeping sets helped the ambitious young keeper to "stand out from

The dawn of an era: Peter Shilton leads the way in the logo stakes.

the crowd," and "Shilton cut quite a majestic figure in his all-white Leicester strip," according to the authors of *Glove Story*, which focuses on goalkeeper culture and collectables. There were also other natty versions of the 'PS' jerseys in red, blue, and black and amber, as well as a startling *Thunderbirds*-style design the authors unearthed, this time in black with a broad red and green diagonal sash.

Shilton's all-white kit is one of the things I remember from my very first outing to Filbert Street in January 1974, another being West Ham United's Clyde Best, one of the English game's few black players, belting the ball past the goalie in front of the massive Double Decker stand. Not that everybody was as wowed by the goalie's lustrous new outfit as much as this eight-year-old schoolboy. According to Shilton, whenever "I'd dived, people would say, 'Oh, it used to look a bit of a mess,' which was a load of rubbish, but it just gave them ammunition again to have a go. I think some person said it was like a clown's outfit for the kids."

Later that season, the keeper's pearly get-up came under more serious scrutiny. Shilton was between the sticks as usual during City's defeat to Liverpool in an FA Cup semi-final replay, illuminated under the Villa Park floodlights. The white outfit is often cited as the reason why the Reds' number seven was able to spot him off his line and lob the keeper from 30 yards. Shilton refutes this theory and says, "There was a real long ball down the middle, and I remember seeing Kevin Keegan running through, and this ball was dropping down with snow on it, and I think Kevin was being closed in by a couple of defenders. I started to come out because I thought the odds are 98 per cent certain he won't try a volley first time, which history proves he did. And the great Jimmy Hill made a comment that he thought Kevin Keegan had looked up, saw me off my line, and chipped it over me, which I thought was quite ridiculous at the time. It wasn't the chip, it was a fierce volley. And so, people did start to take advantage of the fact that it was different, but to me it was unfair to do that."

Following the success of both the Shilton and Leeds United replicas, Bert and John realised they were on to something, and the pair began looking around for other clubs to sponsor. But they trod carefully, particularly in the North West and London where Umbro was all powerful. Through a network of retailers, the Cheshire company provided clubs with a bespoke service, including supplying Adidas footwear, by dint of being the West German boot makers' only UK distributor at the time.

Even so, according to Bert, his Wigston firm was the country's leading supplier of the generic, blank teamwear still used by most professional clubs. This put Admiral in pole position to move quickly, which it did by signing up existing customers Brighton & Hove Albion, Kilmarnock, Luton Town and Port Vale – along with Queens Park Rangers.

The west London club now cut a dash in broad horizontal hoops, coolly augmented by shorts sporting a single thick stripe. But it was at Vale Park that Admiral's designers first made a shocking impression by quite literally wearing their American-inspired sports influences on their sleeves. The Valiants' stripy new outfit was an apparent homage to baseball, if not to Elton John's outrageous stage attire, or perhaps mint humbugs. A goal kick away across the Potteries, Shilton's new club Stoke City had also jumped aboard, with a revamped home strip that attracted far less fuss. But if City's traditional red and white home stripes lacked pizzazz, a dazzling array of away colours provided ample compensation, with dramatic multi-striped sashes decorating the jerseys – including an unforgettable black and turquoise on bright yellow option.

In his book, *Kit Man: All for the Shirt*, Bert recalls how Luton Town were "itching to create a new image," and he describes how Admiral helped the club to become more recognisable by changing its identity. The team's traditional, minimalist white and black playing colours were superseded by a far racier orange and navy outfit with stripes. The overhaul also included a new, modernised club badge, which, in Bert's words, "created a lot of publicity" for the Bedfordshire team.

It's a hackneyed phrase, but these really were halcyon days for those in Admiral's sphere, providing opportunities to mix with famous players and

celebrity fans. Neville Chadwick handed me one of the photos he took during a visit to Kenilworth Road. "We never had to ask the players to smile," he said. "Sitting right in the centre was the famous comedian Eric Morecambe, who was the director of Luton Town, and he kept them smiling with his jokes all the time. Eric, right in the centre, there."

Admiral also approached clubs outside of the top tier, even though they generally had smaller fan bases, offering less potential for replica kit sales. As Bert explains, "Harry Swales, who was a well-known football agent with an involvement with Leeds United, came to see me. He said, 'If you've got any work you want me to do...' I said, 'Well yes, go out and sign up all the lower divisions, the Second, Third and Fourth Divisions.' And he did quite a big job on that, and of course the deal was sometimes just a free kit, because up 'til then, years previously, a club would have to pay for its kit." As a marketing strategy this policy worked brilliantly, but proved less successful as a business model, which we'll come on to later.

For now, though, the firm's stock was rising, and we were afforded a glimpse into the future of an evolving relationship between clubs and suppliers, still in its infancy. Admiral was also Newcastle United's kit manufacturer, who had demurred from a having a full Wigston makeover in favour of sticking with their traditional style of outfit that remained unbranded. But when a Malcolm MacDonald-inspired Magpies muscled their way past Burnley at Hillsborough to reach the 1974 FA Cup final, Bert and John saw an opportunity to cash in. It resulted in a run of 'youth' and 'small man'-sized replicas that found their way to a number of Tyneside outlets. Famously, a photo of two Geordies in the crowd on Cup Final day is now recognised as the first documentary evidence of fans wearing replica kit at any match – having squeezed their adult frames into tight-fitting black and white striped shirts for the big occasion.

The object of Admiral signing up as many teams as possible was of course to get its adventurous new strips and naval logos noticed by children. "We did research in the schools, particularly locally here in Wigston." Bert clearly knew his audience, and he made no bones about who his company was making their kits for. "We had to know what would sell. We would design a kit that didn't belittle the tradition of the club, and then we would think, 'Well, will it sell? Will it sell to kids?'"

Rob O'Donnell was seven years old and living in Wigston when the new designs first began to appear on the market. "It was so unique, the football kits used to be very bland, very plain. And then suddenly Admiral came along with their badges, and bigger collars with the lines on them. It was revolutionary in its day. Suddenly, kids were exposed to a new, exciting football kit that they'd never had before. There were Umbro kits out there but they were very plain, very dull. At that point they were always second best. You'd watch Liverpool on *Match of the Day*, and it wasn't Admiral, at the end of the day."

Bert's prediction about young fans wanting to collect football shirts in the way previous generations saved cigarette cards certainly applies to Rob, who has amassed an impressive array of jerseys. Fishing out a favourite replica shirt he wore as a child, he holds it aloft for inspection. "West Ham would've worn just a plain white shirt before this, but then suddenly you've got the big collars and the colour and the badges. It was fabulous, a brilliant shirt."

By the middle of the decade Admiral was incorporating scores of tiny nautical badges into its designs, and logo taping appeared down the sides of sleeves and shorts, as well as around sock tops, along V-necks and atop of collars. Most bizarrely of all, the little logos punctuated a pair of epaulettes on the Leicester City jersey now in Rob's hands. "And that one I remember getting for Christmas," he says, carefully unfolding what clearly remains one of his most prized possessions.

The wonder and awe inspired by the new replica strips was not solely confined to LE postcodes. "My best mate was a big Man United fan. When he came to school that day sporting this great white shirt with the black stripes going down the front, I was a bit jealous – far more style than my plain Liverpool Umbro strip." Visiting Peris Hatton's North Wales home is like entering a 1970s sports shop. Laid out for my benefit is an array of vintage replica football kits, many in their original boxes and packaging. Ever since he bought his first jersey as a child in the late 1970s, Peris has also been collecting replica shirts – of all manufacturers, not just Admiral.

"Without any doubt, looking through some of the designs that came out, Admiral stole the march on everyone." Peris is gleefully holding up a child's version of the white away shirt supplied to Manchester United. His appreciation remains undimmed of what remains a hugely popular and iconic jersey. One that instantly recalls the swashbuckling football played under manager Tommy Docherty. "This effort from 1976/77 for Manchester United, again having these asymmetric stripes, broke all the design moulds. And to complement that, what a great present to have on your birthday, or on Christmas morning, to get the matching tracksuit. And with this you could get the shorts, which were badged up, and the matching socks as well. Nowadays, you take for granted all these items, but back then, in '76, '77, '78, these really were the first kits of their kind."

Those children running around in Admiral kits, and perhaps equally importantly those that weren't, knew they had an official club strip on their backs. Identical in every way to the ones worn by their heroes on the pitch and on TV. "So it enabled fans to really closely connect with their club, in a way that arguably they'd never done before" says John Devlin. "So if you go to the park after school in an Admiral shirt, you could almost think for a moment that you *are* that player."

It's a significant point, and one also identified by fellow football-strip aficionado Peris. "When you put it on you just think, 'Wow, I've got a proper shirt here.' You finally had a shirt with a team badge on. Gosh, we felt special, we felt proud. I wanted to be identified as, 'I support this team', not the team that wore similar colours – and that, for me, is the difference Admiral made at the time." The genie was well and truly out of the bottle. "It caught everyone's imagination.

Overnight, it seemed we had this special kit with the badge on. And from three or four or five of us wearing the football shirts, it almost became unfashionable to go to school or be on the playground without a football shirt on."

As another indicator of who the new designs were really aimed at, Peter Shilton told me, "It was the start of the players having to wear kit, probably they didn't want to because it was too bright. And, all of a sudden, certain players who were used to plain kits were probably not agreeing with having to wear the kit; but the clubs were making money." At Leeds and Luton the players benefitted directly from Admiral's sponsorship, with the cash from replica sales being paid into a shared pool. Meanwhile, at QPR, Admiral's cash was claimed by the club secretary instead, prompting a revolt in which, 'the players thought they were entitled to a share, and refused to wear the kit', according to *Football News* magazine. Apparently, the Loftus Road stars only called off their threatened strike after the club's hierarchy backed down and agreed to share their kit bonus.

Looking back, it appears the early to mid '70s was football's commercial tipping point. Seemingly on the cusp of modernisation throughout the 'swinging '60s', the game finally experienced a financial gear shift during the following decade. When my dad first started taking me to games around this time, an oft-repeated refrain I'd hear was, "It's not a sport any more, it's a business." Sentiments echoed by former England striker Mick Channon, who told me, "The whole world changed, from the '60s when I started, through 'til the late '70s. The commercialism just wasn't there, but it's gradually come in. Admiral could go along to a club and say, 'Look, we will pay you this large sum of money', proportionally speaking now, 'for the exclusive rights to supply your kit.' It was never heard of before that time, but I can imagine that a large cheque would sway a lot of the club's opinions."

That's exactly what happened over the next few years as Admiral took advantage of an unprecedented array of money-making opportunities suddenly opening up to the firm. For Bert, surveying the virgin territory ahead of him, he admits it was a matter of getting through as many club doors as possible. "No merchandising, very little marketing, and the retailers in sports, they were very happy in that situation, because when we first started changing the kits perhaps every three years, there was a big outcry from the retailers who claimed they were being stuck with the stock of the old kits."

These were mere gripes though, simply the first shots fired in the coming battle between the game's modernisers and its Corinthian old guard. Admiral critics' greatest ire would be reserved for the perceived desecration of one of football's sacrosanct totems: England's pure white jerseys.

Whether what happened next is best described as fate, destiny or just pure luck, is up for conjecture. A momentous act of serendipity perhaps, triggering a chain of events that neither Bert nor John could have possibly foreseen or ever imagined. In October 1973, as they were exchanging contracts on a groundbreaking new sponsorship deal with Don Revie, the fate of the national coach he would soon replace was also effectively sealed.

England's inability to fashion a victory in their final 'win-or-bust' qualifier signalled the end of the side's 1974 World Cup campaign, and manager Alf Ramsey's position. It was a night not easily forgotten by Norman Hunter, as we've already heard. And Peter Shilton remains similarly haunted.

On a bitterly cold Wembley evening, Hunter's missed tackle on the halfway line allowed Robert Gadocha to break free on the left, and set up Jan Domarski for a low shot that squirmed under Shilton's dive. England equalised soon afterwards and, in a heavily one-sided game that they had been expected to win comfortably, Ramsey's side created a string of good chances without reward. Wave after wave of frantic attacks were thwarted time and again by a combination of heroic defending, inspired goalkeeping and desperate misfortune. Besides four goalbound efforts scrambled off the Polish line, Mick Channon's seemingly legitimate 'goal' was disallowed for a harsh handball decision against Allan Clarke. It clearly wasn't going to be England's night. Keeper Jan Tomaszewski managed to get in the way of everything else that was thrown at him, and his woodwork also came to the rescue twice as Poland hung on for 1-1 draw.

It was a result served up with a large dollop of humble pie after Brian Clough had famously called the ŁKS Łódź shotstopper "a circus clown wearing gloves" live on TV before kick-off. Commentator Hugh Johns described the fruitless draw and subsequent fallout as "one of England's blackest days," while the *Daily Mirror* declared it 'England's Night of Tragedy'. Only Martin Peters remained of the team that had lifted the Jules Rimet Trophy in the same stadium just seven years earlier, and Ramsey's time was clearly also up. The Football Association's next appointment, it was agreed, should be a moderniser with fresh ideas: a coach like Don Revie.

Cook & Hurst's prospects and the future of its sportswear brand changed irrevocably in the summer of 1974. John Griffin was now operating as Admiral's MD, and he remembers his first conversation with new England manager Don Revie vividly. "'I want a complete change.' He said he wanted a new strip; he was not going to sing the National Anthem, he was going to sing 'Land of Hope and Glory'. He gave me all this profile, and he said, 'There will be an international meeting.' I think it was in about ten days. He said, 'So you've got to come in and show us what you've got.'" John was acutely aware of what was being asked of him and his team, as well as what was at stake.

But selling Admiral and its designs to the FA would be no mean feat. The grey mandarins running English football's governing bodies were hardly renowned for their openness to change. In the run-up to England's 'must-win' game against Poland, Ramsey's request to reschedule a few domestic fixtures the weekend beforehand was met with a point-blank refusal from the Football League. Chairman Alan Hardaker reportedly reminded the World Cup-winning coach that, "It is a football match, not a war." This was the type of environment that Bert and John realised they'd be walking into when facing the FA's International Committee, offering to brighten up and add their own logo to a jersey that had remained unaltered and unadorned for the entirety of its 98-year existence.

Back in Wigston, John had less than two weeks to prepare a set of samples, and was busily "getting several heads together in the factory, the designers, supervisors and myself actually deciding how much we could get away with – the amount of change that the hierarchy in Lancaster Gate would accept. Anyway, we got a good collection together, and I was pleased with the garments that I was able to show them."

Despite its conservative reputation, there was a genuine desire for change among some, if not all of the FA's bureaucrats. Revie's appointment was supported by the new General Secretary Ted Croker, who reveals in his autobiography that he was "excited" by the coach's track record. Even if some of his ideas, like the introduction of 'Land of Hope and Glory' as rousing team anthem ultimately offered little of the former and none of the latter. Despite Revie's encouragement, Bert and John travelled to London with a certain amount of trepidation, and were aware that other manufacturers, such as Dunlop, had also been invited along to bid. They also knew they'd only get one shot at pitching to the all-male board, led by the notoriously brusque Harold Thompson.

Bert's worst fears proved unfounded, and he told *Football News* magazine that the FA "were up for it really, the timing was perfect." And, as was becoming a common occurrence, he managed to benefit from another slice of good fortune. "Ted Croker and Don Revie were quite keen for us to get the contract, because they knew how successful we'd been so far, so we'd put the kit in front of the committee, they liked it. One of the committee stalwarts was Len Shipman who was chairman of Leicester City, and he said, 'Mr Patrick's a Leicester lad, with a Leicester factory, he employs Leicester people, and that's good enough for me. I want to see him have the contract.' The others didn't disagree. Revie told them that at Leeds we'd looked after the club, and there'd been no problems, so really it was a *fait accompli*. Fortunately, the chairman wasn't there, Sir Harold Thompson, who – years later, I realised – might have caused problems for me. He was a real traditionalist."

Crucially for the Admiral bosses, it was agreed without any serious objections that their company's own logo would also appear on the chest of the new shirts opposite England's Three Lions badge. "They looked over them, and I ended up actually having to model one and stand on the table," recounts John, who became

INSIDE THE FOOTBALL ASSOCIATION HQ AT LANCASTER GATE...

"the first person to wear the new England kit."

Having cleared the first hurdle, the two Admiral bosses pressed on by outlining their offer; but negotiations proved trickier than anticipated, says Bert. "Very difficult, I had to really pull the stops out, and of course I didn't want to make it too much of an offer in terms of money because I really wanted to get on to a royalty situation."

Sweet FA: England sign with Admiral, Sheffield, 21st October 1974.

Admiral offered England similar terms to those they had agreed with Leeds United, but this time the annual fee was increased to £15,000, and an additional five per cent sales bonus was agreed for the next five years. Further add-ons, dependent on how successful England would prove to be under Revie, included £10,000 for qualifying for the next World Cup finals, and a further £50,000 bonus for actually winning the tournament in Argentina. The International Committee ratified the agreement and Bert announced to the press that Admiral had won the contract, "purely and simply because we had made the best offer."

John says he didn't have to wait long to find out whether the pair's latest deal would prove successful or not. Within minutes of the meeting breaking up, "Matt Busby came up to me. 'You know lad, you ought to come and see us, because we're bigger than England,' he said. 'If you come up to see us in about two weeks,' he said, 'tell my secretary you're for a good day.' And I just couldn't believe it."

Adding Manchester United to Admiral's roster of teams, which already now included England and Leeds United, would indeed prove another major coup for the manufacturer. It was another early indicator that the red, white and blue touchpaper had been lit – and was about to lead to an almighty explosion.

CHAPTER 4
All I Want is You

In the BBC's time-travelling drama *Life on Mars*, John Simm's Detective Inspector Sam Tyler is transported back to the Manchester streets of his childhood. All leads on the *Get Shirty* investigation took me back to the Leicester suburbs of 1974. Like many 1970s-set productions, *Life on Mars* went big on wing collars and garish brown and orange patterned wallpaper. Many factual accounts use a similar shorthand to depict an era of shortages and bitter pay disputes, but I remember it only as a great time. I can recall nightly power cuts, most likely because they were the signal to start playing shadow puppets by candlelight, once the telly and everything else had ground to a halt. Coverage of Northern Ireland's 'Troubles' and the deadly Birmingham pub bombings stick in my mind, as does the mysterious disappearance of Lord Lucan. Then there were those terrifying public information films warning against the perils of 'dark and lonely water' and deadly electricity pylons waiting to strike with 66,000 volts. Around the same time, psychic spoon bender Uri Geller was responsible for thousands of unexplained cases of misshapen cutlery in school dining halls across the country.

It was a time of rising home ownership and consumer spending, during which my own family also moved out of rented accommodation. To mark our new upwardly mobile status and to ring the changes, Mum announced that from now on we would be sleeping under 'continental quilts' rather than blankets. An infinitely more successful idea than the Smash instant mashed potato also being trialled in the Wells household. The glorious *Porridge, Rising Damp* and *The Sweeney* made their TV debuts in 1974, as did *Opportunity Knocks*-winning schoolgirl Lena Zavaroni, performing 'Ma! He's Making Eyes at Me'.

It was also the year my sister and I were taken along to see the Wombles perform their top ten single 'Remember You're A Womble' from the back of a flatbed truck, my sister proudly wearing a Womble-style *faux* fur bomber jacket, bought from C&A especially for the occasion. The hirsute rubbish collectors from SW19 weren't the only visitors to hit town on the back of a lorry. I also harbour vague memories of a pungent, dead 70-foot whale being paraded around the local area for people to gawp at. I haven't a clue as to how or why, but I do also remember walking up to inspect the unfortunate beast in closer detail, after spotting it parked up overnight behind a bingo hall.

More importantly, after months of pleading, my dad had started taking me to Leicester City games. No longer would I watch forlornly as the family 'Caribbean turquoise' Ford Anglia disappeared into the winter gloom every other Saturday. On reflection, I think perhaps I was taken along as compensation for the family missing out on a three-year return to Cyprus following the Turkish invasion. A postponement that saw my dad swap Mediterranean sunshine for the rain-soaked and equally war-torn streets of Belfast. Still, there were some advantages to my family staying put in Leicester, chief among them being regular visits to Filbert Street when Warrant Officer Wells returned from his posting 'across the sea'. Thank you, Dad.

1974 was also marked by a dispute at the city's Imperial Typewriter Company headquarters, which attracted the attentions of the national media as well as far-right agitators. Two years earlier, Uganda's President Idi Amin had expelled most of the country's Asian and European populations, resulting in around 6,000 refugees settling in Leicester. Many found work at the Litton-owned factory, where the sacking of 40 Ugandan workers sparked a three-month strike due to grievances including 'bad working conditions, alleged racial discrimination and unpaid bonuses,' according to Leicester historian Stephen Butt. The action was exploited opportunistically by the National Front at local elections, where they managed to win almost 20 per cent of the votes by falsely claiming low-paid immigrants were taking local jobs.

It was also a significant year as far as the managers and workers at Cook & Hurst were concerned, with the firm having landed the biggest contract in its history. The licensing deal struck between Admiral Sports and the FA to produce and sell replica England kits was a watershed moment, both for the company and for sportswear generally.

It was a deal described as "revolutionary" by former England striker Mick Channon, who says manager Don Revie was determined to replicate the success he'd achieved at Leeds, and set about transforming the England set-up from top to bottom. He "wanted to change everything – the system, the preparation to a game, the kit. He wanted a new broom swept clean. And Admiral happened to be in the right place at the right time."

For a business that had been making limited runs of underwear for the clergy just a decade earlier, it was an extraordinary achievement and a wonderful piece of business. A defining moment that made people sit up and take notice of a company that was still very modest, operationally at least.

Football kit historian John Devlin says, "The first England deal with Admiral really shook things up," because it's one thing to change the playing strip of a domestic club like Leeds United and quite another to alter the traditional nature of the national side's strip. "Look how these pure white, unadulterated jerseys had been changed and designed, for them to be coming out with these brightly coloured blues. Gone was the navy blue that always accompanied the England shirts. We're looking at a bright royal blue, we're looking at bright red as well – and the response wasn't good. They were often referred to as 'clown strips' at various times by the commentators and the pundits. It wasn't a popular move, but again it was beginning to become about generating income, there's no doubt that the Admiral deal did that."

Apart from a different type of collar, the new England strip was more or less the same design as Leeds United's yellow away strip, launched earlier that year. Designer Paul Oakley describes the template as "subdued," and compared to how he would go on to restyle England's outfit six years later, it most certainly was. As well as changing the outfield strip, Wigston's creatives also introduced a distinct goalkeeper's kit, which retained its yellow jersey but was now adorned with a button-up wing collar, two black stripes along the sleeves and black elasticated cuffs. And instead of wearing the same shorts and socks as the rest of the team, England goalies would from now on wear black shorts and socks with yellow trim.

According to Paul, Admiral's thinking centred around the creation of a concept or a philosophy as much as a new set of football strips. "No one else had done it, and no one else was relating the product to a brand. You just assumed that they were made by

somebody, and that's it. You didn't care. But then it became part of the identity, so the brand became part of the England identity. And so if you supported England, you supported what they wore and what they wore was Admiral, and therefore it was all part of the same image."

Photographer Neville Chadwick, who worked out of the same building as Paul, concurs, and says, "Admiral and England went together. And if they were talking about Admiral, they were talking about England."

The most obvious and visible example of Admiral's association with the FA was the prominence of its name and logo across England's teamwear. The track tops players warmed up in were emblazoned with the word 'Admiral' writ large across their chests, and the company's trademark emblem covered the back of the jackets. The nautical logo also popped up on holdalls, and Bert told me these received lots of exposure under the Wembley floodlights whenever a physio ran on to the pitch to treat an injured player – with bags placed strategically alongside stricken players, often in full view of a live television audience for minutes on end. It afforded the little-known Leicester company a huge amount of kudos that helped to open even more doors.

SOCCERSTYLES 1975/76

Traditionalists were of course appalled, both by the very act of England entering into a sponsorship deal of any kind, and by the look of the jazzed-up strips. *Football News* magazine reported that, 'bringing such dealings into the untarnished limelight of the England national team was... unheard of and unnecessary'.

Former players turned tabloid columnists lined up to have their say, including Danny Blanchflower in the *Sunday Express*, who claimed, "We cannot approve of a manufacturer's name emblazoned across the England strip. If the FA took £200,000 at the gate, surely they can buy a strip of their own." According to Jimmy Greaves, the "break with tradition" was "hideous" and "they look as if they're playing in pyjamas. I hate it."

With a wry smile, Bert remembers "the press were very critical," but says he was surprised by Greavsie's outrage, "because Jimmy had a sports shop, and was buying lots of the kit," from Admiral. Some criticism was aimed directly at the Wigston firm for having effectively monetised the national team jersey – or so the argument went. Previously, any child could run around in a plain white T-shirt and pretend to be playing for England; but this was no longer the case.

Admiral's kits were meant to look different, of course. That was the whole point, as John Devlin explains: "When the kids saw these new designs, and saw the way it was marketed, to look exactly like their heroes, they weren't just wearing any old plain white top. It was a completely different look. It was dangling this carrot of exclusivity. You had to look like these players. So the price rise, that was part and parcel of it."

The main bone of the contention in many people's opinion was the cost of the branded kits, with a complete set of jersey, shorts and socks retailing from between £9.25 and £12.50, or about a third of the average weekly wage. It was certainly beyond the means of many families, including my own, and Paul says he had a certain amount of sympathy for parents with football-mad children. "It was fair comment that it was expensive relative to a cheap white shirt you could've put on and said was an England shirt, but obviously the manufacturing costs were higher and the sponsorship fees had to be paid by somebody. We have to remember that people weren't used to paying for that. But as we know today, kids just love replicas and branded goods." They were fairly smitten 40 years ago as well, and despite there being less expendable income about, the new England jerseys proved best sellers.

Bert too concedes that his critics had a case, up to a point, when it came to the cost of the kits. "You usually find you have to pay for fashion, particularly if it's exclusive, and we were letting it be known that we were putting money back into football, particularly when it came to the England deal, because that's what the members of the committee were saying: 'Admiral are putting money back into the game.' And really nobody, particularly in my industry, had done that before."

On the same theme, Richard Benson told *Esquire* that before the Admiral deal came along, the FA had fallen woefully short of its earning potential. "In 1973, England earned £24,000 in commercial enterprises and royalties that, 40 years

later, would see commercial enterprises making a reported £27 million." And he attributed the catalyst for that rise to the first Admiral deal.

The furore over kit prices prompted legendary *Sunday Times* editor Harold Evans, renowned for his campaigning and investigative journalism, to dispatch a couple of reporters to Wigston.

John told me, "They were trying actually to understand the 'rip-off', as they said. So the only analogy I could make was, 'Do you like Tom Jones?' And one of them said yes, and I said, 'Well, if his next album comes out, will you buy it?' He said, 'Yes, I will.' But I said, 'If another album comes out with cover versions, much cheaper, will you buy that?' No, he wanted... I said, 'Well, you know, think on this.' And I excused myself. It was a Friday afternoon, that was the only thing I could think of to get rid of them."

Whilst Admiral was taking flak for the cost of its kits, John points out that retailers were being given a free pass. "It wasn't fair comment and nobody really has tried to explain it. We, as a company, we bought the components in, and we made the garment, and we costed the garment out, and then we put on a percentage for England, which was five per cent. And then – nobody really challenged this – it went to the retailers, who put 60 or 70 per cent on it, and all the media didn't touch the retailers. We had a recommended selling price but some of them went their own way. In their own area they sensed they could get more money, because the demand was instant."

Bert and John maintained that all publicity was good for business, even negative coverage, but I suspect both were taken aback by the howls of disapproval towards the end of 1974. The pair's relationship with Don Revie had of course paid off spectacularly but it also fuelled speculation that their alliance was in some way tarnished. By bagging the lucrative England kit contract, seemingly so easily and so soon after the Leeds deal, surely meant some sort of impropriety must have occurred? This suspicion arose despite public reassurances from Ted Croker, who told reporters that all business had been conducted above board, dismissing suggestions Revie had benefitted personally.

Denying any wrongdoing, the Yorkshireman told *The Guardian*, "I've never taken a penny from a sports goods company in my 15 years at Leeds, nor since I took the England job." The paper described him as 'one of the first people in England to recognise the commercial opportunities the game offered', and claimed that in accepting sponsorship, the FA's £250,000 five-year contract with Admiral had 'helped pay for Revie's salary, which had increased from the £8,000 paid to Sir Alf Ramsey to around £22,000'. A lot less than he'd been offered to stay at Elland Road, Revie replied pointedly.

Reiterating the point he had made earlier, John told me, "I was asked time and time by media how much did we pay him, and we paid him nothing. At Leeds, anything that they could get was for his players, and the same with England. He was very straight, and he gave [Admiral] two great opportunities."

Mick Channon was picked regularly for England by Revie, and he has an interesting and revealing take on his old boss's character. "Don Revie was a smashing bloke, I mean he was obsessed, he was football nuts. He was no different to Ted Bates or Bill Shankly, his life was football. And the only thing that mattered were the players and having the best for them. And listen, I had a lot of time for him; but you always knew, what can I say? He was always aware of where there was money to be made, whether it was in the Admiral kit or whether it was in moving to another club. He knew what footballers wanted, and basically he knew what the commercial side of the business wanted. He was probably ahead of his time in that sense, where he was the first manager that was aware that there was money to be made outside of football, and that's not a criticism."

Wembley Stadium, October 1974

England's new Revie era began on the pitch under the Wembley lights in the autumn, with both manager and Admiral taking their bows before a European Championship qualifier against Czechoslovakia. Optimism was as high in Wigston as it was at Lilleshall, where the squad was filmed earlier in the week being put through its paces dressed head to toe in heavily branded training wear. Images of the new playing strip had already been revealed beforehand amid much excitement, certainly among younger fans. The launch had included a photograph of a beaming schoolboy proudly wearing the full England kit in all its glory. Nobody had seen the kit before that photo-shoot, confirms Neville Chadwick: "My young lad, he was ten years old, Mark. He modelled the junior kit and we took him on to the local park, photographed it in black-and-white and colour, ready to send out to magazines and to local papers."

Children's replica England kits had already proved hugely popular, and coverage of the team's first outing in the outfit would surely boost sales further, ensuring they became one of the year's most sought-after Christmas presents. On the day of the game, Nev and his business partner John Plant arrived at Wembley around "three o'clock in the afternoon, just to photograph all the new Admiral kit in the dressing room of the England team. It was all laid out all around, everybody's kit and the boots and everything, and we were there just to photograph that. And then we stayed on to cover the match."

Captain Emlyn Hughes led his side out later that evening, accompanied by a booming rendition of 'Land of Hope and Glory', which Don Revie had decreed would now be England's rallying cry. Among the 83,000 crowd, John Griffin remembers "the walk out. And it did feel good, really thinking, 'What the hell have we started here?'"

Illuminated under Wembley's bright lights, England looked magnificent in their vivid red, white and blue outfits. Alongside the team, Nev was busily firing off shots of the players in their branded track tops. "It was a groundbreaking moment," he says, and "the fact that we were the Admiral photographers, we were allowed into the centre of the pitch to photograph the line-ups. And also into the centre when they did the handshake and the tossing of the coin, while all the other photographers had to stay back by the goals."

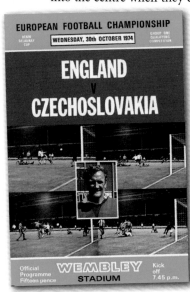

This exposure was subject to a certain amount of tut-tutting in the press, but from both Revie's and Admiral's perspective, the occasion was a huge success, as England ran out 3-0 winners. Goals from Mick Channon and a brace from Colin Bell in the final 20 minutes got Revie's first tournament campaign off to a perfect start. Even arch critic Brian Clough admitted the new coach "had done a superb job," even if he couldn't quite bring himself to mention his old nemesis by name.

"Then we drove back to Leicester, did all the processing, sent pictures out that night for local evening papers' use the next day, and also for national papers. We finished at four o'clock in the morning." And that, says Nev, "was our first day's work with the England team."

Kevin Keegan spoke out in favour of the new-look outfits, while others including Hughes were reportedly less enamoured with the rebrand, and it wasn't long before the wider mood soured. Firstly, UEFA stepped in to put a stop to England advertising the Admiral trademark on players' track tops at any future European Championship fixtures. By this time, many within the press corps had also made up their minds about the new boss and his innovations following a goalless draw against a modest Portugal side at Wembley. Five months after the Czech win,

under the banner 'England expects', sportswriter Frank Keating's verdict was in: "Revie's antics with Admiral – it was a shaming triumph for lucre when his first England team set forth at Wembley with Admiral plastered all over their backs... But for all his worthy record with Leeds, he needs to silence the buzz that is gathering around the international arenas, the insistence that he's a born loser."

The noise would build ever louder in the coming months, and the sponsorship deal Revie helped broker was often used as a stick to beat him with, irrespective of results. Channon says the sponsorship controversy was huge, and one the players were fully aware of at the time. It was "a massive shock to the system, Admiral coming in and shaking the whole sportswear business up. And it hit us like a whirlwind."

Another player who started for England that October night was Norman Hunter, who told me he had welcomed the change because he'd already experienced the benefits of wearing Admiral's lightweight fabrics. Not that Channon necessarily agreed, citing a very unusual injury he sometimes picked up whilst on international duty. "The quality wasn't there, it was shit compared with Adidas and Umbro. They weren't good, I always remember that some of them, it was like plastic. You run in them and you'd be so sore you'd want to get out the bloody things. And when you run, it just chafed your tits, basically. You come in at half-time, you have to put Vaseline on 'em. It did get better. But the

initial Admiral gear was crap, let's get it straight."

Channon acknowledges that there were benefits to clubs signing up with Admiral in the early days, most notably no longer having to wear the same set of shirt, short and socks for an entire season. "When I first went to Southampton, the old strips they'd be taken away, washed and they'd be out again next week. [Admiral] revolutionised the whole thing, they gave the sportswear people a kick up the backside. As I say, to start with, their quality was shit; but it got better as they got on, obviously, as they would do. If you can't learn from the feedback you'd be getting from professional footballers, because we were the biggest moaners, groaners, whingers you could ever come across."

Most ex-players I spoke to hadn't been paying too much attention to the impact Admiral was having on the sport, and why would they? Because, as Channon pointed out as I left his office, "The kit was just what you wore on the day, really. As a player you didn't take any notice of it, did you? Until they start roughing up your tits and things like that."

The former Saints striker is right, of course, Admiral's designer kits hadn't really been produced with professional players in mind, they'd been created for children to wear, including young fans like John Devlin.

The company's sales force "had access to every child in every playground," he says, thanks to blanket coverage of the national team, despite its recent failures to qualify for major tournaments. "In all the magazines at the time, colour TV that was just coming out, the marketplace just exploded for them. They had such visibility. That shop window, if you like."

With his nose pressed firmly up against the glazing was Rob O'Donnell, and hundreds of thousands of schoolboys just like him. "It was so revolutionary, it isn't like a new pair of trainers," he announces excitedly. "This was a massive change in design, a huge step. And so I think that was the appeal, it was so different to what was out there before."

Clapping eyes on these early Admiral kits during his formative years clearly had a profound effect on Rob, judging from his remarkably impressive collection of football shirts. Stored in crates and sealed in plastic bags, several are carefully unwrapped for my viewing pleasure, and laid out across a table for closer inspection. Reaching for a very well-worn piece of off-white polyester, he says, "I think England was probably the biggest one. Everybody wanted the England kit, that was the Holy Grail. But it was very expensive, I think it was five pounds at the time."

Despite the prohibitive cost, the headstrong young O'Donnell was clearly determined to get his hands on this most prized of playground possessions. He tells me about his wealthy auntie who lived overseas, and who always left £5 for her young nephew when she came to visit: "I was thinking great, I'm going to have my fiver and I'd get the England kit, so I was desperate for her to leave because then off I could go round to Roy Sports in Wigston." On the day his auntie said her farewells, seven-year-old Rob raced home from school, "and I can still remember looking on the mantelpiece and there was three pound there, and I thought, 'Oh, God.' I couldn't afford the England kit."

Despite the financial shortfall, all was not lost. Rob's mum had friends who worked at Cook & Hurst, including a woman called Sheila. One of the staff perks was access to the factory shop, which sold faulty and rejected garments cheaply, including, very occasionally, England shirts. "For weeks and weeks I was asking about England kit, and every day it wouldn't come. I finally come home one day and my mum says, 'Go upstairs, 'cos I've washed your tracksuit.' So I went upstairs and went to put my tracksuit on. I thought, 'Well it's still muddy, so how could she have washed it? What's going on?' So anyway, I was getting undressed and as I put my tracksuit on, there underneath was the England kit."

There's still a look of wonder on Rob's face as he tells this story, staring down at the small, itchy piece of fabric in front of him, 40 years on. "So, that's the England one, which I just wore to death. You've got something every kid wants, it's just a fantastic feeling. It was like gold dust, getting England kits because of the money, fantastic. I can still see it now, and I can still smell it to be honest with you. There was a smell to the Admiral kits, polyester or whatever it was." In my school, as in Rob's, "there were very few people that had them," but for the lucky kids that did, they'd rarely be off their backs. "You'd just wear it forever, you'd wear it every day, and it'd have to be washed that day if it got muddy because you'd need it that night." Just as Bert Patrick had predicted, the humble football jersey's transition, from a functional piece of sportswear to a desirable, premium fashion item, was gathering traction.

Perhaps one of the more surprising facets of the replicas' appeal was how the colourful new shirts appeared to transcend football's tribalism. When Bobby Brown first started working for Umbro in the mid 1970s, he remembers reporting back to his bosses to tell them there were kids running around Glasgow's parks in the tops of English First Division sides and Wales.

John Devlin had no qualms about coveting jerseys belonging to other nations or clubs either, such was the allure of Admiral. "I think there's this kind of authenticity about having the manufacturer's logo on the jersey that prior to that point hadn't existed, and I remember this as a little 'un as well – looking at the shirts, thinking, 'Well, I want that, not only has it got the club badge on it, it's got the company that made it on it.'" Such exclusivity may have come at a high price but that didn't make the jerseys any less of a "big deal" as far as John and thousands of other kids like him were concerned. "Some might say it gave parents another thing to worry about, in terms of supplying their child with the kit. But of course back then the kits didn't change that often... but they were certainly very, very popular."

Traditionally, it had always been the exception rather than the rule for children to own expensive toys and sports equipment, despite the hefty price tags. Admiral's early replica shirts were arguably to 1970s kids what pricy electronic devices are to today's youngsters; but it's a difficult comparison to equate in a world where most consumer needs are only a click away. Even if you don't have the budget for the real thing, there's a global marketplace at your fingertips that will most likely be able to sell you a cheaper, near-identical alternative. That wasn't the case in 1974. Not only was there less expendable income at the time, there also wasn't anything else around that came close to a 'real' England shirt.

As a consequence, Admiral was inundated with orders straight away, and demand soon outstripped supply as its factories struggled to produce enough football kits – a recurring problem with capacity that would hamstring the firm and its ambitions in the coming years.

Sadly, I never managed to track down Rob's fairy Admiral godmother, Sheila, but I was lucky enough to speak to several other women who worked on the factory floor. Everybody I spoke told me how busy they were once the 'football orders' started rolling in and, unlike other local employees, the workforce were never told to reduce their hours. Most also mentioned former supervisor Jean Atton, who appears to have fulfilled a role as tough taskmistress and Mother Hen, all rolled into one. Once interviewed for a television piece, she told ITV's reporter, "You've got a tremendous team work here, good workers. Because I believe there's only one way in doing a job, and that's the right way." Under her guidance, a group of her best machinists, referred to by Bert as 'Specials Department', was entrusted with producing the player-issued kits while the rank and file toiled away on the fiddly children's-sized polyester strips. Then, as now, players' kits were usually made to higher specs, either of cotton or a more generous cotton/nylon mix.

Machinist Jill Langton was a member of Jean's elite cadre. Whilst leafing through an old Admiral annual I've brought along to jog her memory, she tells me she, "loved them, proud when we did them. I told everybody I made that England kit," Jill says, pointing at an image of a bubble-permed Kevin Keegan. "We were a part of history, and glad to be part of the start of the revolution of football kits. It was exciting." Making the new England kits created a buzz around Wigston, and there was some kudos attached to working for Admiral, she adds. There was also a pride in seeing their collective work on national TV every weekend, but "I didn't make that one, there's a little stripe out," chuckles Jill, pointing to an imaginary screen.

"No other company was doing things like this," chips in former overlocker Mandy Hutchins, nodding towards the book in front of her. "Bringing a bit of sparkle and glamour to the kits, and I think that's what appealed to people."

One of the benefits of landing high-profile football contracts meant the company was able to attract more experienced employees. "It wasn't making stuff for Marks & Spencer," says John Griffin, by way of explanation. "We'd recruited a lot of people from the factories around, and it was a very good atmosphere." The phrase 'it was like a family' is often overused but it's one that continually crops up during my chats with ex-employees, including John. "It was nice, everybody

Admiral employees enjoy 15 minutes of fame at the local Saffron Lane athletics track.

was in good humour," and when work began on making the England replicas, "I would walk around at least once every week and stop and talk with various girls on the line. And they'd ask me questions, 'What was it like?' And they liked the involvement. So we had a very nice workforce, and they would do overtime because very often we were pressed for very quick responses."

Never ones to miss a photo opportunity, Cook & Hurst's bosses always encouraged the likes of Don Revie and assistant Les Cocker to tour the Wigston factory. "And I would do that whenever I could, make Revie go round and say 'hello' to the girls," John recalls.

Jill and Mandy remember Peter Shilton being paraded around on one occasion, with the staff under strict instructions not to ask for his autograph. Giggling at the memory of it all, the two women said they desperately tried not to stare, or worse still, burst out laughing as the keeper was wheeled past them.

John's recollection of these occasions is a little more earnest, and he believed seeing photos of these visits in local papers was good for morale. "It was just another aspect of getting the people in the factory interested. That they weren't just flogging away every day, and it was a nice diversion. You'd get opinions on what was being modelled."

Warehouse staff and machinists were also regularly used as impromptu models for catalogue photo-shoots. It was a way of saving money, doing away with the need to hire professionals. But also, more charitably, it was indicative of the 'mend-and-make-do' attitudes of those times. One of the colour prints Neville Chadwick showed me featured three young women decked out in Admiral-branded T-shirts in the colours of Manchester United, England and Wales. The smiling trio of workers genuinely appear to be having a good time.

"They enjoyed having a break from work at the factory and spending the morning in the studio," Nev tells me. "It's good actually that they used models from the factories, because I think in those days – certainly the staff that I remember working with – they were very proud of what they produced. This was very much made in England, and indeed made in Leicester. And there was a huge amount of prestige and pride that there were factories in Leicester that were producing fabric for the England team."

It would be easy to dismiss these accounts as misty-eyed recollections from

yesteryear, or as a series of hackneyed clichés about a mythical golden age in industrial relations. But I do believe there was, and still is, a genuine pride in what Admiral's workforce manufactured, and in the quality of the garments they produced. More than one former machinist told me these were "the happiest days of my life," and I believe them, because there is a dignity and purpose that work can sometimes offer.

When Jill started at Cook & Hurst in the late 1960s, the company was still making underwear, and at first she thought designer football strips were another passing fad, destined to go the same way as two other East Midland exports: Raleigh Choppers and Space Hoppers. "When they got England, you realised how big it was. There wasn't anything like it, but at that time you didn't realise how big it was going."

Nobody did, Jill, least of all the people running the company. How could they? But Bert and John, along with the rest of the football and sportswear worlds, were about to find out.

CHAPTER 5
Golden Years

"It had that integrity that it was for the sport," says designer Lindsay Jelley of the Admiral revolution promoting originality and inventiveness. "It was very much for the teams and the players, and I'm pleased to be able to say that as well, because the company had a good feel to it. It was an exciting place, and we were pushing boundaries – but in my view for the right reasons."

As with any effective form of communication, visual or otherwise, clarity is paramount. The primary purpose of a football strip is to differentiate one set of players from another, and to ensure that those playing, officiating and watching can tell one team apart from the other. That's it, everything else is fashion. Not that it's quite that simple, of course, as a club's identity and traditions are intertwined within the very fibres of its playing strips. After World War II, most professional clubs in Britain had more or less settled on a recognisable colour combination and a style of jersey, whether it be plain, striped, halved, hooped or contrast-sleeved. The limitations of manufacturing options led to several teams sharing the same basic templates, which remained fairly stable for the next 30 years – give or take the odd ambitious manager.

One of Don Revie's first acts after taking over at Leeds United in the early 1960s was to change the team's playing colours from blue and gold to all white. The early innovation was part of an extraordinary transformation that would propel a struggling 'rugby town' club into one of Europe's most successful club sides. A feat that would eventually lead to the Yorkshireman taking over as England boss, with Admiral Sports gliding effortlessly behind in his slipstream. By the beginning of 1975, the brand appeared to be well and truly 'on its way', with sales of reigning champions Leeds' replica kits exceeding all expectations.

But it was the England deal that "lit the blue touch paper," according to Bert Patrick, and when those sales took off, he knew he'd captured the spirit and mood of the time. "I realised that it could work, so the thing then was to start moving quickly into other clubs," he says, now talking with the same purpose and enthusiasm that propelled his company forwards over 40 years earlier.

Doors were suddenly opening at club after club: Coventry City, Luton Town, QPR, Sheffield United, Stoke City, West Ham United and, most significantly, Manchester United. Before long, the First Division was looking far more dazzling, and spurred on by the need to create an array of distinctive new designs, an unprecedented period of alchemy ensued. Admiral conjured up an alluring menagerie of football strips displaying sashes, chevrons, yokes and wing collars, often in bold, bright colours. This was picked up on by design magazine *Creative Review*, which noted how 'Admiral took a drab, utilitarian garment that was the height of machismo and transformed it. Tough, hairy footballers were suddenly turning out in the kind of gear that even glam rockers of the time might think twice about.'

This met with the hearty approval of Admiral's target demographic, which included a seven-year-old Peris Hatton. "The designs were just completely different to anything else that we'd seen before – very plain and simplistic, which really didn't identify who you supported. But when Admiral burst onto the scene, in school playground or PE days, we were allowed to wear our football kits, and it was great from week to week to see who was going to be wearing what. It was the talk of the playground, really."

Another significant introduction was the liberal use of the Leicester firm's own logo. Rivals Bukta and Umbro had been discreetly adding their own badges to track tops and keepers' jerseys since the late 1960s, but from now on Admiral's approach was to be far more overt. The company was, after all, effectively paying for advertising space on playing strips and training wear.

"We were really brand specialists, I suppose," says designer Paul Oakley, "and actually putting branding on formal kit, which was unheard of at that time, was quite an exciting thing to do." Paul had recently set up a creative agency, renting a studio above Neville Chadwick's premises on Long Street, opposite Cook & Hurst's factory. With his swept-back hair, Paul carries the urbane confidence

of what I would have guessed a senior creative art director looks like. Sipping an afternoon gin and tonic while relaxing effortlessly into his chair, Paul's character would surely be played by Bill Nighy in a feature film about Admiral's exploits. And it's no surprise to hear Paul say he hit it off immediately with Bert, or that he found him charismatic and fun to work with. The pair set out to create unique identities for the teams they were now sponsoring, according to Bert.

"We wanted to give individuality to a club, an ownership in its kit, not Manchester United running out with a similar kit to what Nottingham Forest wore." The clubs themselves usually bought into the concept as well, and Admiral would often end up as the sole kit supplier. "The clubs were obviously haphazard, they were buying their shirts from one place, their tracksuits from another, their bags from somewhere else," says Paul. "So offering them a complete package made sense probably to the clubs as well as to Admiral."

"I did that one; yeah, that's one of ours; that's another one," says Lindsay Jelley, pointing to an imaginary screen. "I remember my little cousin; I'd go, 'Oh, I've met him. 'Oh, and I've met him,' and he'd go, 'You've not met *him*, have you?' I hadn't got a clue who it was... now, if Bryan Ferry had walked in, I'd have known *him*."

I first met Lindsay after an article appeared in the *Leicester Mercury*, where I requested former Admiral employees get in touch to help with research. The artist's creative force and mettle seem as strong now as when she responded to another appeal in the same paper 40 years earlier, this time for a designer 'due to continued expansion at Admiral Sportswear'.

"I'd finished at Loughborough Art College, doing the fashion degree... and bear in mind my mother was a designer and my aunt was a designer. They were very particular about what I should wear for my interview, and I remember I wore a small blue hat and a dress. And they were right, because I was told later that I was the only person that turned up in a hat."

Lindsay obviously made a favourable impression to land her "dream job," and among the cuttings she's kept all these years is a letter confirming her successful appointment, which includes confirmation of her pay: £40 for working a 37.5-hour week.

"It was brave of them to take somebody on straight from art college, trained as a designer, who didn't know anything about football. I've only realised lately how that was a definite gamble."

I asked John if he'd taken a risk employing Lindsay, who he refers to as "the young lady from college" throughout our conversations. "I didn't think so, actually. I thought she had the skills but also her personality, and she was able to speak to people at clubs. So, I thought she was a pretty good, rounded person. I'd had two previous designers but they'd really been in the business too long. But the young lady from college, she had an open mind. She wouldn't say, 'Oh, I don't think that'd work,' she'd go away and see if it could work, or make it work. So, she was very good."

Lindsay's appointment was clearly a good fit, and she too fed off the enthusiasm and creative energy pulsing through the Long Street factory. "Revolution, it just felt that everything was happening on the crest of a wave, and there was a good feeling in the company. Right from walking in the front door, it felt buoyant and felt innovative."

To get the young designer up to speed, Lindsay played Eliza Doolittle to Bert's Professor Higgins during an outing to Filbert Street. "My first football match, I went with Mr Patrick in his Rolls-Royce, and we turned up to the directors' box, it was great." The Admiral boss explained the laws of the game, she remembers, and, "he had to tell me what a yellow card meant, and which way they were going

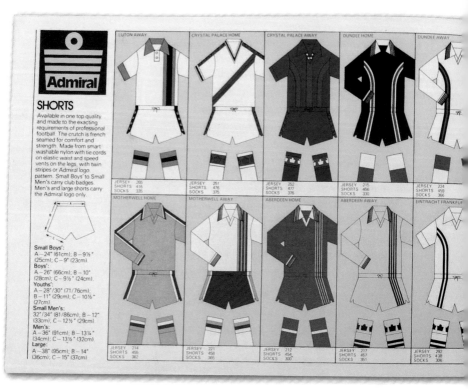

and the offside rule, all that stuff." Lindsay can't recall much about the match itself but admits, "it was wonderful, I had a great time, but I have to say I never really became a big football fan."

Bert and John demonstrated a real knack for spotting talent, but also realised they needed to 'break the mould' for their venture to succeed, by coming up with something radically different to what was already out there. A challenge that Lindsay was more than prepared to take on. "I didn't know anything about football," she admits, "so I had no baggage from that side of it. I wasn't going to think of the history or anything that had gone before. So, anything that was presented to me was a clean slate. I was just taking it forward, and I think that probably was a good strength."

Eventually, after leaving the fashion world behind, Lindsay returned to college to study fine art, graduating with three degrees, including an MA from Nottingham Trent for which she was awarded a distinction.

When I next meet her, it's in her studio close to the city's Queen Street 'Cultural Quarter' and Curve Theatre. I entered Lindsay's world of brightly coloured canvases and paint-smeared palettes armed with my own props: a 1978/79 Admiral 'Professional Soccer Kit' catalogue and a '60s copy of Martin Tyler's

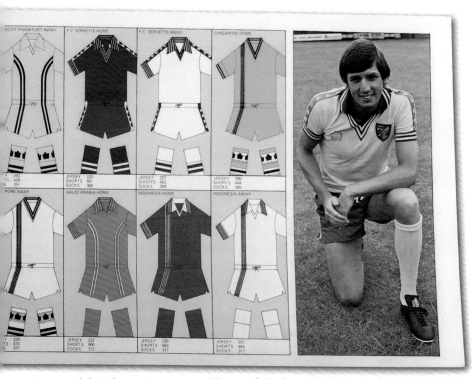

Soccer Club Colours. I encouraged her to flick through the latter first, and she immediately recoils in mock horror at the blandness of it all.

"Hell, look at that," she announces, pointing to a drab row of blank identikit templates. "Look at how ordinary and very plain these are, and then you take it to where Admiral wanted to go. Look at the difference." Comparing the two contrasting publications side by side makes it apparent just how radically different those early Admiral designs were. "It was really pushing the boundaries, weren't we?" she says, looking at the Admiral brochure and then back across to the '60s directory. "Because I hadn't worked in football or sportswear before, I had nothing to compare it to, so it didn't strike me as strange. But now I realise it was really quite at the forefront."

Colours are so central to the aesthetic appeal of football, explains Lindsay, that it makes sense to exploit that vibrancy – and that's exactly what she did. "Oh, excellent, that's a nice colour isn't it? I loved colours, still love colours," Lindsay announces with glee, pointing to a line drawing of a tracksuit. "They wanted it to be different from everybody else. There was a limit to the repetitions that you could do, and it still have the oomph the club wanted as a new kit. And in those days the printing facilities, you had many more limitations than you've got now, but within those limitations we came up with a whole variety of different shapes.

I remember that one," she adds, pointing to a chevron splashed across the front of West Ham United's home shirt, her right index finger jabbing excitedly as it moves across page after page. "I remember these as well. There it is, makes me smile even now. And that one. As I'm just flicking through them, they all bring back such different memories."

Even the sportswear firm's generic 'economy range' of kits could often be souped up with a little craft. "We used to think a lot about the socks, which were quite an important part of it." This time Lindsay's pointing at the international team strips, a reminder of the brand's reach beyond these shores.

"Singapore, yeah, that was a nice kit. You see, you could make a fairly plain kit a bit more snazzy by putting good socks with it."

An imaginative name also helped, and Bert's 13-year-old son Shaun would pitch in with monikers to make strips sound more exciting. He plucked out the names of exotic-sounding cities, such as 'Santiago' and 'Louisville', at random from the pages of an atlas. Shaun told me he'd often accompany his dad into work on Saturday mornings, when Bert would catch up with opening his mail, while Patrick Jr rummaged around, looking for any jerseys he could lay his hands on.

As previously mentioned, the decision to shake things up wasn't entirely driven by a desire to push the creative envelope, and neither was it solely a ploy to generate publicity. It was more a case of practical business decisions proving to be the mother of invention. A generic claret and blue jersey could belong to any number of clubs, including Aston Villa, Burnley or West Ham United. But by coming up with a unique chevron design, somewhat similar to an upturned Citroen grill, Admiral's claret and blue shirt was clearly identifiable as a West Ham shirt, and West Ham only – a unique style that could only be reproduced legally by the Wigston firm.

"There were one or two rocky times" at the very beginning, remembers John, before telling me about an early test case that Admiral fought tooth and nail to win. "Litesome, a company owned by Dunlop, copied [the England shirt] and were going to sell it and were undercutting us, so we took out an injunction." Citing the 1968 Copyright Act, Admiral won their battle, and "Litesome had to burn the garments that they made."

Bert told me the company had poured an awful lot of its resources into what in effect was a "make-or-break" legal action, revealing that had the hearing gone the other way it would have sunk his business. But lessons were learnt and, from then on in, he says Admiral made sure its designs became ever more elaborate, not least to deter counterfeiters.

The only real instruction to designers on the Admiral payroll was to make sure they stuck to the same home colours. But even then there was a certain amount of leeway, and if a team played in red and white, these colours could be applied in a variety of different combinations, including adding stripes. A third colour, introduced sparingly, was also permitted, just so long as the overall aesthetic remained red and white. Besides that, Lindsay was unencumbered. "I wasn't in any way tied to what they had traditionally used, because I didn't know what they had traditionally used. I was a fashion designer. But apart from those things that were set in stone, you'd probably try and change everything, that was the game."

It's a point reiterated by fellow designer Paul Oakley, who told me, "I would design them on paper – we only had paper in those days, and magic markers. Of course they'd give you parameters, and then you'd see what you could get away with. And you just pushed the boundaries as much as you could."

It's fair to say some managers and chairmen embraced their Admiral makeovers more willingly than others, with a creative tug-of-war or even a battle of wills occasionally ensuing. "The clubs obviously wanted to retain their previous image as far as they could, but they knew they had to change it to some extent, otherwise it wouldn't become Admiral's kit," says Paul diplomatically. Even when both parties recognised that they would sell more replicas with outfits that appealed to kids, there was a balance to be struck so as not to alienate older supporters, or indeed club directors. "Man United, they were very, very traditional, and really didn't want us playing around with it too much, so there were tweaks, really, to the plain red and white and black. Other shirts like Southampton and Sheffield United were just red and white stripes. I sort of put stripes within stripes and stripes on stripes. So, I was maintaining their original image, but changing it slightly." The latter two revamps are great examples of what Wigston's creatives did so brilliantly and effectively well with just a few simple embellishments.

Unsurprisingly perhaps, negotiations between supplier and customer were not always straightforward, and the terms of their joint agreement sometimes differed in interpretation. "You'd get the bigwigs come in, and I remember they'd go into my boss's office, and they'd have an argy-bargy," recalls Lindsay, who clearly wasn't averse to fighting her own corner. Smiling broadly, she tells me, "There was this real battle that I had once, it was scary," whilst thumbing through an Admiral catalogue to help jog her memory further about "things kicking

Red with White Trim
Red
41
Aberdeen
Brechin City
Doncaster Rovers
Liverpool
Scunthorpe United
Stirling Albion
Canada
Congo
Dubai
I F.C. Kaisers- lautern (W.G.)
Olympic (B.)
V.K. Mechelem (B.)
Vittoriosa Stars F.C. (M.)

The dull old days: one colour and style fits all.

off" over a Pantone colour chart. "Motherwell," she declares, pointing at the Dossers' kit from the late 1970s. "I do remember there was a bit of a battle, because he wanted this certain tone of red and yellow that I really didn't like, and he wanted something vibrant and all this, and I just really hated what he wanted. And we definitely had a major battle on that."

The 'he' in question was Motherwell manager Willie McLean, elder brother of a Scottish footballing dynasty, including brothers Jim and Tommy. It's not hard to imagine how Willie and the Fir Park board reacted to being schooled in design by a young English woman of limited football knowledge. "I think they wanted a very bright red and a real yellow, which other teams obviously had got; but I didn't want them to have it. And *that's* what they had, and I think that looks very nice," adds Lindsay, laughing loudly, pointing triumphantly to the maroon and gold soccer strip in front of her. "I have to say right now that I think the Motherwell kit looks really good, so I must have won the battle."

Bert was fully behind the more elaborate creations, not least because it made them easier to copyright and more difficult to counterfeit. They also inevitably attracted more publicity but, as already mentioned, getting some of the design department's ideas past the clubs themselves was sometimes difficult. When it came to tracksuits, though, Lindsay says she was given pretty much *carte blanche* to do what she wanted. "You could actually be a bit more adventurous, so this was very much something that I used to like doing." Not least because tracksuits were often used as 'Trojan horses' with which to introduce more outlandish ideas into playing strips. "With the tracksuits, we felt that you could push them along a bit and get them to try something else, and then hopefully they'd like it and go a bit further. And that was exciting."

JOE WARK

Other skirmishes involved the use of Admiral's own nautical logo, according to Lindsay. "I think it was a case of one side trying to get the Admiral logo everywhere they could, and maybe the manager would say, 'No, that's too much, we're not doing that.'" Here, Lindsay has a certain amount of sympathy with the clubs, and grimaces when I ask her about the Admiral trademark. "I didn't like the logo. It's just the limitations of the shape. It had to be incorporated in a good way, and I think we pretty much did it. But, me personally, I wouldn't choose to work with that logo, I'd like something a little more streamlined. But, equally, it stood out. It served the purpose of a logo."

Despite her misgivings, Lindsay is quick to point out that as a mark it worked brilliantly well. "The first thing that really shouts out at me," she announces, leafing through a series of action shots within the pages of *Shoot!* magazine. "Such a good, distinctive logo, and it went everywhere."

Paul remembers battles over the firm's trademark as well, and says, "The Admiral logo was always a bone of contention for the clubs, and there were countless arguments over what size it could be." Holding his hands wide apart, he tells me, "Bert would've had it about that size, right in the middle of the chest, if he could've done." He reveals that he would often make the logo "larger than possibly you even wanted it yourself, just so that they'd reduce it down to a size that you wanted," such was the dance played out between studio and boardroom. "We probably thought [Admiral's logo] would have parity. The clubs were always going to defend their own image as well, and really wouldn't want to be superseded by the manufacturer. Which, at the end of the day, that's what you are, the manufacturer of their kit."

Not that any such misgivings stopped Bert and his team from promoting Admiral's own identity at every opportunity, and the fact that they managed to effectively secure equal billing is remarkable in itself. Particularly when you consider the likes of Manchester United hadn't even worn their own club crests on their shirts up until 1972. The firm was also quite cute in where and how they placed their badge on outfits. As the Football League only allowed a single manufacturer logo on the chest, this was circumnavigated by badges appearing on collars and within stripes as logo taping.

There were other considerations, of course: the challenge was to create strips that looked good on TV and showed up well in press photos. Even if an idea worked well on paper, it didn't necessarily transfer successfully as a product or as a costume that's constantly in motion, viewed from a multitude of different angles. It's a challenge Paul picks up on, telling me, "You have to remember here that I did the graphics two-dimensionally, and then I'd do a number of variations. I might've done ten, and they may be slight variations on it, or they might've been completely different. One would be chosen, or maybe two, and then that would go to Admiral's design department, and then they'd make sure that it worked in manufacturing terms. Then they'd make it up, and it'd be presented." Typically, a set of prototypes or samples of each design would be made up, and these would be offered up to a club board or manager. "I'd also look at it again to make sure that it'd be doing its job in terms of being a brand. Bear in mind what the cameras

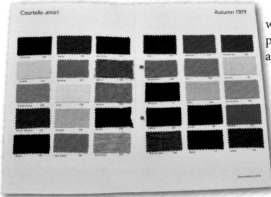

were doing, and the way they were positioned, and so we could try and push the Admiral brand as much as possible."

The end-game here, from Admiral's perspective, is best summed up by Lindsay. "It had got to look good on the television to boost replica kit sales."

This visual appeal certainly wasn't lost on myself, or on other young fans like John Devlin. "The idea of exploiting this arrival of colour TV, where kids could watch *The Big Match* or *Match of the Day* and then go out and buy those colours – that was a big draw. To have those richly coloured designs that were attractive to children."

The Admiral designers worked wonders with the limited options available at the time. "Don't forget that textile machinery in the following years became much more sophisticated and could do all sorts of things," Bert told me. Despite investing heavily in new plant, "the chevrons and the stripes were popular because of the limitations of the machinery." There really wasn't too much that could be done with the actual fabrics themselves. "If we wanted to produce stripes on fabric, we could produce them horizontally, like for QPR, but vertically for Stoke. You virtually had to turn the fabric round to make it in a shirt, and then it wouldn't stretch properly, so that restricted the designs."

One area where there appeared to be very little restraint, which becomes more pertinent later on in Admiral's story, is an apparent lack of fiscal cloth cutting. Wrangling over budgets is a source of constant tension in many creative industries, where artistic ambitions are often stifled by production costs – but seemingly not in the samples room where Lindsay worked.

"That never came across to me. That became a bit of a shock when I then went on to work in different areas of the industry and suddenly the financial thing was put on to you; but no, I was never told to economise." Perhaps it was the pioneering spirit of the times, with Bert and John giving their designers free rein in order to maintain momentum. Or an indicator of giddy excitement that would see the company lose focus later on. Either way, it certainly helped inspire some outrageously extravagant and striking football strips.

"The mid '70s onwards was Admiral's baroque period," enthuses John Devlin. Referring to the 'Wigston period' between 1974 and 1980, rather than the early 17th-century European arts movement. "It was so lavish, so flamboyant, there was an arrogance, a swagger: wing collars, taping, stripes, sashes, yokes. They took a football uniform and turned it into a work of art. It was just the perfect accompaniment to '70s football – '70s football fashion. It was the way that Admiral changed the whole way the game looked."

Not that those tasked with making up these elaborate costumes were always as enthused as young devotees, explained Jill Langton. "Tramlines were my nightmare because they used to bend," the machinist adds, before telling me she hated adding the vertical stripes to these outfits because they were so difficult to line up "on that curve bit, and then you had to keep them really straight."

West Ham's tracksuit was equally difficult according to Mandy Hutchins, because its chevrons would pucker and didn't always stretch the way she wanted them to. Despite these challenges the two women said they always looked forward to working on each new design, Jill admitting it was "exciting when another one came in because you got bored. We loved it when a new one came in."

Spread out across the paint-splattered trestle table in the middle of Lindsay's studio are the various Admiral catalogues and annuals I've brought along for her perusal. Publications containing a series of colourful line drawings, of the type more often found within a book about tropical birds. Spanning the entirety of the '70s, the pamphlets are a barometer of where the decade began for Cook & Hurst, and ended for Admiral Sports. Thumbing through the well-worn pages, Lindsay examines the images in front of her, before looking up to deliver her verdict. "I don't think I've really got a favourite. Actually, for me, I don't like the more ordinary ones. I don't like the ones that are just following the same as what's gone before, so I obviously was trying to break with tradition. I've not ever even thought about that until this moment, looking at this brochure. The ones that I don't like, they're the ones that were the same as they always had been."

In essence, this is what Admiral was all about. Replacing off-the-peg uniformity with bespoke Long Street tailoring. The overriding attitude is summed up by John Devlin, who says the strips were "bold, aggressive, arrogant, flamboyant. Maybe, following the fashions of the time. The perfect kits for the perfect time."

FRANK McLINTOCK (Manager)

Admiral became a glam rock/punk hybrid, if you like: the New York Dolls of sportswear. A spirit not only endorsed by Lindsay but acted upon with great gusto. "I think we were breaking the mould, definitely, and it shows because so many clubs wanted Admiral to do the kit. So of course we were way ahead. And I think the – how could you say it? – the *chutzpah* of giving all these different colours. The clubs probably thought, 'We never thought of that before, we've never been offered that before, let's go with these people.' I'm sure that's what happened."

This 'can do' attitude transferred from the top down, with Bert and John often turning up at clubs unannounced, like pushy door-to-door double-glazing salesmen.

ROGER GIBBINS

And John Devlin believes this approach contributed to their success. "I think Admiral were very lucky, really, that the era they operated in was a time when managers still had a certain degree of power."

Further into the decade, as more clubs came on board, the pressure to come up with distinctive new styles became constant, driven by a commercial need to stimulate demand as much as originality. It's clear Bert wasn't afraid of courting controversy, and readily admits he even encouraged it. "We wanted people to sit up, we wanted the newspapers to comment, and they did." Publicity, either positive or negative, was good for business according to the Admiral boss, and one of the easiest ways to ruffle a few feathers was to dramatically change the look of a team's playing strip.

TREVOR BROOKING

The demands filtering down to Long Street's first-floor samples room were loud and clear, according to Lindsay. "What would stand out for them on TV, and what would give a certain notoriety as being different – and that would generate the sales to the kids."

Reminding me of his background in journalism, Bert says he knew what

"newspapers wanted," and duly obliged. He wasn't prepared to pass on any titbits of gossip from inside the FA, but he was more than happy to give the media something else to feed on: chocolate.

By and large, Admiral stayed true to the traditional colours of their clubs' home strips. After all, why alienate the very supporters you wanted to sell kits to? However, the away strips were considered fair game, and were susceptible to what John Devlin describes as a certain amount of "muscle-flexing." "It was an even greater chance for Admiral to say, 'Right, we're going to use another colour – let's do it in this, let's make this design.' So they really took the bull by the horns."

In 1978, the cloven-hoofed beast in question was brown, when Coventry City unwrapped their coca-coloured 'tramlines' away strip. It was based on a template also sometimes referred to as the 'egg-timer' or 'hourglass', that married up stripes down the length of a single-colour kit – a style much beloved by Bangor City, Dundee, Manchester United, Ross County and Wales, as well as Eintracht Frankfurt and Saudi Arabia, further afield.

On this occasion though, the transition from Sky Blue rinse to brunette bombshell wasn't to everybody's taste. "Coventry's was a baddie, no doubt about it," says former Admiral supplier Greg Cross, inhaling sharply. Everybody else

I ask about the infamous kit reacts similarly, as if recalling a particularly nasty crime scene.

Football shirt collector Peris Hatton is still aghast. "It's just not right. I think brown and orange are 1970s Britain. I just think that a brown chocolate football shirt just took it too far, even for me."

When I tell Bert some people still consider it one of the worst football strips ever produced, he beams with pride. "I introduced that because I believed that Coventry would have a lift from it, everybody would be talking about it, and it was quite a good success, in sales."

Admiral even managed to spin the name of the strip according to John Devlin, presumably to make it more palatable. "It was officially known as 'chocolate' at the time; 'brown' probably didn't have enough glamour to it, or lavishness. But it's a great example of how Admiral took hold of their marketplace."

Some commentators have speculated that the great football innovator Jimmy Hill was behind the idea to adopt such a divisive strip. The Sky Blues chairman certainly signed off on the deal, which turns out to have been a commercial marriage of convenience between a club in need of a sponsorship windfall and a manufacturer desperate to offload several rolls of fabric ordered too hastily.

Interestingly, brown was on the FA's list of proscribed kit colours due to the potentially camouflaging effect of mud, and this is where Ipswich Town manager Bobby Robson joins the story. John Griffin was in negotiations with the Portman Road boss with a view to striking a kit deal. "Ipswich is a bit of graveyard for selling stuff, but they were on Anglia Television a lot. So, that's what appealed to me." Admiral's MD knew he needed to come up with something eye-catching to help boost sales, but Robson wouldn't entertain the idea of introducing stripes, or 'decorations' as the Blues boss put it.

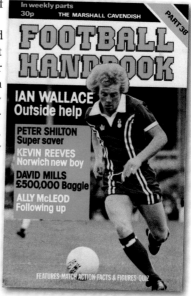

Robson appeared more open to changing the club's away strip, though. To the point of expressing more than a passing interest in an autumnal range of fabric swatches dangled under his nose, according to John – who, by his own admission, may have "jumped the gun" somewhat upon leaving Ipswich that day. He returned the following week with made-up samples of Town's new away kit, but only after placing a very large fabric order.

"I thought I was home and dry" he told me, raising his eyebrows. But Robson's enthusiasm had dampened by the time he accompanied John up into the stands to watch a couple of players run around in the prototype strips. "He said, 'Hmm,' and then he said, 'I'll get you a drink,' and he went away for about a half an hour. Then he came back and he said no." The Ipswich boss's team was in the middle of a particularly bad patch of form, and he was worried he'd be told, "You look like shit and you're playing like shit." On his return to Wigston, John hit the phone, ringing around the company's roster of clients, desperately trying to offload the unwanted reams. Leicester City and Sheffield United were among the clubs to turn him down flat, and the fabric remained untouched and unloved in a corner of the warehouse. That is, until an irate Jimmy Hill called the Long Street offices demanding to speak to John immediately.

Hill was one of the first club chairmen to sign up with Admiral in 1975 and struck an initial deal that would see Coventry City being paid £7,000 per year.

Bert and John didn't expect to make much money from City's replica sales, but were keen to drum up business to help encourage other clubs. The following year, Admiral signed up West Ham United and agreed to pay the Londoners an annual fee of £10,000. The Hammers were a bigger and better-supported club, and the two bosses expected to sell more kits and merchandise to United's fanbase. The club's televised European Cup Winners' Cup final appearance against Anderlecht provided the catalyst for the deal.

Not that any of this reasoning placated the Sky Blues chairman. "Hill found out about this and he went mad. He said things like, 'How could you do that, and give us less?' The furious call was the answer to John's prayers. "And so we argued a bit, and I just had an idea. I said, 'Well, okay, I'll give you the same amount but I want to change your away strip.' And he said yes, and I told him what it would be, and I'd got a sample – brown, sky blue and white – and he said yes, he okayed it."

United, you're looking good.

Admiral Sportswear
AVAILABLE FROM YOUR LOCAL SPORTS SHOP

A few years later, Hill reportedly blamed the chocolate-brown strip for making his club the butt of 'dogshit kit' jokes forever more, and when I relay this news to John he jokingly adds, "Coventry supporters were after my blood for years and years and years." But during the course of the intervening decades, the club's brown strip has attained cult status, and is viewed retrospectively with a certain amount of affection, if not altogether pride.

Appropriately enough, it's also the same colour as Marmite, and its ability to divide opinion remains undimmed. Designer Paul Oakley says, "You loved it or hated it. I'm not sure I knew many people who loved it, but I suppose there's a sort of perversity in liking it."

Surprisingly perhaps, other sportswear firms appeared indifferent to the waves being made in the East Midlands – initially, at least, according to Bert. "There was great resistance when we started making designer kits. Umbro and Bukta thought we were on a loser, they didn't even bother to compete." The Wilmslow firm were particularly dismissive, according to former Umbro sales director Bobby Brown, who says he was being repeatedly told not to worry about Admiral as "they'd be bust in six months' time" – a stance that would of course change dramatically over the next few years. Despite Bukta and Umbro's reticence,

Admiral's success hadn't gone unnoticed. West German footwear giants Adidas were taking a particularly keen interest in Britain's growing replicas market, though at the time any move on their part would undoubtedly jeopardise their relationship with its UK distributor, Umbro.

By the summer of 1975, Bert and John took stock of what was an extraordinarily successful and momentous 18 months for Admiral Sports. The company had signed up the country's 'Big Three' teams in Leeds United, Manchester United and England, prompting numerous other clubs to also fall into line. The two bosses took great satisfaction from watching one of its flagship clubs reach the 1975 European Cup final, when UEFA's end-of-season showpiece pitched Leeds United against fellow European heavyweights Bayern Munich in Paris. The game was played before a packed Parc des Princes crowd and – far more importantly, as far as Admiral was concerned – a worldwide television audience of millions. Led out by former manager Don Revie at the behest of Jimmy Armfield, 'Don's team' took to the field in their Admiral-branded track jackets and all-white strip. Conversely, the European Cup holders walked out on to the pitch in an Adidas-sponsored all-red outfit, with the supplier's distinctive trademark three stripes and logo on full show.

Leeds lost the final in highly dubious and suspicious circumstances. Those who played in the City of Light that evening still describe it as a game that United 'would never be allowed to win'. Peter Lorimer's volleyed goal was disallowed for an apparent offside, while Allan Clarke was denied a clear penalty after being brought down by Franz Beckenbauer as he bore down on goal.

Bert and John realised instinctively that this was no longer about Leeds vs Bayern or even England against Germany. This was the first skirmish in what would soon escalate into a sponsorship war between Adidas and Admiral. Worryingly, the outcome didn't augur well for a campaign Wigston was ill equipped to fight, let alone win.

CHAPTER 6
Glass of Champagne

By 1977 Admiral Sports, driven on by owner Bert Patrick and managing director John Griffin, had without doubt hit zeitgeist gold. It seemed as if every other club in Britain was turning out in a strip festooned with nautical badges. Ergo every football-mad child in the land either had or desperately wanted one of Admiral's prized jerseys. Including this writer, who was sadly still in the latter camp. It wasn't just kids clambering to get their hands on their designer strips, either, according to Bert, observing that modern players were also fashion-conscious young men aware of their celebrity status.

"Remember, these are the days when many consider themselves veritable 'Beau Brummells' off the field, and they dress in all the mod gear and fashions," he told *Football News*. "Many want to look the part at play, and they want the latest, independent strips." The now-defunct periodical reported Bert as saying that while Spurs' hierarchy was resistant to change, "some of their present players have actually asked me to do what I can do to get the club into a new strip. Change the image and put new life into them. Unfortunately for those players and myself, I have been unable to convince the club of any need for a strip change. But we are still negotiating."

Bert makes a good point, and in the wake of football's £20 maximum wage being abolished, a generation of 'baby boomer' players was becoming more aware of their own value. Especially those individual enough to attain 'entertainer' or 'maverick' status. Some players even had the temerity to employ agents for the first time – not that the presence of such interlopers was welcomed, let alone encouraged, by the clubs themselves.

Bert's persistence also clearly paid off, as Wigston's designers eventually created a very stylish Tottenham Hotspur kit once manager Bill Nicholson had moved on. It's impossible to look at this strip without imagining Ossie Ardiles and Ricky Villa running out on to the White Hart Lane pitch under a blizzard of ticker tape.

Meanwhile, dealing with Spurs' South London neighbours at Selhurst Park proved far easier, as the Admiral bosses were effectively pushing at an open door. Fellow innovator and American razzmatazz enthusiast Malcolm Allison began a Crystal Palace rebrand after taking over as manager in 1973. 'Big Mal's' own homage to Catalonia involving a change of team colours from claret and blue to a distinctly Barcelona-looking style of apparel. From now on, Palace would be known as the Eagles rather than the Glaziers, and the fedora-toting cigar smoker also had his players' nicknames stitched on to the back of their track tops, which meant 'Shuffler' and 'Hustler' could be seen warming up next to 'Blockbuster' and 'Road Runner' on a match day. Allison had left by the time Palace unveiled their Admiral-sponsored outfits – a gleaming all-white strip lit up by a striking red and blue diagonal sash, inspired by an away kit introduced by the outgoing boss earlier that year. The stylish home jersey attained instant cult status, and many fans still rate it their club's best ever shirt.

Despite Mick Channon's earlier nipple-rash gripes, many other sports stars considered Admiral's teamwear an improvement on what was already out there, because its playing kits were designed specifically for athletes. Footballers too were latching on to the benefits of Wigston's lighter-weight fabrics, and whereas previously jerseys had been supplied on a 'one size fits all' basis, Admiral offered a range of sizes.

"The kits were a bit more slimline, much more fitted, and the material was better," says Peter Shilton, "and that was the start of producing better quality kits, really."

As word spread among changing rooms, previously closed doors began opening, remembers Bert. "Managers became much more receptive because the players were putting them under pressure: 'Boss, why can't we have an Admiral kit like so-and-so's got?'" The badgering, he acknowledges, wasn't down to aesthetics and comfort alone. Royalty payments from replica-kit sales tended to be paid into a players' pool, and was considered a very welcome bonus. Individual player endorsements and lucrative sidelines like newspaper columns and personal appearances then tended to be the preserve of higher-profile players, better able to sell the 'Great Smell of Brut' or Cossack hairspray.

By the middle of the decade, 84 of the 92 English Football League clubs were now wearing a manufacturer's logo on their shirts, whether it be Adidas, Admiral, Bukta or Umbro. More often than not, any proposed kit deal meant signing up a manager as much as the club. Industry insiders have told me it was common practice for bosses to receive cash as a 'contribution to kit design'. Or, as it was delicately put to me, deals otherwise tended to collapse because 'financial terms were not agreed'. Despite '70s football's unsavoury reputation for brown paper envelopes stuffed with cash, Bert is adamant that there was nothing underhand about his company's dealings with its roster of managers. But he agrees that adding "the boss" to the payroll as a consultant was good practice, and helped avoid any kit "issues" further down the line. "We would pay them a fee, and we would make sure that it was above board. There was no question of bungs. They were paid an agreed fee,

which was usually the same, and that would be cleared through the tax situation the usual way."

It was a smart move on Admiral's part to involve club coaches, explains John Devlin. It ensured that whenever players "came out on the pitch for the pre-match warm-ups, they'd be wearing tracksuit tops with massive Admiral logos on the front or the back. When the trainer came on, there would be a bag placed when he tended to an injured player – Admiral logo, very clever product placement that hadn't been seen before. So again it was Admiral really pushing the boundaries. It was all above board, but they were incredibly canny in terms of getting their brand out there. It was an extraordinary, bullish way of doing business." I was told by another interviewee that if the aforementioned holdalls ever appeared in shot during a televised game, physios could expect to pocket a £50 cash bonus for a job well done.

Despite their earlier successes, Admiral's bosses trod cautiously while drumming up new business. The country's football club boardrooms were a myriad world of local businessmen, protective of their own interests and alliances, only too willing to adopt a grievance or easily take offence. Bert and John went after chairmen and clubs they believed would be amenable to change, or at the very least meet with them to explore the possibility of a tie-in. Discretion was paramount if they were trying to poach a club currently being supplied by either Bukta or Umbro.

On one such occasion, John arranged to meet Watford chairman Elton John in a remote countryside hotel. But the Admiral man's cover was immediately blown by the Watford owner's grand entrance across the lobby in a huge fur coat and platform boots, much to the delight of the other guests. For clubs with less resources, the biggest incentive to striking a deal was of course money, and how much of it they'd see. From Bert and John's perspective, they needed a team big enough to sell a sufficient number of replicas to cover costs and turn a profit.

"A lot of the lower [league] clubs and the management of them, at director level, they were more pragmatic," remembers John. Their attitude was more along the lines of "Yeah, we've got to do something different," to help boost club coffers.

Access to some top-flight clubs could be trickier, particularly those in the North West with close ties to Bukta or Umbro. The two long-established Cheshire manufacturers had made their displeasure known from the outset at what they perceived to be flagrant encroachment on to their patch – not least because other kit manufacturers would now also have to pay for the privilege of supplying clubs with their playing strips. And teams now expected to be provided with their own individually designed outfits, to boot.

According to Bert, Umbro's managing director John Humphries resented Admiral's intrusion. "We were most unpopular. And I think they were quick to create problems for us with the retailers. Because they were saying, 'It will mean that you've got to stock just one kit, for one team, and not a red or blue kit for a number of teams. So this is going to increase your outlay for stocking these kits that Admiral are making.' Particularly if they would get stuck with the stock."

Another way for Bert and John to get their foot in the door at clubs was to deal directly with managers, which had worked so successfully at Leeds United with Don Revie. "Managers really did have that complete control over everything. They had direct access to influence what was going on in terms of apparel on the pitch." John Devlin outlines a time in which many managers operated autonomously and effectively ran things from top to bottom. "Clubs were simpler, they weren't governed by external forces, and there certainly weren't the international sportswear rules and regulations that had to be adhered to. So managers were able to make suggestions, and sportswear companies were able to very quickly respond to those suggestions."

Legendary agent Harry Swales had been taken on by Admiral to help hoover up some of the North West's smaller clubs. But he also happened to represent some of the area's top players, including several Liverpool stars, who'd let it be known they wanted an Admiral strip at Anfield. Or, more precisely, they were attracted by the lure of sponsorship cash and the win bonuses that would surely follow with any tie-in to the supplier. Alongside Leeds, the Reds were the North's other major powerhouse and, from Admiral's perspective, landing Bill Shankly's team would prove another massive coup.

"The word went out that Liverpool players wanted a change of kit, keeping the red, but they'd seen other teams changing." Bert told me he travelled up to the club's Melwood training ground with John, carrying sets of prototype strips already prepared, confident a deal could be struck that day. "We met the players in the players' lounge, they were all there: Keegan, Toshack, Tommy Smith, Steve Heighway. And I showed them the samples and they thought they were fantastic. And then they said, 'The boss is going to come in soon – Shankly.' And I said, 'Well, we need to model the kit, will one of you...' Steve Heighway was the favourite, so we put Steve in the kit. A few minutes later Shankly comes in, sees Steve Heighway, and he said, 'It's nae a bloody circus, Stevie. What's all this?' And the players just crowded round him, said, 'Look, boss, we want a change of kit. It's good, let's go with Admiral.'"

Shankly examined the mock-ups closely, picking out a style he liked but insisting on certain alterations, remembers John. "We listened to him. And he explained how he wanted a minimum of elastic in the shorts because of no pressure on the stomach, to really restrict any athletic movement." Ironing out an agreement with the Liverpool boss took a long time to negotiate as they wrangled over the percentage of profits the players would receive. Eventually, John says, "We went away and produced a legal contract and he signed it."

It was the "same sort of details of terms of the other clubs," recalls Bert, who was delighted to have bagged another of the English game's big beasts. "A week later, I had a phone call from John Smith, who was chairman of the club. He said, 'I'm cancelling this contract. You had no right to come into my club and get the manager to sign a contract.' I said, 'Well, I understood he was making the decisions about the team.' He said, 'Contrary to what the Great British public think, Bill Shankly does not run the Liverpool Football Club.'"

"So I had to go up and meet him," says John, of being summoned to Merseyside for a dressing-down. It was clear Smith and his fellow directors were wresting control away from Liverpool's legendary manager, in what was to become Shankly's final season in charge. "He said, 'I have an existing contract.' It was with Umbro, and he said, 'You can take me to court and you'll win. But then you'll lose, and nobody in football will want to get really involved with you.' And just that sentence struck home with me. I knew he was right. What he said, I accepted as the case: if you upset Liverpool Football Club, then your competition

would really be able to make something out of that." All good business operators know it sometimes pays to be pragmatic, and on this occasion John chose "discretion as the better part of valour."

During my research for this book, I tracked down three crates of Admiral ephemera discovered in the loft of former production manager Paul Gough. Among the brochures and order books unearthed from this time capsule was an array of different garments, including a few unfamiliar one-off prototype kits that, as far as I'm able to verify, never made it into production. Buried at the bottom of one of the boxes was a fairly plain all-red strip with a white collar and cuffs that looks like the sort of 'minimalist' Liverpool mock-up described to me by ex-employees. This wasn't the actual sample taken up to Melwood by Bert and John, as logo taping was some way off when Shanks left Liverpool; but it provides yet more fuel for the endless speculation on how the Reds would have looked, given their own bespoke Admiral treatment over a number of years. A finished version of this style eventually emerged, also in red, when it was repurposed as England's training kit.

Sadly, this treasure trove of memorabilia didn't unearth any emerald gems. For around the same time as the on-off Liverpool deal, the Admiral bosses also made a similar approach to Glasgow Celtic boss Jock Stein, which involved creating a set of green and white track tops. This proposed sponsorship also faltered – and these weren't the only deals that slipped through Bert and John's fingers.

Often, these initial meetings were held at a football club's offices or sometimes at nearby hotels, but it wasn't unusual for further negotiations to take place in Wigston. "I think the glamour was more intrinsic than the actual premises, and clearly managers and footballers would come there, and I don't think in those days the expectation of glamorous offices actually existed." Which is fortunate, given Paul Oakley's less than flattering description of the Cook & Hurst premises, that he remembers as being somewhat shabby.

But what the factory lacked in glitz, it more than made up for in character, and the old place had a rather surprising trick up its sleeve, capable of disarming the toughest of negotiators: a sauna and a sunbed. "Yes, it was quite unusual with the sauna in the basement, and the tradition of having the lunch meeting going on with a sauna, which brought a few people down to earth, especially those who had been rather pompous during the meetings in the first place, and then found they had to actually take their clothes off, and their pomposity disappeared very rapidly." Bert is rightly proud of the "dressing downs" he managed to engineer, and his story's also a reminder of just how novel his approach to business was in 1970s Britain. "Don't forget, not many people did this sort of thing in those days, and we had a fridge with some nice cold wine in it, and we'd have our meetings there. I'd get a phone call from a manager, and he would say, 'Any chance you're going to be in so-and-so, I'll be down in the Midlands. I'd love a sauna,' because that's what they did in those days, it was very fashionable." For once, Bert's slightly underselling himself, as a workplace sauna was positively the height of sophistication at a time when most people's idea of *savoir faire* was a lump of cheddar and a piece of tinned pineapple on the same cocktail stick – as brilliantly realised in Mike Leigh's 1977 television play, *Abigail's Party*.

Not that every manager or club official succumbed to the steaming charms of hot coals and cold water in a Wigston cellar, of course. There were also some battles John didn't even bother contesting. "The chairman," he announces with a resigned shrug. When I push him for further details, he tells me that Admiral was invited along to a meeting in Birmingham to discuss a possible deal with Aston Villa. "I didn't bother going. It would've been a good club to have, but already we were told we couldn't change the design, so that was that." Even an initial chat was deemed pointless, says John, such was Doug Ellis's reputation for intransigence. Another club that escaped the firm's clutches early on was Glasgow Rangers. "We made a good offer," says John, and came up with a "very strong" minimalist-style strip, but the Ibrox club turned the manufacturer down. Albion Rovers, Clydebank, Dundee and Ross County did commit, however, along with a resurgent Aberdeen on the cusp of greatness. Yet, despite these successes, it was always going to be hard to make serious inroads north of the border without either Celtic or Rangers on their books, as John acknowledges.

The schmoozing didn't always end once clubs had committed pen to paper. In some cases, it even had to be cranked up a notch, and John diplomatically points out that certain relationships needed more "maintenance" than others. Admiral's sponsorship of the FA pretty much looked after itself, as did their agreement with Leeds United. An occasional visit to Elland Road for a congenial chat over a cup of tea with Jimmy Armfield kept things ticking over,

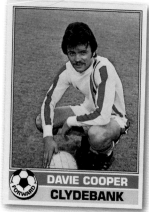

DAVIE COOPER
CLYDEBANK

and the coach also gave his blessing to a revamp that saw United's minimalist all-white strip transformed by logo taping along its sleeves and shorts at the start of the 1976/77 season.

"We had people like Lawrie McMenemy, Jimmy Bloomfield, quite a lot," Bert Patrick says. "In fact, our brochure one year, that went down very well, had a full-colour back cover with all the managers that were working with Admiral." Here, a montage of photos surrounded the outline of the company's logo. Other coaches featured in the catalogue included Dave Sexton, Keith Burkinshaw, Mike Smith, Tommy Docherty, Gordon Milne, Jimmy Armfield, John Lyall, Harry Haslam, John Bond, Frank McLintock, Ron Greenwood and Terry Venables.

Arguably the manager with the highest profile at that time was Manchester United boss Tommy Docherty. He was certainly the most important coach as far as Admiral was concerned. Snatching the Old Trafford contract from under the noses of Umbro was considered a major coup, and according to John, it was "the golden nugget" that proved more lucrative than the first England contract. Bert concurs and says, "It was a huge deal, in that although the England deal was big, Manchester United would sell throughout the world. They travelled the world out of season, playing matches, and they were hugely popular in places like South East Asia." Domestic sales were also suitably impressive as United's renaissance under Docherty continued apace. The Scot had steered the Red Devils back to the top flight, and his young, swashbuckling team was now challenging for both the First Division title and the FA Cup. For Admiral to capitalise on that success, they needed 'The Doc's' full co-operation, explained Bert. "He'd always wear a sweatshirt with 'Admiral' right across the chest; he would make sure that the trainer, when he ran on the field during a match, would be carrying the Admiral medical bag."

When I bring up the subject of Docherty with John he offers a shrug and tells me, "Manchester United did need watching." Several local sponsors had a solid rapport with the club, and he was made fully aware he was operating in "Umbro Country," as he called it, such were the efforts made to undermine Admiral's standing among United's directors.

Bert and John realised they needed to be cautious, particularly when it came to rebranding the club's playing strips and respecting United's traditions and heritage.

"I was thinking, we won't get much change on the home jerseys, immediately you think of that." John says he made sure he'd spoken to the company's North West sales rep at length before putting any prototypes in front of the Old Trafford board. What the designers back in Wigston came up with wasn't too dissimilar to what had gone before. Thin red stripes were added to the white collar and cuffs but the overall effect meant United retained their familiar-looking red shirts, only with a single Admiral logo on the chest and shorts. The changes were accepted by Matt Busby and the Edwards family, and a similar deal to the terms of the England and FA contract was agreed. Admiral would pay United £15,000 per year plus five per cent of sales, for five years, as well as a number of bonuses dependent on how successful the team was on the pitch. John had been expecting the United's hierarchy "to say, 'We want more than England,'" but instead left with what he knew was a very good deal for the company. His elation didn't last very long though, as on his way out of the meeting he was intercepted by Docherty, who none too subtly started talking about porcelain figurines. "He said, 'Do you travel a lot, John?' I said, 'Yes I do.' He said, 'Well, my wife loves Capodimonte.'" John ignored the comment but realised what was being implied, and told me he didn't have long to wait before he was "brought to heel" by The Doc.

As was the case at other clubs, Admiral's designers were given a freer rein with United's change strip, resulting in a radical makeover. The template remained broadly the same as the red home shirt but with three asymmetric black stripes running down the length of the white away jerseys. A striking modification that chimed perfectly with United's cavalier playing style. But if you thought this looked mind-blowingly futuristic, wait until you saw what had happened to the tracksuit: a red two-piece based on the 'tramlines' template, featuring connecting white and black vertical stripes running down the length of the body. If Colonel Ed Straker from Gerry Anderson's *UFO* TV series had been a football coach, he would have worn this outfit. John had his own reservations about the tracksuits though, as some players complained of looking like 'skeletons' when warming up. Despite his misgivings, Admiral's makeover proved a resounding success within the club's boardroom, with replica sales proving hugely popular at home and abroad.

But within weeks of launching, John's diplomatic skills were about to be called into action, with the Manchester United contract seemingly in danger of being cancelled. "All of a sudden, in early October, there was a panic because the *Manchester Evening News* ran a big article that said, 'Where was the real, true red of United, where has it gone?'" John says it was being claimed the paper's evening sports edition wasn't the only *Pink 'Un* in town, with United's traditional shade of dark red looking a bit rosier that it should – and, perhaps not unreasonably, the finger of blame was pointing directly at Old Trafford's new kit suppliers. "So I went up and I saw the manager after training. I said, 'Well, how is this happening?' He said, 'They can't wash, those ladies can't wash.'" Docherty was firmly laying the blame at the laundry room's door. He also distanced himself from his players' failure to wear their Admiral-emblazoned tracksuits during televised games, as per the club's agreement with its sponsors. But fortunately, Docherty was able to offer a solution, recalls John with an eyebrow firmly arched. "'Manchester United are a very, very busy club and there's so much happening, you'll need somebody to look after your interests. Somebody ought to look after this laundry business for you.'"

Following his chat with the Scot, the Admiral boss talked to United's kit man and visited the women who washed the club's strips. A bunch of honest workers he described as "salt of the earth" people. Arriving with three bottles of sherry – one of which was opened immediately to liven up their hot drinks – John set about trying to find out the cause of the problems. "After about two-and-a-half cups of tea we were the best of friends. And I said, 'What's happening?' And they said, 'Well, we do everything as per instructions,' but they said, 'We reach a stage where we have to stop the machines...' And they alleged that the manager would come down and would throw one or two buckets of bleach into the machine on top of the jerseys." Following the women's revelations, John returned to talk to Docherty. "I went up and said, 'You know, you're perfectly right, somebody should look after us.' I said, 'You can have a consultancy, but it's

got to be above board, and it's £1,500 a year.' But he said, 'Can I get a bonus for getting to the Cup final?' So I said, 'All right.' There was a contract drawn up, and the washing improved immediately."

A few weeks later John attended an awards dinner at Manchester's Piccadilly Hotel where he was sat between WBC light-heavyweight boxing champion John Conteh and Docherty. "He said, 'Have you got my money?' And I said, 'Yes, but I'd like to eat first.' So eventually, at coffee time, we went out. It was a typical wet night in Manchester, we're standing on the fire escape staircase," overlooking the city-centre skyline. Such was Docherty's reputation that a Mexican standoff ensued, with John refusing to hand over the cash he was holding until the Glaswegian had signed the contract he was offering up to him in his other hand. Acting out the exchange, played two floors up under the night drizzle, John says the impasse was ended with the words, "Tommy, sign this for me, and I'll give you this."

Maintaining the Old Trafford contract necessitated regular visits to the North West, but it was well worth the effort, says John. "The club were generating so much business for Admiral," and selling more shirts than England. "Mega. Much, much more business," because Manchester United were featured on television more. "Every four weeks I'd make the journey there, and I'd see Les Olive first, then I would maybe see Matt Busby sometimes in the nearby golf course, and then I would see Louis Edwards on his own, and then I would see Docherty and his staff, two or three, on their own, and they were all in various parts of the ground. So you were tiptoeing through the egos." But Docherty was earning his consultancy fee, according to John. "There was a lot of carelessness and people wearing competitors' T-shirts, which we didn't want, especially in hotels. There was a lot of little things that could go wrong, which would affect us." The Scot "would see that the players were wearing the kit; he would see that they were wearing the tracksuit, because players, they're pretty absent-minded and there's lots of distractions even in a big dressing room like there used to be at Manchester United. There used to be a lot of showbiz people there." It was an environment the wise-cracking Scot relished. He "was always good for a quote" and "would appear for 15 seconds to 30 seconds on TV during the week, and he didn't want to be paid in money, he wanted to be paid in champagne."

Whenever I visited Neville Chadwick's Long Street studio, I always came away feeling like a lucky contestant on a quiz show in which every round was about 1970s football. As Nev plucked out random images from a box of prints, I would try to name the player or team as quickly as I could. This time, it's a photograph of the victorious 1976 FA Cup-winning Southampton side. "I remember that very well," Nev says, "because my partner and myself went to this photocall and we actually took the kit with us, because it had only just been made up, so the rest of the photographers were there waiting when we got to the ground in Southampton."

Nev and John Plant's trip to The Dell came about after Lawrie McMenemy's Second Division side had just reached the final, beating Crystal Palace at Stamford Bridge in the semis. The following week, Bert and John had ironed out an agreement with the Saints manager, who had agreed to switch from Umbro to Admiral, even though the Wigston bosses didn't think their replica kits would sell particularly well. But the prospect of Southampton walking out at Wembley alongside fellow finalists Manchester United, with both sides decked out in Admiral strips, was too good an opportunity to miss. The supplier agreed to pay the club £7,000 a year, for three years, as well as a small bonus in the unlikely event of them actually winning the FA Cup. United had finished third in Division One and were the bookmakers' heavy favourites against an ageing Saints side that had finished 25 places below them, in the second tier. Some observers were wildly predicting that Docherty's free-scoring side would hit double figures.

"It was the perfect showpiece" for Admiral, according to John Devlin, "and as was often the tradition, the new kit would be unveiled on FA Cup final day."

United had won the toss over the colour clash and opted to wear their usual red, meaning the Saints would now revert to their second strip. A bold new yellow and blue outfit which included, for the very first time, logo taping in contrasting colours along the sleeves. The Wigston creatives had seamlessly incorporated multiple tiny nautical badges into the very fabric and design of the kit.

When unveiled alongside both teams' newly designed track tops, the new look "caused quite a bit of criticism in the media, that the spectacle of Wembley was an Admiral show," recalls John Griffin, before quickly adding that, "I didn't take any notice of it." But football's authorities and BBC *Grandstand* executives in White City certainly did, becoming increasingly nervous about 'product placements' creeping into their broadcasts.

As phlegmatic as ever, John remained unperturbed by the growing furore as he set off from Wigston on the eve of what was set to be a glorious Bank

Holiday weekend. In the boot of his Jaguar XJ-S were two sets of strips that he would deliver to both teams at their respective hotels on the outskirts of London. Specially made for the occasion, they were embroidered with a small FA Cup trophy and a 'Wembley 1976' insignia. "We had to be very careful, actually, with big-game kits. So we took it down, and in any case I had to meet Docherty to give him his bonus for getting to the Cup final." The Manchester United party was staying at Sopwell House in St Albans, close to the London Colney training ground, and a short detour off the M1 for John who found himself sitting in the hotel lobby alongside the BBC's *Match of the Day* editor Mark Murphy, also waiting for an audience with Docherty – who was otherwise engaged in his suite filming a television commercial for Gillette razors.

John remembers the atmosphere around the team's base as being strangely subdued. "The United players were very withdrawn, and then, of course, the manager was just over the top about himself." As he describes being summoned to see the The Doc, John begins shaping his hands into a dome: "In Docherty's room there was a big pile, like that, of money." The size of a beachball, lying on top of his bed. "Bonuses. It's the advertising and the exposure that you get between winning the semi-final and actually going to Wembley. So there was a big, big exposure factor. And he cashed in on it." Docherty's overconfidence was unbearable, according to John, who was handed a glass of champagne on arrival. "It just sort of annoyed me, he was so cocksure. He was part of the machine that made a tremendous amount of our turnover. But just in that instance, I thought, 'Oh, to hell with it.'"

John took his leave from Hertfordshire, driving south across the capital and over the Thames to the Selsdon Park Hotel in Croydon, where Southampton were ensconced. Still annoyed by Docherty's arrogance, he admits that "by the time I got across there, I thought, 'Who do I want to win?' And I wanted Southampton to win." The omens of an upset were encouraging, with the South Coast club staying in the same location as the Sunderland team from three years earlier, who had pulled off one of the biggest Cup final shocks against mighty Leeds.

The mood among McMenemy's group couldn't have been more different to the atmosphere John had just left: "Southampton were more appreciative. They recognised us when we went in, and Harry Swales was there, so he introduced us to some players and they were quite grateful about what we'd put into the pot." A fee of around £400 was paid into the players' pool, according to Channon. The following morning, John thought he'd try his luck at pocketing his own bonus, placing a £5 bet on Southampton, at odds of around six or seven to one. But I suspect seeing Docherty's face at the final whistle gave the Admiral man far more satisfaction than his winnings.

Handling Docherty's ego hadn't been the only issue to deal with in the run-up to the Cup final, according to Bert. "The big problem had been that just prior to going down to those camps, I'd had a phone call from the BBC director of sport to say, 'I understand that both teams are going to come out at Wembley on Saturday with 'Admiral' emblazoned on the front of their tracksuits?' And I said, 'Yes, that's correct.' He said, 'Well, you can't do it.' I said, 'Why can't I do it?' He said, 'Because the BBC can't allow it. We're not allowed to show advertising.' So, I said, 'Yes, but I've got a contract that says the players will wear the 'Admiral' across the tracksuits.' So, he said, 'We won't be able to film the match if we don't reach some sort of conclusion with you.' And I thought to myself, well there's no way they're not going to film the match, so I said, 'Look, leave it with me for 24 hours, and I'll see what I can do.' And what we actually did was, we put the 'Admiral' on the back of the tracksuit jacket, and that when the players came out the tunnel, the cameras were behind the players, and of course we got wonderful exposure, both teams, in tracksuit tops."

Looking back at footage of the two teams emerging from the Wembley tunnel, Bert really couldn't have choreographed the entrance any better if he'd tried. Even the team of ballboys surrounding the pitch were clad in his firm's branded tracksuits. May 1st 1976 was declared 'Admiral Day' in the People's Republic of Wigston, as the shock result garnered worldwide headlines, and placed Admiral Sports firmly on the map. In front of 100,000 fans and a live television audience of millions, Southampton pulled off one of the great FA Cup giant-killing triumphs when, deep into the match, Bobby Stokes raced clear of the Reds defence to

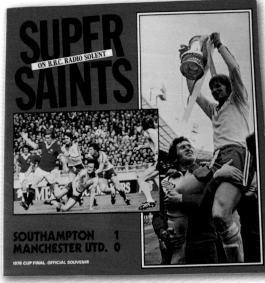

hit the winner past Alex Stepney – earning his teammates a joint £700 bonus into the bargain.

Following the celebrations, "I got a phone call from the BBC on Monday morning, thanking me profusely for co-operating with them," says Bert. It was hard to escape the feeling that this was a watershed moment for both broadcasters and sponsors alike. On this occasion, the two parties had successfully muddled their way through to their mutual satisfaction but sport's commercial axis was tilting. Australian media tycoon Kerry Packer was limbering up to launch his own World Series

Cricket tour, or 'Flying Circus', and would soon be playing televised matches in competition with official tests. Closer to home, football's administrators were edging closer to accepting shirt sponsorship, with Hibernian and Bukta paving the way the following year. The fact that Admiral was involved in these early negotiations is a good indicator just to how far the company had come in

such a short space of time. Bert had always undoubtedly been shooting for the stars, but it was clear his Wigston outfit wasn't always the well-oiled corporate machine it aspired to be. Mishaps, such as Leeds United running out in a set of strips in which their smiley club badge was affixed upside-down, happened from time to time. And a common disappointment among young fans was seeing the transfer of their club's crest fade further away with every passing laundry wash.

More inexplicably perhaps, neither Neville Chadwick nor any of his regular freelancers were dispatched to cover the 'Admiral Cup final'. How such an oversight occurred is unclear, but at its heart Bert's Wigston operation was still very much a provincial, family-run business – albeit one greater than the sum of its parts, which gave it the confidence to punch above its weight. "I don't think Adidas realised how small we were," Bert admits. "We were a major competitor of Adidas and Umbro, and I don't think they realised that."

Leading up to the Cup final's 3pm kick-off, I was hunkered down at home, glued to the television. Coverage had started at 11am on both BBC and ITV, and I would excitedly flit between hosts Frank Bough and Dickie Davies so as not to miss anything important, such as the 'The Road to Wembley' highlights or an interview with a star player in which you'd discover the identity of the team's 'joker'. There might be an appearance of a celebrity fan from 'the world of light entertainment'. And it was vital to catch the coverage from inside the team coaches as they made their way towards the Twin Towers. I didn't always care for the players' inspection of the playing surface, for some reason, and from here on in the matches themselves could often to be anti-climactic. But if I had to conjure up a quintessential FA Cup final in my mind's eye from that era, it would be the 1976 tie between Manchester United and Southampton. A true 'David vs Goliath' battle, on a gloriously sunny afternoon, and all with an added Admiral bonus, for good measure. It was the '70s football kit equivalent of jam roly-poly with a dollop of custard and a liberal sprinkling of hundreds-and-thousands.

Another cultural reference that stands out in my mind from that year was

Abba's ubiquitous hit single 'Fernando'. One of the reasons I remember the song, or the chorus anyway, was because it was always being sung by our new neighbour; but that wasn't the reason my housecoat-clad mum took a dislike to Mrs B. To my eleven-year-old mind, the blonde woman next door seemed incredibly glamorous, breezily coming and going in her boutique-bought chiffon dresses. To the more trained eye, she was 'all fur coat and no knickers', apparently. My older sister and I liked our new neighbours, though, and for very different reasons. Mrs B's only son was slightly older than Sue, and he would regularly lend her Marc Bolan and David Bowie records, which she would play endlessly. So by osmosis my musical education began also, but there were other benefits of living next door to the Bs. That summer was the hottest for 30 years, during which sweltering days our bohemian neighbour would regularly sunbathe topless on her patch of brown lawn, within view of my sister's bedroom window. Shamefully, my eleven-year-old self not only took advantage of this observation post but also charged my mates 10p for a furtive glimpse of my neighbour's reddening torso. A fledgling racket that was shut down one Saturday when my parents arrived home early from a shopping trip to discover a queue of neighbourhood boys lined up along the hallway, eagerly clutching their pocket money.

Other seismic events of 1976 included the launch of Leicester City's new Admiral kit. Not that City's new look attracted much of a fanfare, and even the club itself didn't seem to think it was that big a deal. The announcement in its own official yearbook was confined to half a dozen lines buried in commercial manager Stuart Crooks' musings about the upcoming campaign. Even when the season kicked off in August, Crooks was far more interested in bigging up the club's

175 STEVE KEMBER

revamped 'matchday magazine', barely mustering a sentence about the sponsored kits. "In a few weeks' time we will be coming up with a cover design that includes the lads in the new Admiral strip." And that was it. No other mention apart from two adverts listing local stockists and a price list. The players themselves seemed a little more enthused, trotting out into the centre circle in their colourful new track tops, before copying one of Leeds' old PR stunts, waving to all four corners of the crowd.

Despite such overt displays of glamour, I still had to process the actual look of Admiral's latest offering. It was of course unique and different to anything the company's creative minds had come up with before; but also it was a little confusing. There was no coveted naval logo on its chest, or tramlines running lengthways, or even any logo taping along the sleeves. Instead, a tiny row of Admiral badges wrapped around each shoulder, which commentator Barry Davies reliably informed viewers were called "epaulettes." Holding up his much-cherished first replica City shirt, Rob O'Donnell says, "I can still remember now looking in the *Leicester Mercury*, and I saw this around the arms on the new kit, and I thought they were little foxes. It was only when you saw it up close that you saw it was the Admiral badges."

What's striking, looking back at the club's literature from that time, is all the messaging about straitened times and cash-strapped finances. City's hierarchy clearly hadn't yet cottoned on to the eventual money-spinning potential of replica kits, even though this was a couple of years after the deals with Leeds United and

England. Maybe it's a reflection on how slowly commercial wheels were still turning in some quarters, or else on the purchasing power of supporters of less-glamorous sides. Paying £5.75 for a 'youths' jersey that its wearer may quickly outgrow was an awful lot of money, particularly when the previous, unadorned royal-blue jerseys could be picked up for £1.50. To put these prices into context, the charge of admission to stand at Filbert Street that season cost 70p for my dad and 30p for me. One of the new Admiral tops cost the same as a junior's entrance fee for an entire season. Not that their exorbitant price tags made City's new shirts any less desirable, of course. But sadly the following few Christmases and birthdays came and went without its arrival.

Wembley Stadium, October 1976

The weather that year remained unseasonably warm deep into the new season. Not least for England boss Don Revie, whose honeymoon – if he truly ever had one with the press – was well and truly over following his team's failure to qualify for that summer's European Championship finals. Not that any of that dampened my mood when Dad announced he was taking me out of school early to watch England take on Finland's part-timers in a World Cup qualifier at Wembley. I recall the drive down the motorway and navigating our way through a bustling mass of expectant supporters, as well as clutching my newly purchased England 'silk' scarf and clambering up a terraced bank towards the colossal Empire Stadium. We had bench seats along the side of Wembley's lower tier, accessed by a short concrete staircase off its circular concourse, and with each step nearer, the noise inside the amphitheatre grew ever louder, until I was stood atop of the gangway looking out into the vast bowl in front of me. It was like entering a scene in a science-fiction movie just before a spacecraft is about to land. My reaction prompted smiles and nudges from my dad and his mates, as I stood transfixed gazing out in disbelief upon 90,000 people wrapped around

a luminous baize forcefield. To most other observers, that evening's game didn't generate anywhere near as much wonder and awe. But I was simply mesmerised. Just a few yards in front of me, incandescent in their gleaming white Admiral jerseys, were England's star players. A Kevin Keegan-led side huffed and puffed its way to a 2-1 victory over an assortment of teachers and postmen, but ultimately came up short. England's inability to score more goals against the Finns proved to be their undoing. The following year, Italy qualified for Argentina '78 ahead of England on goal difference, by which time Revie had already departed.

Another major development of 1976, besides a national ladybird infestation, was a shift in playground allegiances. During the long, hot summer months, a new sportswear kid arrived on the block, sporting a very stylish crew-neck T-shirt with contrasting collar and cuffs, in a combination of highly sought-after colours. Most importantly, there were three stripes down each arm and an Adidas trefoil logo on its chest, making the German manufacturer's 'California' T-shirt that year's must-have item of clothing. Its status was cemented by its ubiquitous presence on the BBC's *Superstars*, during the filming of which Kevin Keegan took a tumble on the bike track, and Stan Bowles almost shot himself in the foot. Literally.

And Adidas's T-shirts weren't only selling to kids, having made the leap from sportswear to fashion accessory via the covers of lifestyle magazines. The growing popularity of the three-stripes brand hadn't gone unnoticed in Wigston. "It was worn by everybody – people playing tennis, workmen wearing it, and I was convinced actually that God was a German." John Griffin's antenna was twitching, and he realised Admiral was faced with a formidable competitor looking to extend its reach. Off the back of a highly successful Montreal Olympics, Adidas was looking to expand beyond footwear into clothing, and it had the commercial clout to support its goals. Just the sort of financial backing that Admiral lacked.

"I'll tell you another club we didn't get, we didn't get Nottingham Forest," reflects John ruefully, musing over his dealings with the club's new manager

Brian Clough during 'Old Big 'Ead's' erratic 44 days in charge of Leeds United. But it was Forest chairman Brian Appleby who made an initial approach, knowing John from the time their paths had crossed in the textiles industry. Appleby asked Admiral to "do something for us" at Forest. "So I said, 'Well, how are we going to be able to work with Clough?' He said, 'It's possible, yeah, it's possible.' So I got some stuff together, and the chairman got an appointment for me, and I think it was the Thursday afternoon I went over after lunch. And I was shown into a room, waiting, and then the door opened and Clough came in with the guy from Adidas."

John suspects Clough was cannily playing the two manufacturers off against each other to inflate their offers. "I showed him some designs, and he said, 'Yeah, yeah, that's great.' And I said, 'And they've been made in England.' So he said, 'How much would you offer us?' I said, '£30,000 a year.' He said, 'You go away and put that in writing, young man.' So I had the letter and I gave it to him, and I said, 'There you go.' So he said, 'Right, we'll be back.' But then they went away and they [signed] their Adidas contract. Adidas had got them for the next three years, and that was that."

The West Germans certainly backed the right horse to help them launch their British club strips. Wearing the company's trademark three stripes, Clough guided his newly promoted side to the First Division title, followed by back-to-back European Cup wins. It afforded Adidas the type of exposure Admiral had enjoyed with Leeds' success earlier in the decade. Only now the field was more crowded, and the stakes were climbing ever higher.

Sportswear's tectonic plates were definitely shifting. By the time the Manchester United sponsorship deal came up for renewal, chairman Louis Edwards was asking Admiral for much more money than before. "We were selling so much Manchester United merchandise, and the opportunities were there for other accessories, that we had to take it because we knew it would get bigger and bigger – and it did." Bert also knew that if he didn't pay the asking price, there were now other manufacturers who would do so in a heartbeat. It wasn't just Adidas muscling in on the replicas market, and Wigston's bosses were acutely aware they could also be gazumped by the likes of Bukta and Umbro as well. Following a day of negotiations at Old Trafford, John arrived back in Leicester on the evening of his firm's annual dinner dance at De Montfort Hall.

Bert recalls, "He came to me and said, 'Do you want the good news or the bad news?' I said, 'The bad news.' He said, 'It's going to cost you £100,000.' He said, 'The good news is that they want to carry on with us.' So that was the first big lift from what we'd been paying previously." A jump from £15,000 to £100,000 within three years, and very much a foretaste of what was about to come.

CHAPTER 7
Pump It Up

"It's remarkable," says John Devlin of a previously unknown Leicester hosiery firm's effect on the football strip world. "We've got to remember how small Admiral were in relation to other sportswear companies. But they really were making such massive impact at that time."

It's dull and overcast outside on the afternoon I meet up with the 50-something football kit aficionado to talk about the beginnings of the replicas market. We're chatting in my local pub which, aptly enough, doesn't look like it's seen a lick of paint since the mid 1970s. In forging ahead with its radical new sponsorship deals, and by proving that selling official football shirts to young fans was a lucrative business, Admiral unsurprisingly provoked a reaction from other suppliers: as John says, "'Hang on a minute, we like the sound of this deal. Let's see what we can do.'"

During 1976's long summer heatwave, Umbro had launched its own range of 'designer' strips, while Adidas was making further inroads into the UK market. And with only so many football clubs to go round, a replica kit 'arms race' was hotting up.

"At that time, the sportswear firms didn't believe that adults would be interested in wearing these strips. It was something for children to almost play being their heroes, rather than a symbol whereby any football supporter could show their loyalty to their club." John and I both belonged to Admiral's target demographic, and by the middle of the decade every football-mad kid in the land either had, or desperately wanted, one of their shirts. "It raised everybody's game," he says of the deals to sponsor England and a host of top clubs. The likes of Umbro and Bukta "reacted as you would expect, and they began to look at their own deals, look at what they could do, starting more visible branding on the shirts. All of a sudden they were racing to catch up with this business model that Admiral had created, and before you know it, the football kit world changed dramatically, almost overnight."

Following Cook & Hurt's failure to 'go bust after six months', as predicted by Wilmslow executives, Umbro adopted a similar approach to its East Midlands rival. Safe in the knowledge that it had a larger production base, including five factories in the North West, and the financial muscle to offer clubs bigger and better deals than Admiral could afford. The intention all along had been to wait and watch, and if Admiral's sponsorship model

didn't fail, Wilmslow would try to squeeze its Wigston competitor out of the market by upping the ante. Into the second half of the decade, both Umbro and Bukta were redesigning and copyrighting their own kits, and marketing replica copies in children's sizes. 'It's going to be a sparkling season,' announced Umbro proudly, launching its revamped strips at the start of the 1976/77 campaign. The full-page advert in *Shoot!* magazine implored you to 'Look at those diamonds' gracing the sleeves, shorts and socks of Bristol City, Everton, Derby County and Manchester City kits. The manufacturer also added solid logo taping to its Blackpool and Scotland outfits, while Arsenal and Liverpool's own kits remained comparatively sober, but it was obvious both belonged to Umbro's stable thanks to heavy branding.

When May's FA Cup final came around in Jubilee year, Wigston's marketing team no longer had a monopoly on Wembley events, despite the return of Tommy Docherty's Manchester United. They lined up in relatively modest Admiral hoodies opposite an obviously Umbro-sponsored Liverpool team on course for the Treble. And this time it was United who upset the favourites, thanks to Lou Macari's deflected shot spinning off Jimmy Greenhoff's chest into Ray Clemence's net – and so the FA Cup went to Old Trafford. But Umbro's executives only had to wait four days before they could celebrate with their own 'choice of champions', this time in Rome where Liverpool beat Borussia Mönchengladbach to lift their first European Cup.

The Cheshire firm may have been late to the party, but Umbro was clearly intent on making up for lost time. The following season, its tiny rhombuses were retooled and this time appeared as double diamonds on the strips of Bolton Wanderers, Cardiff City, Chelsea, Hearts, Morton, Partick Thistle, Stoke City, West Brom and Wolves. "At the time they were considered a bit outrageous but, looking back, this fairly simple template," Hammond & Silke judge, "has a relatively restrained and classy look about it." Yet despite the popularity and success of its souped-up new replica lines, Wilmslow's chiefs were now also looking nervously over their shoulders. Adidas had also entered the UK market, in a move that put strain on a previous arrangement with Umbro whereby the two companies kept out of each other's core business.

The respective founding fathers, Adolf Dassler and Harold Humphreys, had joined forces in the 1960s to sell each other's products. A reciprocal agreement existed whereby Umbro had exclusive rights to market Adidas boots in Britain, while Adidas promoted and distributed Umbro clothing in West Germany. This relationship fractured once Adidas began supplying three-striped garments directly to UK suppliers and "now, all of a sudden, the partners were head-on competitors," says Barbara Smit ominously. The pair's mutual collaboration had completely unravelled by the 1980s.

While Umbro launched its 'sparkling' collection that summer, Adidas pressed on by kitting out Queens Park Rangers. The following year in 1977, the names of Birmingham City, Dundee United, Fulham, Ipswich Town, Middlesbrough,

Nottingham Forest, Notts County, Preston North End and Wrexham were added to its burgeoning roster. These early Adidas template kits were fairly simple, adorned with the company's distinctive three stripes and an unfussy crew or V-neck collar.

"Very boring," was John Griffin's blunt assessment of the Germans' initial offerings, and he also dismissed Umbro's efforts for copying Admiral's use of logo taping. But despite his observations, he was also quick to acknowledge that, "Our product wasn't quite right, and Adidas were getting more and more teams."

As replica kits grew ever more popular and sales increased, John Griffin says this created a dilemma for his own sales reps. "You'd bump into directors from other clubs, and they would say, 'It's my grandson's birthday, do you think you can get me so-and-so?' And you're on the spot. Here we go again, another freebie." Most other ex-employees I spoke to received similar requests from family and friends, telling me proudly that their own kids "would be the first ones to have them in their school. Even if he didn't like the teams, he wanted their kits. He did pretty well in the playground." Other workers recalled brazen neighbours and passing acquaintances turning up on their doorsteps with requests for kits. Fortunately, Long Street had a factory shop selling discounted 'seconds' to its employees, but it wasn't unknown for garments to be smuggled out illicitly. Many of the women I spoke to admitted to helping themselves to an occasional shirt or track top over the years. Sporadic bag checks were introduced, but word soon spread on such days, and workers would slip into the toilets to find a better hiding place for their contraband, with coat sleeves being favoured by many smugglers. The biggest threat to getting caught was often schoolboy excitement, with some recipients wearing their ill-gotten wares to school even before the jerseys were available in the shops.

"I don't think anything came of it, I don't think anybody realised," a former machinist told me, recalling the time her son showed off his newly acquired England jersey despite his mother's strict instructions not to do so. "I think we'd have been sacked probably, 'cos they weren't for sale, not then."

To a certain extent, Admiral's kits 'sold themselves', and Bert told me he preferred to generate his own news coverage, but the company did also advertise in magazines such as *Shoot!* and various matchday programmes. The marketing sent out some fairly sophisticated messages, whether intentional or not.

"Admiral created something that wasn't there before," says Rob O'Donnell. "They created this need, where kids needed football kits. They desperately wanted these latest designs, whereas before that wasn't the case. Anybody would be happy going around in any blue shirt if you were a Leicester or a Chelsea fan. As long as it was blue, it was fine."

John Devlin describes Admiral's "some might say cynical approach" when discussing the company's marketing strategy. "The adverts nearly always just featured children, and again it was really pushing this as a new way that you can follow your team." Some ads, as I remember only too well myself, were less than subtle. "There was a certain amount of emotional blackmail involved. There was a classic advert, 'Show your team you really care', the implication being that if you didn't buy the official Admiral replica jersey you weren't really a true supporter." Another advert I distinctly remember featured a group of boys around my age outside a corner shop, all suavely decked out in a range of replicas under a strapline: 'Our kit is just up your street'. As with all youth tribes, the implication was simple: if you don't dress like us, you can't be in our gang.

Our kit is just up your street

Whether you support a top soccer club or national team, or you are just interested in looking great, — Admiral is the kit to be seen in! Just go up the street to your local sports shop and take a look at the range of fantastic Admiral clothing and footwear. Now!

Admiral If it's Admiral-it's professional.

Rushing down to a newsagents to buy a copy of *Shoot!* magazine was an integral part of many young fans' Thursday-morning journey to school. Each edition contained readily available posters in the form of full-page action shots and portraits that would often be torn out and pinned on to bedroom walls by evening time. Rob O'Donnell remembers becoming increasingly drawn to the "fantastic pictures of these new kits," once Admiral arrived on the scene. His own recollections chime very much with my own, and I'm instantly able to visualise specific photographs he mentions. "I can still see the Norwich City kit – Martin Peters, you can just see the picture of him sitting there. And they were so different that you just wanted to study the pictures and see where the Admiral badges were."

The first time I meet Rob, I bring along a poster that we both had on our bedroom wall as youngsters, a montage of action shots featuring many of the clubs on Admiral's books, with an illustration of each team's strip as a border. Rob knows it only too well. Having studied the chart intensively as a child, he easily identifies and points out each kit. "Leeds, I think that was the first one. I remember England, Leicester, Tottenham, Luton was a big one, West Ham – they had fantastic designs and I always remember those in the brochures. Aberdeen, that was another because they had the white stripes, about six white stripes down the left side. Crystal Palace was another one."

Many of the photos mentioned above, as well as all of the images that appeared in a series of Admiral annuals, were taken by Neville Chadwick and his team. With his business partner John Plant, Nev would study the coming week's fixtures and pick out the best games to cover. Ideally, matches in which both teams would be wearing Admiral strips. During international breaks, the focus would be on star players turning out for England and Wales. "They'd got to be prominent, and we selected the pictures for the advertising material with the advertising agency boys who were doing the designing of the brochures and the adverts." Picking up a transparency of an image taken at a Home Championship game, the snapper places it on to a beaming lightbox and nods approvingly towards it. "This picture would probably be in the short list, because it shows both teams with the Admiral kit on, and a reasonable action photograph. I'm not saying that that one would be in, but it would be on the shortlist." It probably was, because the image of Gerry Francis and Terry Yorath battling it out at Ninian Park feels very familiar. "We were looking for good action pictures because the annual was for children as well, and they wanted to see good action pictures, not just the Admiral logo. Nothing looked better than a first-class action picture with the Admiral logo on both teams."

The Sun newspaper's sports editor, Frank Nicklin, was enlisted to produce The Admiral Book of Football each year, and it was quickly established as a Christmas-present staple alongside the Shoot! annual. It was essentially the same format as the latter publication, only heavily weighted towards Admiral-centric photos and articles. "Frank Nicklin and Bert, myself and my partner would spend the afternoon in the studio projecting all the pictures that we thought were good enough for the football annual." Together, they sifted through around

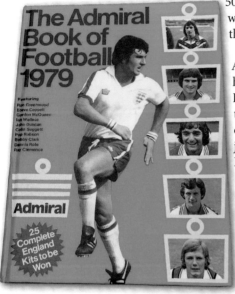

500 photographs that would eventually be whittled down to the hundred-odd images that made it into each picture book.

All of Cook & Hurst's press releases were handled by Terry Harris at East Midlands Press Services, conveniently based on the top floor of Nev's premises diagonally opposite the Long Street factory. After jointly setting up Oakley Young Associates, Paul Oakley also began renting a space there as well, and was soon taking on design work for Admiral. According to Nev, "the whole building was full of Bert's advertising, press people and photographers, we were all together there. If we wanted a business meeting between photographers and press and the designers and Bert, we could fix it up within ten minutes, and spend the morning talking where we were going and what we were doing."

There's a degree of cottage-industry charm in Nev's retelling of those early days. It's a time he certainly looks back on fondly. Operating informally on a shoestring budget, he was typically given less than 24 hours' notice to photograph the latest line of merchandise. "We hadn't got the time to employ models, you've got to book them up a week in advance. A lot of our pictures were taken the next day: 'We need a picture for an advert, can you do it tomorrow?' sort of style, so we used to use quite a few local people." As mentioned previously, when Nev says "local people," he means Admiral employees. "We'd go across the road and have a word with Bert, and he would say, 'I know just the girls you need for these pictures.' So we didn't have to walk around and say, 'That one would do, and that's a nice one.' Bert had already done that for us."

These impromptu photocalls would very often take place in local parks or at the nearby Saffron Lane athletics track. Leicester City's Filbert Street stadium was used for a Wales photo-shoot and, perhaps less surprisingly, for the club's own kit launch. If there's a better set of photographs that incapsulates that moment in time, I have yet to see them. The images feature a trio of young women with big hair, sometimes pouting towards camera, and occasionally in a state of undress: *Carry On Admiral*.

Carry On Admiral: one of Neville Chadwick's outtakes from Leicester City's new kit photo-shoot in 1976.

"Bert asked me to organise it, and the club said, 'Right, you can do it tomorrow,' sort of style, on the pitch, with their new kit. But I needed models and I could only get two models at such short notice. So there was a girl who worked at Leicester City in the office, she stepped in to be the third model." Working on his own without an assistant or art director, let alone a stylist or make-up artist, Nev rattled off a series of colour and black-and-white images. "And that was the result of the photocall," he says, handing me a monochrome print of a young woman with a blonde bob, seemingly caught by surprise putting on a pair of blue shorts. Advertising clearly works, as I did eventually buy the white shirt she's wearing.

Nev's Admiral work sounds a far cry from today's multi-million-pound sportswear campaigns, and the closest he got to a foreign location was a roundabout outside Heathrow Airport. The image in question is of Manchester

United's Lou Macari showing off a pair of Admiral-branded football boots. Nev had been chasing the elusive Scot for weeks and eventually pinned him down, albeit very briefly. Macari was in-between trips but agreed to be snapped in transit if the photographer promised to be "quick." Stepping out of the terminal building for his allotted "ten minutes," the only thing Nev could spot with any green foliage for a backdrop was a busy traffic island being orbited by vehicles. The smiling Scotsman was duly snapped in a United shirt, presenting the aforementioned footwear to Nev's camera – all the while being pointed at by curious holidaymakers.

Excitement in the days leading up to my 12th birthday had been building steadily, with the expectation of my grandma buying me a tracksuit. Indeed, the garment did materialise; but sadly it wasn't one adorned with a nautical badge or three stripes. Worse, instead of royal blue, it was bright pillar-box red. Initially, I refused to wear the thing but was left in no doubt that the garment wasn't "going back." And besides, "the more you wear it, the sooner it will need replacing," so the argument went. Like every other kid in the area, I practically lived in a 'trackie' outside of school – with 'practical' being the salient point. The wear and tear of playing out all day meant you 'got through' these catalogue-bought outfits fairly regularly, but they were also easily replaced. They certainly weren't considered costly or precious. So perhaps it's inevitable how criticism followed as Admiral's 'designer' clothing became more sought after.

Children's official replica club kits and tracksuits were undeniably expensive, regardless of whether they were made in the East Midlands, the North West or indeed Bavaria. And it was argued, not unreasonably, that this put pressure on parents. Sewing a badge on to a plain jersey was no longer going to do it for most youngsters when the 'real' shirts were now out there and available.

"It was dangling this carrot of exclusivity, you had to look like these players. So the price rise, that was part and parcel of it because it was an officially produced Admiral shirt, and it had that brand on it." John Devlin shakes his head, recounting his own parental shopping horror story. "I used to have a Liverpool shirt that Mum bought me from the market with a sew-on badge that you put on. It wasn't quite the same, and kids, as children are today, you knew it. Even back in the '70s you knew you didn't have an official shirt on – and it's a big deal for a child."

Then there were the lucky kids, of course. "There's always a rich kid in class, isn't there?" announces Peris Hatton with an eye roll. "We were all quite jealous of this lad because every week he'd come in a different strip. He was quite a good player as well, but he'd come in the all-yellow Admiral Wales kit. I remember that day, because we'd never seen it before and we were all sort of, 'Oh, what's that kit?' They weren't cheap. To buy a full strip at the time would probably cost about £12, which in 1977, '78 was an awful lot of money."

HOUSE OF COMMONS

LONDON SW1A OAA

As more and more clubs signed up to sponsored kit deals, the debate about the cost of replicas was reignited. But this time Admiral wasn't the only manufacturer caught in Fleet Street's crosshairs. Umbro, Bukta and Adidas also came under scrutiny, and not solely from crusading columnists. In February 1977, Prices Under-Secretary Mr Robert MacLennan announced that the replica kit business was being investigated by the government's Prices Commission. It followed a speech made in the House of Commons by MP Roy Hughes, chairman of the All-Party Sports Group, claiming "star-struck" children were "paying through the nose" to dress like their heroes. By exploiting the 1968 Copyright Act, he argued that sports manufacturers were using the country's top players as "walking adverts" to sell their overpriced shirts.

"One of the principle offenders appears to be the Leicester firm of Cook & Hurst, the chairman of which is Mr Bert Patrick and their trade name is Admiral. The attitude of that firm is arrogant." The right honourable gentleman for Newport also named and shamed Umbro, Bukta and Adidas for what he termed "undesirable practices" on their parts. "The price of the products is excessive. It is about double that of similar products without an emblem. It is if the biblical incantation 'suffer little children' has been taken literally."

"That hurt a bit, because I didn't think I was arrogant," Bert told me. But he says he simply accepted the criticism as a part of the rough and tumble of doing business – and, sure enough, the affair blew over without government censure. Besides, tweaking the tail of the tabloids was part and parcel of the game as far as Bert was concerned. "Parents were being persuaded by their children to buy records, which weren't cheap; skateboards, that became very popular, in fact that affected our sales, and they were expensive. But my answer was always, well, 'We are one of the few organisations putting money back into football.'"

The following year, the BBC waded into the fray, taking a look "at how replica football strips were becoming popular" in an episode of *The Risk Business*. Reporter Judith Hann told viewers that "nearly all of the 92 Football League clubs have some sort of deal with strip manufacturers." She went on to explain that "Manchester United's away strip by Admiral costs £10.30, and that's for a young supporter. And Southampton's strip, again by Admiral, £11.70." Warming to her theme, Judith then holds aloft a plain unbranded blue shirt before adding,

"But you could get this one from Bukta for only £5.43. That's over 100 per cent difference in price for trivial changes in design and little or no difference in quality. And there is a second wrinkle, clubs are persuaded to change their strips from time to time, even yearly in some cases, and no self-respecting fan would be seen dead in last year's kit."

Oh Judith, there's an awful lot to unpack here. But perhaps the reporter did have a point...

"They were too expensive, you just couldn't buy them," says Rob O'Donnell. "Not many people had them. So it was a massive purchase." He told me his seven-year-old self would look longingly through "brochures with these fantastic kits that were available at the sports shop, and you'd be flicking through them and thinking, 'Wow, I'd love to have that kit.'"

Fortunately for Rob, the former Wigston schoolboy's mum had found a way around the high prices with the help of family connections. The legendary Sheila would prove to be Rob's fairy godmother once again. "Everybody was trying to get the kits. So, we were lucky enough to know people within Admiral, so your mum would come home with a kit one day and it was just, wow! Suddenly I get home and I've got a Crystal Palace kit, fantastic. You just didn't know what you were going to get. But being in Wigston was great because you'd get all sorts to wear, and you'd be on the park with the latest one."

Rob holds aloft another child-size shirt, this time in white adorned with claret and blue trims and logo taping, that I immediately associate with the 1980 FA Cup final – and also the Cockney Rejects' appearance on *Top of the Pops* that year, the punk band all dressed in Admiral replica jerseys as they mimed along to their cover of 'I'm Forever Blowing Bubbles'.

"That one was supposed to be for my brother. But I think he wore it once, and I was desperate for it, so she took it in a couple of inches so I could go out and wear that one. That was an amazing one to get. Not a fan of West Ham but a fan of the shirts, definitely." It was easy to put club allegiances to one side, says Rob. "It was more about the kit because it was such a new thing. Suddenly there's badges and the Admiral logos, and so if it was Crystal Palace or West Ham you didn't care at that time."

For those unfortunate enough not to know a 'Sheila', there was always Ralph's Hardware. Our local ironmonger would occasionally sell rejected and slightly faulty Admiral tops at knock-down prices, but you had to be quick. Whenever word spread of a delivery, kids would jump on their bikes and descend en masse at the affable brown-coated Ralph's shop, with pocket money to burn.

Gary Silke was another beneficiary of what I suspect may have been a Leicestershire-wide retail experience. "This early version of TK Maxx was created – highly desirable labels at affordable prices. We would dive into the box and rummage around for brightly coloured treasure... Norwich, Sheffield United, West Ham, Tottenham and Manchester United kits, all bearing the jaunty yellow Admiral badge." Ralph's own bargain bucket was always brimming over with Norwich and Southampton cast-offs, I remember. That is until another, far more exotic line of clothing turned up out of the blue.

When Admiral won the UK concession to licence North American Soccer League shirts, imperfect 'seconds' started turning up at Ralph's aforementioned emporium, as well as at other outlets across the county – and overnight,

Leicestershire's playing fields were alive with kids running around in the tops of bizarre-sounding teams such as Philadelphia Furies, San Jose Earthquakes and Tampa Bay Rowdies. There was a dizzying spectrum of colours and badges to match. And, unsurprisingly, Rob O'Donnell was beside himself with excitement. "Suddenly this array of fantastic, new-designed American kits came out, with pictures on the front and different-style arms. That was the next level. That took you again to a situation where you wanted more and more kits."

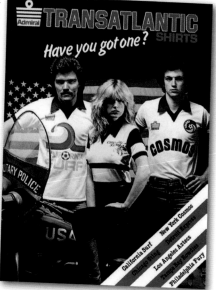

Once kids like Peris Hatton got their hands on one of the precious shirts, they'd virtually never take it off. "We all wore them all day every day, and it was sort of dragged off us by our parents to go into the washing machine."

My Ralph's Hardware story would be easily trounced in any game of Admiral Sports Top Trumps by Dave Tazzyman. As a pupil at All Saints Primary School, around the corner from the Long Street factory, Dave appeared as an 'extra' in at least two local news reports. Visiting TV crews occasionally approached the school's headteacher seeking help with their filming, and a hastily arranged football match would often be filmed in a local park involving eager young volunteers. In one clip, Dave and a bunch of his mates even made it into Admiral's foyer, where they were filmed helping themselves to a pile of free posters, notionally being handed out by an overrun, bubble-permed receptionist. The stuff of dreams.

But if I thought Dave Tazzyman had struck it lucky, then Dave Harris had won

one of Willy Wonka's golden tickets, with unfettered access to the Chocolate-Brown Factory. The very nerve-centre of all things Admiral became Dave's Saturday-morning playground courtesy of his best mate, whose mum was a cleaner at Long Street – except on Saturday mornings when she was supposed to be sweeping up, she preferred to play bingo instead. The problem was easily resolved by the woman co-opting her son and Dave into carrying out her weekend cleaning duties. A task with which they were more than happy to oblige. Around the same time, the British Museum's Tutankhamun exhibition was attracting thousands of visitors a day, but I can't imagine for a second that those Edwardian explorers could have been as excited as the two 12-year-olds creeping along that factory's empty, unlit corridors. Dave says he would stand in the middle of a workroom looking around slack-jawed at the multicoloured splendour of the rolls and reams surrounding him. He freely admits the pair spent as much time scouring for "souvenirs" as they did "cleaning," but regrettably always came away empty handed.

Despite growing pressure from Adidas and Umbro, business in Wigston was booming, and Admiral had an impressive client list that included a host of top English and Scottish clubs, plus several European and international teams. But rather than consolidating his business, Bert decided to take the fight to his competitors. "I thought, well, the German market's a lucrative market, so let's have a crack there." The company duly opened an office in West Germany – Admiral Sportbekleidung – which was akin to "parking my tanks on Adidas's lawn," he adds mischievously. The distributors Admiral was dealing with "didn't particularly want to import direct from the UK, they wanted to import from a German-based warehouse, so we were investing, investing, investing. And of course Adidas, I'm sure, didn't like us encroaching on their territory."

Bert took evening language lessons to help him succeed in Germany but readily admits it was a tough market to crack. He describes the reaction of the Teutonic sportswear industry as "frosty," and particularly so when Admiral exhibited at trade fairs in Munich and Cologne.

Lindsay Jelley remembers one West German excursion vividly, as a 20-year-old. "We had a big stand and all the tracksuits, we took two models – it was fantastic for me, a great trip away." Ostensibly, she was going along to launch a new range of terry-towelling tracksuits but, "of course, the other mission was to get ideas and market research and all that, which we did."

An act of corporate espionage required a certain amount of *chutzpah* on the young designer's part. Security around some of the exhibitors was tight, and the likes of Adidas were very particular about who was allowed on to their stands. Lindsay laughs heartily, recounting how she was able to sashay past officials and charm delegates into showing her their latest designs and fabrics, which she would commit to memory before hurrying off to the ladies' toilets. Once ensconced inside a cubicle, she would then hurriedly fill a sketchbook with all that she'd gleaned.

Lindsay's clandestine efforts notwithstanding, Admiral's foray into West

Germany was a disaster. Of all of the country's top clubs approached, only Bundesliga side Eintracht Frankfurt signed up with the firm. After less than a year, Bert pulled the plug on his European operation. "So, I had to come out of Germany with my tail between my legs, eventually, because we just couldn't eat into the market."

Fortunately for Bert and Admiral, plans to open a manufacturing plant had already been shelved, but the company still lost £250,000 on the misadventure.

293 EINTRACHT FRANKFURT AWAY
ALL SIZES

292 EINTRACHT FRANKFURT HOME
ALL SIZES

Unperturbed, it wouldn't be Bert's only overseas excursion. Domestic labour shortages and attractive startup incentives in the Republic of Ireland soon persuaded him to open a factory in Ballina, County Mayo. Once again, the project ran into difficulties, despite an alleged offer by local IRA commanders to 'kneecap' anybody threatening to go on strike, and a local Catholic priest blessing the new factory. Not only finding but being able to train and maintain a reliable workforce was the undoing, this time. Bert cites absenteeism along with recurring problems – including batches of jerseys with only one sleeve – as his reasons for abandoning the Ballina sojourn.

"Don't forget we were not a big organisation administratively," he adds by way of explaining the setbacks. And it's true, the original Cook & Hurst company was still a relatively small manufacturing operation. If Bert wanted to compete with the likes of Umbro and Adidas, he needed to scale up and expand his manufacturing base, which experience now showed was probably easier closer to home.

Admiral moved into a state-of-art 50,000 square-metre open-plan factory just a mile away from Long Street on the Chartwell Drive Industrial Estate. A second unit directly opposite operated as a dispatch office, which was also used for storage, while Long Street was now primarily used to house the accounts department and the team making up prototype samples.

After settling into its purpose-built premises, the company still appeared to be on an upwards trajectory. Orders were rolling in, and clients were entertained on yacht trips aboard the *Admiral Sport*, moored at Poole Harbour. And Bert looked every inch the successful entrepreneur, driving around in sports cars and a Rolls-Royce Corniche.

As Paul Oakley told me, "The cars were always a bit of a joke, really, even by the standards of the day. The Lamborghini, I think it was an Espada, and the Aston Martin Lagonda were probably two of the most hideous supercars ever made."

Even so, it's hard not to be childishly impressed by Bert having bought the latter straight off the stand at the Motor Show in Birmingham.

ADMIRAL SPORTSWEAR
Head Office: Long St, Wigston Magna, Leicester LE8 2RQ, England. Telephone and Telegrams: 881302 Telex 34; 159
Sales Office and orders: Telephone 889311

EDITORIAL for the Wigton Advertiser

Admiral Sportswear of Wigston have taken to the water.
A fast Coastal Patrol Boat, commissioned and built by Fairey
Marine Ltd of Hamble near Southampton, was launched in the
traditional style by Birmingham sports retailer, Harry Parkes
at Poole Harbour Yacht Club.

Attending the ceremony were employees and customers of the
Wigston company and a reception was held afterwards in the
Poole Harbour Yacht Club house.

By the second half of the decade, it was clear to all concerned that the replica kits market was not only sustainable but here to stay. As were the merchandising spin-offs following in its slipstream. "Globally, probably about a hundred," Bert tells me when I ask him how many football teams were on his books at the company's height. "In our own factories, we'd probably got about 400 people, and I think there was at least as many people again helping us out with production. And we talked in dozens, a thousand dozen [shirts] a week was the norm perhaps, if we were particularly busy. At certain times of the year it would be more than that, producing in our own factories."

Other businesses orbiting Admiral's world also benefitted, including Neville Chadwick's photography studio. "We didn't know obviously where it was going to finish up," Nev says, "but it was gathering pace every year. Each year you'd start off again, and you'd do the photocalls of the football teams, and instead of doing three or four or five, we were finishing up doing ten and 15 and 20 teams. And at the same time it meant we'd got to expand our firm. We doubled the amount of photographers, just to keep up with Bert and Admiral."

Life at the production end was equally hectic. "I used to say, 'Oh, we've got all the football teams in the country,' because that's how it felt," remembers Lindsay. "And you're always coming up with ideas, so it was mad, the whole thing was going at a terrific pace. That's how it felt, but that made it vibrant and exciting. It was a very, very exciting company."

One of the peak thrills came when Lindsay was dispatched to London to meet American film producer Albert 'Cubby' Broccoli and his production team. She was there to discuss Admiral designing costumes for a forthcoming James Bond movie called *Moonraker*, starring Roger Moore as 007.

It was "all a bit mad," recalls Lindsay, who had to suppress a few giggles when dealing with a "ridiculous" French costume designer. "All that he was banging on about was the 'fab-ric' should be 'sex-y' and all we wanted was the logo." The tie-in foundered on Admiral's insistence that its own trademark stayed in the picture – a request the producers weren't unreasonable to turn down, acknowledges Lindsay, because "if you've got people landing on the moon, I can see that an Admiral logo wouldn't quite look right."

Nevertheless, Admiral did make it on to the silver screen. *Yesterday's Hero*

was a football feature film written by Jackie Collins. It starred Ian McShane as washed-up star striker Rod Turner who – may contain spoilers! – makes an implausible comeback for 'the Saints', culminating in a match-winning FA Cup final appearance against 'Leicester Forest' at Wembley. The actors were kitted out in a rebadged version of Southampton's yellow away strip, and the climactic scenes intercut with actual footage from the 1979 League Cup final between the 'real' Saints and Nottingham Forest.

"It was a whirlwind," Lindsay enthuses. "I'd turn up for work and you'd just never stop, and there would be different things coming at you from all directions. There was a lot of pressure, but I think that was part of the excitement of it, and there was a lot of pride in it, too. I remember times when somebody would come in for a meeting with Mr Griffin, and they would demand a sample *now*, and you'd rustle something up. And I remember times when I'd say, 'No, I've got to press it...' 'No, we haven't got time for that.' And it would just go down."

Working to deadlines was occasionally stressful, Lindsay admits, and voices were occasionally raised, but never at her. "You wanted the momentum to continue anyway, the factory had that feeling about it. As a boss, Mr Patrick was quite inspiring. I think they both were. They made you feel like you wanted to produce more, and so you did. They came to me and said, 'Lindsay, we need something in these colours...' Away I went, loved it. Happy days, mad days."

To sustain momentum, the company needed to maintain cordial relations with its workforce and its union, as stalled negotiations and intransigence were starting to unsettle other sectors. Strikes weren't uncommon in Leicester.

As Bert Patrick remembers, "The unions in the textile industry – you could live with them, but they were still fairly aggressive." But he says he always recognised that the success of the business wasn't just down to the selling skills of its management team or the creativity of its designers. The strips still needed to be manufactured, and this required a proficient and motivated workforce.

One capable of producing elaborately styled, hugely labour-intensive outfits fast enough to meet demand while still turning a profit.

"The important thing was the women machinists, and we had some very, very expert cutters," acknowledges John. "Because fabric is the biggest part of costing, they would get maybe 80 to 85 per cent fabric utilisation, which was good. And initially they'd do it just by their knowledge and their ability to try things out." He remains fulsome in his praise for his former employees, for their ability to quickly get up to speed with different styles. "Seventy per cent of making the garment is handwork, manual, and 30 per cent is mechanical machine [work]. It's amazing," he tells me, while demonstrating with a piece of cloth how machinists would skilfully manipulate garments.

The company's workforce remained fairly stable throughout this period. Employees tended to leave due to personal circumstances rather than to take another job. Even now, Mandy Hutchins admits she'd return in a heartbeat "if

I could go back in time." She tells me how the factory would grind to a halt at 10.55am in order to listen to the 'Our Tune' segment of Simon Bates' Radio One show. More often than not, this was a heartbreakingly sad love story that "everybody ended up crying" over before getting "straight back to work" as a

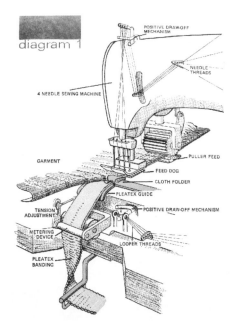

diagram 1

POSITIVE DRAW-OFF MECHANISM

NEEDLE THREADS

4 NEEDLE SEWING MACHINE

GARMENT

PULLER FEED

FEED DOG

CLOTH FOLDER

PLEATEX GUIDE

TENSION ADJUSTMENT

POSITIVE DRAW-OFF MECHANISM

METERING DEVICE

LOOPER THREADS

PLEATEX BANDING

couple's "special song" played out.

The importance of good morale and a happy workforce wasn't lost on Bert. Particularly as he would often call on them to work overtime or to produce a fast-turnaround kit for a specific match. "It was a competitive labour market, in the sense that they could easily walk out of our factory into another factory down the road and get a job. So we'd introduce things like a free hairdo every week to the top female operative. She might be an overlocker or a lock-stitcher, and they would really go for it. And then, once a month, the one that had probably got more than one award would get a perm. And it was quite something, in those days."

Nearly every ex-employee I spoke to remembers the workplace camaraderie and the firm's social get-togethers with great fondness. Even if Mandy still grimaces at the memory of being taken to the 'Nautical' pub for her 18th birthday, which she says was celebrated far too enthusiastically with whisky and orange. She has happier memories of the time she took part in the Lord Mayor's Parade with Jill, alongside Bridget Marlow and Hilary Cottam, when they entered the procession on an Admiral-sponsored float. Jill admits she may have gone a bit overboard on the 'monster' theme and says she persuaded an undertaker on Central Avenue to provide an actual coffin. The casket featured as the centrepiece of their flatbed truck set, on which Mandy's Devil, Hilary's Bride of Frankenstein, and Bridget's Dummy, as well as Jill's own Dracula, were paraded around the streets of Leicester. Not only did Jill supply the dry ice and blood tablets, but she also sat up for hours the night before dubbing Bobby 'Boris' Pickett's 'Monster Mash' single, repeatedly on to an audio cassette tape. A track the freshly permed 17-year-old Shaun Patrick remembers as "that bloody record," blaring out of a "ghetto-blaster" continuously on a loop all day. The group's efforts were clearly appreciated by the parade's judges though, who presented Team Admiral with their award for best float, sponsored by the local knitwear firm Ladies' Pride.

As with most other successful lines of clothing that make money, the replicas business attracted spurious imitators looking to cash in. Bert and John had previously fought and won a test case against Litesome by citing the 1968 Copyright Act, forcing the Dunlop subsidiary to burn the Admiral-designed shirts it was copying and selling. But combating counterfeiters outside of the

UK's borders was more difficult. The popularity of British football abroad, and TV shows such as *Match of the Day* meant the Admiral brand and its strips were recognised around the world. Increasing the company's exposure in more ways than one. Sales of its kits, particularly England and Manchester United replicas, started taking off in South East Asia, boosting profits even further and helping to increase turnover by 800 per cent since the start of the decade, according to the *Financial Times*. The same paper also revealed that the firm 'has come under attack from the pirates of the international textile trade' and reported that 'the shirts are being turned out in Bangkok, Thailand and Penang in Singapore's neighbouring State of Malaysia.' The upshot of this piracy was the Wigston firm losing hundreds of thousands of pounds of profits to illegitimate overseas sales.

In his memoir, Bert writes about visiting the region, and the time he was taken to a warehouse in Bangkok where boxes of pirated Admiral shirts were being stored. He recalled how the legal clerk accompanying him threatened the unit's owner with arson by falsely telling him Bert would burn his factory down "if he didn't stop producing fakes." The Admiral boss enlisted the help of the UK's Department of Trade, but neither Thailand nor Singapore belonged to the International Conventions for the Protection of Industrial Property, so their authorities continued to ignore the trademark infringements.

With all official channels seemingly exhausted and its hands effectively tied,

the *Financial Times* reported that the company would fall back on its own innovation. "Admiral is placing more faith on its traditionally fast footwork to counter the pirates. By frequent alterations of strips involving complex design changes, it hopes to stay far ahead of the Far East competition. It also achieves the not insignificant target of constantly stimulating demand at home as schoolboys rush to imitate their heroes."

As competition hotted up on the home market, Wigston's managers sought to become less reliant on selling replica kits alone. After all, an overdependence on underwear orders had led to Bert taking over Cook & Hurst in the first place, 20 years earlier. From now on in, the company would also be targeting non-sports fans and a leisurewear market yet to be fully realised, according to Bert. "My vision was that a tracksuit would become an everyday garment that women, housewives, would do the vacuum cleaning and the housework in, which they did of course." Diversification also meant expanding into other areas of football merchandising, and Admiral's bosses began to add their trademark to all kinds of sundry products. An extensive range of scarves, T-shirts, holdalls and footwear appeared over the coming years, all carrying the naval logo. Once again, the company managed to tap into what young consumers wanted. Branded spinoffs also included eiderdowns and pyjamas.

"I remember the scarves," says Rob O'Donnell wistfully. "It was completely different, because before that there were just normal bar-blocked scarves, and then suddenly you've got Admiral scarves with actual player's faces on them. The start of a brand new era."

"I don't recall scarves very much, but they did get into other things like darts," says Paul Oakley, recalling the British Darts Association commissioning a different line of players' clothing that eventually saw the light of day. Or, more accurately, the smoky gloom of packed working men's clubs. The sport attracted huge television audiences in the '70s and '80s, elevating its stars, such as Eric 'The Crafty Cockney' Bristow, into household names. One of the most popular players on the circuit was the toothless, 5'4" Scotsman Jocky Wilson. He just about managed to squeeze his 17-stone frame into a satin-effect Admiral-branded top that was a hybrid affair, looking something like a bowling shirt crossed with a football jersey.

"They were huge, I can't tell you the measurements," says Lindsay, rocking with laughter, her arms outstretched to reveal the scale of the outfits. "You were used to doing footballers, and suddenly there was this shirt that was wider than it was long, and you had to try and make it look a good design. It was really challenging, that was. Yes, they were big chaps." There's something very British and ultimately quite comical about this particular venture. While Adidas and Nike were battling it out for their market share of the running and jogging boom, Admiral was aligning itself with downing pints, tabs and 'good arrows'.

Some felt such moves spelt trouble, and Paul Oakley believes Admiral was losing sight of what it was good at. "I felt it was a real mismatch to the athleticism of football and the lack of athleticism of darts. Rather weakened the product, as far as I was concerned, [but it went] under the radar for most people because I think the success of darts would've been an even bigger contributor to the failure of Admiral as a serious sports brand."

There was also a move into footwear – training shoes and football boots – that was considered a mistake. The company was spreading itself too thin, it was argued, and was moving away from its most profitable line of business: making replica football kits. There were also issues with the supply chains needed to break into other markets, explains John. "It was impossible for us to expand everything organically. Sources had to come from outside and to give our salesman a year-round range of goods to sell. And okay, the shoes were an attempt, but I knew actually that it wouldn't work. And even in the first order they were late on delivery, which was crucial. I mean, salespeople work very, very hard to get people interested, and then comes the delivery date and we can't make it."

Admiral's capacious darts range included these enviable trainers.

An uncanny ability to spot gaps in the market and seize opportunities had carried Admiral Sports a long way. But a feeling began to emerge of a company starting to drift. Was Bert perhaps losing his Midas touch? "I do think he used to fly off in different directions quite a lot, and possibly have to be reined back by somebody," recalls Paul, the brand specialist. "I personally don't believe you can put your logo on anything that is completely different from your core product and expect it to work."

Bert told me himself that there had been a discussion at one point about selling Admiral-labelled baked beans, such was his confidence in the trademark.

Of more immediate concern to lots of other firms within the textiles industries was holding on to the markets they already had. Support for a 'Buy British' campaign was growing exponentially as more and more knitwear and textiles jobs were lost in the area. Fears were raised earlier in the decade, when Leicester South MP Jim Marshall warned of local manufacturing being destroyed by cheap foreign imports, in a prediction seemingly coming to pass.

Suddenly, some of life's constants in this 12-year-old's world also looked a little less certain in Silver Jubilee year. Even the supply of vinyl singles coming over the garden fence started sounding more edgy and angrier, with the Sex Pistols' release of 'Anarchy in the UK' and then 'God Save the Queen' proof enough

that Britain was indeed changing. As was our teenage neighbour, who now regularly left the Bs' house in a mohair jumper and spiky 'sugar-watered' hair, according to my sister. Saturday afternoons became more menacing as well, and it wasn't uncommon to see gangs of youths fighting on matchdays, or 'Bring Back the Birch' headlines following these weekly acts of 'football hooliganism'. One of the more shocking images from this time was a photo of a young Manchester United supporter called Peter Brookes, clad in a white Admiral away shirt, being led to safety by police and a first aider after being struck by a dart that was now embedded in the bridge of his nose.

Ominously, the summer of 1977 was also marked by the abdication of one of Admiral's biggest cheerleaders, and the man who provided the launchpad for its success: England manager Don Revie. Seemingly, there had been no hint of his intentions just weeks before, as he negotiated a largely successful tour of Latin America in which England, wearing their red away jerseys, emerged unbeaten after three games. Portentously perhaps, the excursion was interrupted by a publicity stunt involving long-term exile Ronnie Biggs, clad in an Admiral shirt, at a team training session on Copacabana beach. Less than a month later the *Daily Mail* broke the news of the England coach's resignation by announcing,

'Revie quits over aggro' across its front page. Its full exposé outlined his reasons for leaving, along with details of the "heartache" the job was bringing into the lives of the Yorkshireman and his family. "Nearly everyone in the country wants me out, so I am giving them what they want." It appeared the press were aware of Revie's decision before his employer, and FA secretary Ted Croker claims he only received the manager's resignation letter after the story had hit the newsstands. Worse, according to Croker's autobiography, the former Leeds boss had already lined up another job, despite FA assurances that his position was safe.

Revie had few friends among sportswriters, many of whom delighted in picking through his unsuccessful reign in forensic detail. Scouting dossiers, bingo nights and carpet bowls were all offered up as reasons to lampoon him. The manager's relationship with Admiral also featured high on his list of failings, and that too was reheated for public consumption. Inevitably, the 'Don Readies' jibes grew ever louder after it was announced he was off to coach the United Arab Emirates, and details of his £340,000 four-year contract were disclosed.

Get into Admiral

If it's Admiral - it's professional

But many former players, including England internationals like Kevin Keegan, lent their support. Mick Channon, who was capped 26 times by Revie, believes the stress of being national coach became overbearing and ultimately made his job untenable. "He wanted to be the best in the world. The pressure he was under to succeed was enormous, and he got to a stage where I feel he got a bit lost, and he would do what the press wanted rather than what he thought."

Revie's departure was a blow but it didn't significantly affect Admiral's relationship with the FA or their contract. Wigston would continue to supply the England team with its playing strips, and carry on producing replicas for young fans. But there would be other departures in the coming months that would hit the company harder, and ultimately impact on its wellbeing more significantly at a time when the future of whole swathes of British industry was beginning to feel more perilous.

CHAPTER 8
Too Much Too Young

"The country had changed. The positivity, the optimism, the wave of culture and modernity brought in by the '60s had started to wane. The economic landscape markedly." John Devlin describes an all-pervasive mood in the late '70s from which Wigston was not immune. Sounding uncannily similar to a song by The Specials at that time, "Too big too quick," is Tim Edson's assessment of his former employer's predicament. The former shipping manager cites the spiralling cost of its sponsorship deals as its biggest worry. Admiral was struggling to offer clubs as much money as its competitors, which was taking its toll. The business had outgrown Admiral Sports, just as the executives at Adidas and Umbro had suspected it eventually would.

The Wigston outfit was still operating from a relatively small manufacturing base despite its previous years of success. Yes, there had been a recent move to a larger, purpose-built factory, and the company outsourced work to other manufacturers to meet demand. But to sustain growth and to compete against much bigger organisations, the company didn't expand nearly enough. That would have involved selling a significant stake in the company to an investor. But for now, and at its heart, Admiral was still very much a family-run business, and remained a company with good ideas, lacking the infrastructure to become a global operator.

"The way that they ran the company, it just wasn't enough to keep their foothold in the market they'd created. More competition was coming in – Le Coq Sportif and Patrick coming over from France." Equally as worrying, according to John Devlin, the likes of Umbro were also leaping ahead in the style stakes. "Other companies starting to become a little bit more bullish, a little bit more adventurous in their designs. It could be argued that they were beginning to overtake what Admiral were doing. You could see some of the designs were beginning to look just a little old hat, a little bit more dated."

Other kit manufacturers appeared to have more cachet among young supporters. I remember chatting to schoolmates, poring over magazine photos of Adidas's stylishly minimalist strips, and wishing our own teams would swap over to "the brand with three stripes." With these first adolescent stirrings of 'brand awareness' or 'label snobbery' came the realisation that some clothes were just 'cooler' than others. Ironically, Bert's stated aim at the beginning of the decade was to turn replica football shirts into fashion items; but having done so, Admiral was now in danger of falling prey to the fickleness of fashion's endless churn. "Admiral, their colours burned so bright," John Devlin notes, "but it couldn't continue, and eventually they began to wane. They'd made such a massive impact into the football world, it was almost like they had just run out of steam."

Leicester's textiles industry, long struggling, was now also in decline and, in many ways, Bert's own 'boom and bust' misfortunes became a microcosm of the UK market. "The clouds were looming towards the end of the '70s. With regard to the textile and shoe industry, a lot of stuff was coming in from South East Asia, and they could produce football kits at a fraction of the price than we could do it with local labour. And that, consequently, was the downfall of the company."

But to outsiders, as well as to most employees, Admiral still appeared to be a company on the up. The firm was never troubled by strikes, and Alec Kilsby, area official for the National Union of Hosiery & Knitwear Workers, described Admiral as "a model company." The firm was still fulfilling orders for a whole raft of top international and domestic sides, as well as for scores of lower-league clubs and lesser international teams. After all, the success of its replica kits had surely safeguarded the company's future for years to come? The turnover of

The Specials: the debut LP, and Mike Roberts' favourite Spurs track top.

foreign exports alone, including many orders to the Middle East, totalled £1.1 million in 1978, and the firm recorded an overall net profit of close to £1 million the following year. Yet despite the impressive numbers and the company's shiny new premises, cracks were appearing in its financial footing.

"Bad management," says Shaun Patrick unequivocally, by way of explaining Admiral's downturn towards the end of the decade. By then he was working for his dad's company as a trainee, and says replica shirts were costing more to produce than they could be sold for. Yet, despite the warnings, his dad insisted on ploughing ahead, reportedly telling his managers to "sort it out and carry on" regardless. Rising overheads were crippling the company, according to Shaun, who says there were now as many admin staff on the payroll as actual machinists, and a once-lean operation had become flabby and less efficient. Opposite the main factory, Tim Edson told me his export office was often piled high with stock lying around for days awaiting dispatch, with seemingly no means of getting it out of the door sooner.

It was also an open secret that large amounts of stock was regularly leaving by the back door. "I would have carried on for longer, but there was something in the air that I didn't like, so that was me gone." Lindsay Jelley's decision to walk away from Chartwell Drive was inevitable, she says. "I didn't want to work there. It was a huge factory, and I think they went through a period of transition there, a point where the company maybe massively overstretched. For the first time, I started to feel that the atmosphere changed." Like other former employees from that time, Lindsay uses the word "leaky" to describe what was once a well-run operation. "When I started, it felt like a very tight ship. The boss was only working two floors away. Everything was communicated very easily and directly, and then suddenly you didn't have that direct contact with somebody working in the next room, it was down the road. It just didn't have that same cohesion any more. I wonder if that was the beginning of the end?"

At this time lots of local business owners were looking nervously over their shoulders. Throughout the decade thousands of textiles workers had taken to the streets to support a 'Buy British' campaign, and ITV's John Mitchell reported from one such march organised by the Hosiery & Knitwear Workers' Union in the city. "In the last year alone, 40 firms have gone to the wall here in Leicester, which is the heart of the industry. That means a loss of 5,000 knitwear jobs, and many more are on short-time working. The reason? British industry just cannot compete with low-cost imports from abroad."

The business of manufacturing and selling replica football kits was also changing, says John Griffin. "Umbro had started to buy tracksuits from China. Adidas are buying tracksuits from China, because of the amount of labour involved in it. And we were still making them in the UK, but [foreign competition] hadn't caught up with us at that point." According to John, making the strips in Wigston was still financially viable, but the company needed to supplement these sales with imports. "I desperately wanted us to produce knitwear at prices that football fans could afford, and the only way I could do that would be to go to China." He says he visited the People's Republic three times to try and set up a supply line but, "I didn't have enough working capital, and that is the crux of the thing. Our financial structure hadn't changed in all the time I'd been there. The owners didn't allow any venture capital into the company. I think they had maybe a mom-and-pop outlook. But they wanted to keep it, and they'd done fantastic, actually running it on credit for 14 years."

The company wasn't without its suitors, of course, and "Admiral was a gem," according to John, despite all the swirling uncertainty. It's a view confirmed by Bert, who told me he'd been approached by a "number of companies" looking to either invest in or purchase his company, including local heavyweights Corah. The knitwear giant was still producing orders for Marks & Spencer but was now also looking at ways to plug gaps in its orders book. Bert sat down with chairman Nicholas Corah and his finance director Frank Bushall to discuss an amalgamation, and to look at ways of harnessing Admiral's creativity to Corah's larger production capacity, in what was a rapidly changing landscape. There was even a suggestion to launch a new clothing line together called 'Mr Leicester,' remembers Bert. "With Corah, we could survive and expand into a considerably bigger outfit than Admiral had been, and take on all comers." But the merger never gained any real traction, and the two companies were left to fight their own separate rearguards. Bert described the day Corah's succumbed to its eventual closure as "inconceivable." The feeling of loss throughout the city was palpable, and the message it sent out was loud and clear: if Corah's could go, then nobody's job was safe.

As far as Bert was concerned, he'd done everything he possibly could to make his business more efficient and competitive. "Our machinery's up to date," he told ITV. "Obviously, I've had to do this over the years on my own and I've ploughed

back profits into that company and bought new machinery. Our new factory at Chartwell Drive is very modern and a very nice place to work in, good facilities." Another option for Bert at that time was to sell his business altogether. "We had several offers over the years to be bought out, which we refused because we said, you know, 'We're making money, why should we sell out?' And though still a family-owned business with limited financial resources, we resisted the urge to enter into talks, preferring to stay as we were: with hindsight, probably a mistake." Having overhauled Cook & Hurst 20 years earlier, Bert tried to resurrect the ailing business once again, believing the move to Chartwell Drive and a fresh pair of eyes would help make the business more competitive. "I employed some consultants, who said, 'Make your factories more efficient.' We thought we were efficient, and that's what we tried to do. We tried to fight it by competing with lower profit margins."

But these new cost-cutting measures and pay reviews would ultimately fracture both a working partnership and a family friendship with John Griffin. Only the two men themselves really know whether the former Corah's man jumped ship or was pushed, and even then the reality has probably become clouded over time. What we do know is that John moved on, and was soon aligned opposite his old boss as a direct competitor – at Adidas.

"I got a job about four weeks later with the biggest sports company in the world at that time. So, life went on." The two men next crossed paths a few months later in Coventry City's Highfield Road boardroom but there was no handshake or reunion. During the course of many conversations with both men, neither mentioned the other directly by name unless pushed, preferring to use the title of 'owner' or 'managing director'. The company appears to have been struggling even before John's departure, but to make matters worse his skillset was never adequately replaced, with Bert preferring to employ people he liked rather than those he needed. But it could also be argued that it didn't really matter who was in charge by that stage. The country was in the grip of an economic tailspin and chronic deindustrialisation, forcing countless well-run businesses to the wall.

The perilous state of the economy meant that textiles firms were no longer facing the prospect of riding out a recession so much as experiencing the death throes of British manufacturing. Throughout the turmoil, there was another possible course of action, or more a moral dilemma as far as Bert was concerned. He could follow Adidas's lead and move his production base abroad and slash his overheads at a stroke. "I was approached by some people who were well connected in the Far East, Leicester people, who said that if I closed my factories down, they could provide all my production needs from the Far East. They were already doing it with a textile product successfully. So the decision was, do I close my factories and make everybody redundant, hundreds of operatives redundant, and go out there? Or did I stay with it and risk the competition from other companies who were having the stuff made out there?" The choice was simple but stark. "I chose to stay with it, and the answer really was the same. We went out of business because we were no longer able to make the profits we hoped for, and we had to make the factories redundant and close them down."

Throughout the first half of 1978 I would compulsively flick through the back pages of *Shoot!* every fortnight, to check the price of Leicester City replicas, which were always ticketed at £5 on the same full-page advert. This routine continued for months until miraculously, just before the summer holidays, the shirts were suddenly reduced to £3.50. Lounging around on the school sports field I convinced myself as much as my companions that now was the time to act, and that weekend I converted my paper-round money into a postal order, duly sent off to Smallcombe Sports in Essex.

Fast-forward a few weeks to July, and the novelty of a 'frothy coffee' at Brucciani's café is enough to lure me 'into town' in the company of my family. The thought of a dedicated coffee shop on every corner was then as fanciful as the idea of grown men parading around in 'children's' replica football tops. Besides, I wanted to show off my new white City shirt, and the day got even better when Dad suggested we pop "down the City" to have a look around while "the girls finish their shopping."

Like many Victorian football grounds, Filbert Street was within easy walking distance of the city centre. On match days my pace would quicken once I caught sight of a floodlight pylon poking out among the rooftops of red-brick terraces, and by the time we'd passed the 'Statue of Liberty' atop of Lennard Brothers' shoe factory, I knew we were just moments away from our destination. We'd turn a corner to find the Main Stand's corrugated blue wall and club car park stretched out gloriously in front of us.

Today though, on this warm, matchless weekend, the back of the stadium is quiet and empty. Unsure what to do once we arrive at the deserted reception, I follow my dad's lead through an unlocked exit gate. Inside the belly of the ground, it's dark and cool, above us the wooden bench seats from which I watched my first matches. Dust-speckled shafts of sunlight guiding us, we make our way silently along the concourse until we emerge from the players' tunnel into the warm sunshine, gazing out across the playing surface. A magical moment.

As we made our way back down the tunnel, we were met by the club's manager Jock Wallace coming the other way. Instead of the reprimand I was expecting, the gruff Scot growled a far more devastating admonishment: "Is that a Spurs shirt, son?" Too awestruck to utter much of a response, the City boss informed me the club had dumped Admiral in favour of Umbro in time for the new season. It was true, as the first photos of Jock's diamond-encrusted team proved a few weeks later, and as retail lessons go it proved invaluable: stockists don't flog things off at knockdown prices without good reason.

Losing City's business was a shame, but it wasn't too big a financial hit as far as Admiral was concerned. Still, its local club's defection did lay bare a more worrying trend. "We were under great pressure, our profits began to slide away. And we just tried to keep ahead of the ballgame, and the payments to clubs were obviously going to go up." Bert watched on, seemingly helpless, as clubs ran down their existing contracts with his firm before announcing a new deal with a different supplier.

"Other firms came in," John Devlin explains, "and Umbro possibly had more financial clout to tempt the clubs into these deals. From that point on,

Jock Wallace and Eddie Kelly stroll in the Filbert Street sun.

it all became about what clubs you could get and what money was prepared to exchanged hands."

Star asset Manchester United was among the teams that migrated over to Adidas. As did Wales, with secretary Trevor Morris using the launch as an opportunity to take a swipe at his country's former kit supplier. "To start with, the new contract is more lucrative than the old one. Secondly, we must say, without wishing to throw any mud, that we were never happy with the other company. We received many complaints from members of the public over the retail price of the kit sold to the kids."

Bert described his comments as "most unfair," telling *Harpers Sport* that Admiral's kit would undergo an independent 'value for money' test at the Hosiery & Allied Trades Research Association to disprove the 'overpricing' claims.

More worryingly, the Midland Bank was also raising concerns about Admiral's business practices, as the company continued to haemorrhage both money and clients. Fortunately, Bert didn't have to look very far for further backing, and with few other options available to him, accepted a rescue package put together by his wife's family. That saw H. Flude & Company, makers of 'Cindy' tights, invest over £500,000 to help shore up Admiral, in exchange for a majority shareholding. Bert was replaced as chairman by Flude's financial advisor Stan Gunby, in a move that also saw Bert's nephew Simon Flude join the board.

Surveying the scene he walked into, Simon told me, "Bert's expertise was in marketing, and he needed help with manufacturing. Would I say that Bert had an excellently managed, high-quality production, efficient factory? No, no, he didn't." Fortunately, Flude's strengths lay in manufacturing efficiency, and the restructured company had also been promised additional investment from a Netherlands-based trading company called Frisol Oil, which had major interests in energy, shipping and agriculture. At a Reform Club lunch, Bert announced that the two companies would be joining forces, to expand Admiral globally and to reach a £30 million turnover target within three years.

From now on Frisol, trading as Admiral International Marketing, would handle the brand's worldwide distribution, marketing and sales, while Simon would run the British set-up and concentrate on the domestic market. He told *Sports Trader* magazine that Admiral Sportswear UK "remained totally financially

Mass migration: the Adidas roster suddenly features seven ex-Admiral teams.

independent and self-sustaining operation in every respect," still owning the brand's UK rights. "Both Bert Patrick and Simon Flude confirmed that the majority of lines carried by Admiral would be manufactured in this country," reported the same publication.

The agreement was exactly what Admiral needed, Simon told me, particularly as it would involve Frisol taking care of international affairs, long a troublesome area. Bert confirmed that he too remained on board, and said, "The rumours concerning Admiral's cashflow problems could now be safely buried," because "Admiral's growth had now been almost guaranteed by the partnership with Frisol and with Admiral's manufacturing parent company, H. Flude and Company."

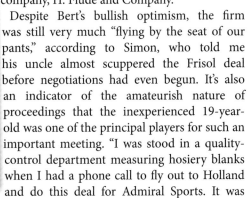

Despite Bert's bullish optimism, the firm was still very much "flying by the seat of our pants," according to Simon, who told me his uncle almost scuppered the Frisol deal before negotiations had even begun. It's also an indicator of the amateurish nature of proceedings that the inexperienced 19-year-old was one of the principal players for such an important meeting. "I was stood in a quality-control department measuring hosiery blanks when I had a phone call to fly out to Holland and do this deal for Admiral Sports. It was crazy, really." A private jet arrived at East Midlands Airport to fly Bert, Simon and accountant Hugh Dixon to Dordrecht, where they were met and driven to Nico De Vries's offices. The initial greetings were cordial enough, but the mood soon soured as the two parties settled down to business and the room's two 'alpha males' locked horns. Bert's pride was piqued having been forced to ask for help, and he was understandably sensitive about "letting go of his baby." Fortunately, Simon stepped in to act as peacemaker and was able to broker a truce. "I can't remember how or what I said. I managed to take the heat out of the situation and steer them both in the right direction to complete the deal. As we walked away [Hugh Dixon said] he felt I had saved the day, saved the deal, [and] the deal we got was the deal we wanted."

The '70s drew to a close as the decade had begun with Britain mired in industrial turmoil and rancour. Following 1978's 'Winter of Discontent', Jim Callaghan's premiership and five years of Labour governance was coming to an end. But the following spring's electoral campaign simply contributed to the country's unease, as the far-right National Front sought to build on previous gains in places like Leicester, where it had won almost 20 per cent of the vote at local elections three years previously. This time, the party mobilised more than 300 candidates nationally to contest seats on an anti-immigration and repatriation platform, by claiming non-white low-paid workers were responsible for high unemployment levels. Football grounds, including Filbert Street, were strategically targeted, and it wasn't uncommon to see leafleting on match days, or hear racist chanting and shouts from the terraces and stands. The NF's campaign culminated in rallies on St George's Day, staged in multicultural areas where the prospect of violence and media coverage was inevitable. In Southall, West London, anti-fascist campaigner Blair Peach was killed and hundreds were injured or arrested during angry clashes between marchers, counter-demonstrators and police.

On the same day, more than 5,000 police officers were deployed on the streets of Leicester, where running battles and missile throwing resulted in 80 arrests, and about half that number injured. Ten days later, Margaret's Thatcher's Conservatives swept to power, offering up the words of Francis of Assisi from the steps of Downing Street. "Where there is discord, may we bring harmony... And where there is despair, may we bring hope."

In reality, manufacturing closures accelerated at breakneck speed and job losses continued to rise unchecked as the new Prime Minister and her government set about destroying the power of the trade unions, and Britain slid into an era later defined as 'Thatcherism'.

There was some good news for workers in Admiral's Wigston and Market Harborough factories in 1979. Bert and the Flude family had managed to keep Admiral Sports afloat, and the business still had one last ace up its sleeve: the lucrative and highly coveted FA contract to kit out the England team. "They thought it was very successful," Bert says of the existing arrangement he'd brokered with the FA in 1974. So much so that, with the deal coming to an end, "they took me out for lunch, and Sir Harold Thompson said, 'This time, Mr Patrick, you better have your pencil sharpened, because you're going to pay more.'" The reported deal would now cost £200,000 a year for five years, and Admiral had beaten off competition from five other vying companies. "They've always supported a British firm, they've wanted a British firm to have that contract, so that was a big help," Bert told ITV, relaying news of the FA's decision.

The new England deal wasn't so much a renewal as a lifeline, and Bert was determined to generate as much revenue from it as possible – not least to recoup the FA's £1 million-plus fee. From now on, it wasn't just the children's market being targeted: the new England shirts would also be available in adult sizes for the first time. Unsurprisingly, it wasn't long before the original criticisms resurfaced, the *Daily Mirror*'s back page 'Strip-off' splash setting the tone as the red-top accused the FA of 'taking commercialism too far'. Bert explained to *The Guardian* that it wasn't in his interests to "rip off" buyers, and told the paper, "If our prices were unreasonable, we would not sell the volume of goods that we do."

FA secretary Ted Croker was "sickened" by the criticism and, springing to his supplier's defence, argued that by choosing Admiral the FA was helping to support the ailing economy. "We have brought Britain into an international market that had been dominated by Adidas. Admiral are now exporting. The balance of payments has benefited, as has the employment situation in Leicester and elsewhere in the country. This has been a deliberate policy."

As before, disapproval of Admiral's latest national offering wasn't solely confined to the deal itself, and much of the confected outrage was reserved for the new outfit's appearance. Particularly the jersey, which Bert had declared "a fashion item" to reporters, telling the *Daily Express* that from now on, "England will be the best-dressed international team in the world." What caused all the fuss was two horizontal blocks of red and blue, above a thinner blue stripe, across the shoulders of the white tops. I must admit, it's a look that puzzled me when I first clapped eyes on it, but the gentlemen of the press were far less hesitant and dived straight in.

"From time to time the Football Association accuses people of bringing the game into disrepute. But who are to be the prosecutors when the FA itself behaves in a manner inconsistent with the game's best interests?" It's fair to say *The Guardian*'s Patrick Barclay didn't share Bert's enthusiasm. The Scot observed that the new strip "looks like a half-knitted pullover; V-necked, with lateral stripes stopping just below the FA badge. The shorts shown had a vertical white stripe down the left-hand side only, presumably to help excited players put them on the right way round."

Among the many shock-horror headlines that greeted the new strip's unveiling in February 1980, Brian Clough used his *Match* magazine column to opine: "The wraps are off England's new strip – and I'm saying now I don't like it. Right now, it has the looks of one of my mother's old pinnies!"

Unbeknown to columnists, or even Admiral's own managers, it's a wonder the new strips ever made it to Lancaster Gate at all. Seventeen-year-old Shaun Patrick, having recently passed his driving test, was given the honour of delivering the FA's new teamwear. Together with his teenage mate, he loaded up a company Ford Fiesta with cardboard boxes and headed for the motorway. Driving into

London was a daunting experience, with each mile nervously being counted down, until the teenagers were forced to confront the terrifying experience of crossing the *Wacky Races* rally that is the Marble Arch roundabout. But once safely negotiated, Master Patrick duly delivered all of his cargo to the FA HQ.

I'm not sure the same can be said about another of the firm's young trainee managers. In the run-up to launch date, Rich Frost was tasked with dropping off the top-secret outfits to a London ad agency, under strict instructions not to let them out of his sight. A quarter of an hour into his journey south, Rich could hear banging coming from the back of his van. He pulled over into a lay-by and said he was initially relieved to discover it was only the sound of the back doors flapping open, and nothing more serious. Until he spotted a trail of England tops stretching back down the A6 for half a mile. Thirty-five years after the event, it's fair to say the experience hasn't exactly scarred Rich. He's laughing as loudly in front of me as I suspect he did at the time. Following a scramble along the hard shoulder and hedgerows he believes he rounded up "most" of the runaways.

England's controversial new jerseys finally made their bow in May 1980. The new look was still a concern to some. "Why the England shirt should have the colours of the Union Jack remains a mystery," declared BBC commentator Barry Davies, when a Kevin Keegan-led side emerged from the Wembley tunnel alongside World Cup winners Argentina, who included a teenage Diego Maradona in their line-up for the friendly.

But Paul Oakley wasn't overly bothered by the scorn being heaped upon his patriotic offering. "As a designer, and as a brand-identity designer, you obviously push things as far as you can. I'm going to take what, in my opinion, makes that an England shirt, as opposed to a white shirt, and that was to take the Union Jack and to apply it to the shirt. And that's what I did." Paul had of course introduced red alongside a paler shade of blue to England's playing colours five years earlier. But on this occasion, he pushed its 'Britishness' far more overtly. "We're used to seeing athletes draping the Union Jack over their shoulders and running around the track after winning, and so the concept of putting that Union Jack on to your shoulders, almost a cape if you like, somehow endorsed that Union Jack British image... and subsequently branded it much more strongly."

The nationalistic choice of red, white and blue was perhaps not as surprising as some imagined. These were the colours of the recent 'mod revival' and an Austin Metro advert that tapped into the 'country's mood,' with cars seeing off foreign competition from the cliffs of Dover. The Oscar-winning film *Chariots of Fire*, with its euphoric Vangelis score, took the patriotism even further. Drawing heavily from advertising, it told the story of two British runners and their triumphant pursuit of Olympic gold medals. Some likened it to state propaganda. According to Andy Beckett's critique of early '80s Britain, *I Promise You a Miracle*, it could "have been scripted by one of Margaret Thatcher's speechwriters."

Forty years on, the flag of St George has been reclaimed by England supporters, and is now synonymous with the team's identity. But back then it was a very different story, as John Devlin remembers vividly. "I look back at it and think, 'Yeah, why were they wearing the colours of the Union Flag?' But again, you need to look at context, you need to look at what nationalism was, what iconography, what colours, what flags were around. The Royal Wedding, it was all Union Jacks." As far as Admiral was concerned, they'd take any help going, and if that meant joining in with the flag waving, then so be it. The company and its nautical trademark were still in choppy waters, and to stretch the maritime metaphor even further, when you're adrift at sea you'll grab any life raft that's going.

The number of people out of work in Britain at the start of 1980 was close to two million, and rising. The worst unemployment figures for almost 50 years, and more than 1,100 manufacturing jobs were being lost every day. Admiral was still employing around 250 people in Wigston and another 50 in Market Harborough, and to a certain extent its workforce appeared more fortunate than most. The unique nature of what was being made at its two factories was seemingly able to insulate them to a degree. But for how much longer? In reality, the company's hopes of survival rested on the success of its contract with England. Ron Greenwood's men were heading to the European Championships in Italy that summer with expectations high, his side among the favourites along with West Germany. It was hoped any success would rub off on to sponsors like Admiral and help boost replica sales.

The company's fortunes were now inextricably linked with the England team's – and it wouldn't just have been the players feeling the pre-tournament pressure, according to John Devlin. "Potentially their future, their economic, their viable, going-forward plans, were resting on what England were going to do. The international kit market was starting to become dominated by Adidas. So again we've got this sort of David and Goliath; this small, Leicester-based English firm battling against the German might of Adidas, with their future at stake."

That June, Bert accompanied the FA's party to Turin, anticipating he'd stick around for the entirety of the tournament. But less than a week after England's first game, turmoil reigned on and off the pitch, and Greenwood's side had been eliminated. Fighting in the stands and streets involving England supporters, combined with heavy-handed policing and the liberal use of tear gas, marred similarly poor performances by the national team. An opening draw with Belgium followed by a narrow defeat to hosts Italy was enough to send England's lacklustre side packing.

In the same week, Admiral's fortunes fared little better. Despite having been bailed out by Bert's in-laws just two months earlier, the company was again in financial difficulties. "I saw it coming, but the shock on the day was bad," Bert told me. "Ted Croker took me to the side and said he'd had a phone call from one of my directors. It was most important I got back to Wigston because the bank were going to request me to appoint receivers."

As *Sports Trader* reported, "Earlier this year it looked as though the future of the company was assured when Admiral joined forces with a Dutch company Frisol. The plan announced at the end of April was to establish the Admiral logo and name throughout the world." What the piece didn't mention was, because of the disastrous state of the UK's financial crisis, banks were becoming increasingly jumpy as an increasing number of industrial businesses were going bankrupt. East Midlands textiles companies were considered especially vulnerable, and as a result lenders began calling in loans, irrespective of individual circumstances.

"The one thing Admiral is never short of, has never been short of, is business." Bert told ITV. "How many companies go broke with a £2 million order book?" he wondered aloud, referring to the Midland Bank's decision asking for Admiral to pay off all of its £1.25 million overdraft immediately.

All the work of pumping a healthy amount of working capital into the firm via the Flude and Frisol takeovers "was torpedoed by a nasty little man at Midland Bank," according to Simon. Flude's initial payment tranche of £250,000 was swallowed up straight away by the bank to pay off a chunk of its loan, even though its managers were aware of the joint rescue plan with Frisol. Unsurprisingly, Frisol then pulled out of their own commitment to invest in Admiral, leaving the company high and dry. "There was no way the business could have survived," says Simon, believing there was little will on the part of the Midland's "vile" manager to keep Admiral afloat, or to save it from administration.

It was a perplexing, infuriating decision, given that the firm still had a full order book, including many sales to the Middle East; but by now Bert knew the game was up. "That was the death knell, really. I had to get the bank to appoint receivers, and they came in. Then people were out to strip the assets of the company, the machinery and everything we'd got."

CHAPTER 9
That's Entertainment

Wigston, June 1980

A week after England's elimination from the 1980 European Championships, Richard Turton's beige Morris Marina rolled into Admiral's Chartwell Drive car park. The balding auditor told the waiting television film crew, "The company's board approached the bank and asked the bank to bring the receiver in, and I'm that receiver. My job's to evaluate the situation and see whether the whole business or part of the business can be sold as a going concern, and therefore some of the jobs saved – or, if not, then of course I've got to close the place down."

Turton also spoke to *The Guardian*, revealing that one of the clauses in the England contract – the carrot with which to tempt to any potential buyer – stipulated that the FA could now withdraw from the deal if it chose to. However, "at the moment it is too early to say what will happen."

Meanwhile, the remainder of the company's pared-down office staff, a self-titled 'Fairy Ring' of managers and reps, knew exactly what was going to happen: they were going to throw a party. More specifically, they were planning a 'Burn a Wales Shirt' soirée to commemorate, or perhaps to obliterate the memory of being stuck with thousands of unsold daffodil-yellow away shirts. Recent demand for the red Wales home jerseys had far outstripped supply, prompting managers to increase production of the away tops, making the reasonable speculation that Wales supporters would also rush to buy their country's second strip. Except it wasn't just football fans buying the kits but music lovers as well. Reggae devotees in particular were attracted to its red, yellow and green Rastafarian colourways. The year before, Errol Dunkley had appeared on *Top of the Pops* dressed in an Admiral 'tramlines' tracksuit, minus the Wales badge, miming along to his hit single, 'OK Fred'.

There were around 30 attendees at the gathering organised by sales rep Don Munro, including Shaun Patrick – which didn't go down too well with Patrick senior, according to his son. By 9pm, following drinks inside the warehouse, the ceremony had moved outside to a yard backing on to a railway line. With the gathering illuminated by the large neon 'Admiral' sign aimed at passengers on British Rail's London to Sheffield line, a single lemon Cymru jersey was offered up for sacrifice, doused in lighter fuel and set alight, before being tossed aflame into a metal skip. Whether it appeased the gods of sportswear, we'll never know, but it certainly raised a cheer from those assembled.

Light the yellow touch paper: the offending Wales away colours.

There were also "some tears" to mark what everybody recognised was the end of an era, but the overall mood was by and large celebratory. An acknowledgement of what the firm had built up and achieved over the past decade by those gathered. And now those remaining employees stood around a smouldering piece of scorched polyester rather than a raging pyre. The perfect metaphor for where Admiral found itself.

Ever since the receiver's arrival, a publicly upbeat Bert Patrick told reporters that "offers to take over the company have been pouring in," along with yet more kit orders, reaffirming that the company was very much "still alive and kicking." He believed Turton would most likely accept an offer "within a matter of weeks."

According to Bert, it was vital that he offer his services to the receiver, to help attract a new buyer. But he may not have appreciated the Sisyphean task facing both men. The factory was still making garments to fulfil orders, while existing creditors lined up to be paid – and suppliers now demanded payment up front. Additionally, any incoming cheques were hastily snapped up by Turton, and used to reduce the bank's overdraft.

The receiver was only really interested in clawing back as much money as he could, believes Simon Flude, and was "much more concerned with what the machinery was worth than what the [actual] business was worth."

Turton's first duty was to the Midland Bank, of course, but he wasn't simply flogging off the company's fixtures and fittings at knock-down prices. People were losing their jobs. Following an initial round of lay-offs, further redundancies were scheduled to help make the company's £1.5 million asking price "more attractive." Any potential buyer, "whilst recognising the global marketing reputation of the Admiral name," would baulk at the thought of inheriting a large workforce, it was reasoned.

"Terrible" is the word Bert uses to describe how he felt, seeing his former employees cast aside.

Alec Kilsby, the area official for the National Union of Hosiery & Knitwear Workers, told ITV that his members had deferred an agreed pay rise to help their employer, and expressed his shock in more forthright terms. "I was appalled when the announcement was made, absolutely appalled. The peoples' faces when they were told the details, and were told, 'All right, within a month or so, unless a buyer can be found,' the whole factory would be closing down. All jobs would be lost. The look on their faces was absolutely shocking. People were dumbfounded. There wasn't any questions asked, people were numb."

Admiral Sportswear.
Long Street, Wigston. Leicester LE8 2BQ
Telephone 881302

Thirty-five years on, the group of machinists I meet in a lunchtime pub, a few minutes' walk away from their old factory, are still as puzzled. Unlike other workplaces, Jill Langton tells me the firm remained busy, and the staff were never put on "short-time," which was common elsewhere. She admits that made the shock even greater, because "nobody" in her group of workmates "saw it coming."

As the factory's union rep, Hilary Cottam heard the devastating news first, in Bert's office. She had absolutely no inkling of the statement about to be delivered, and says was even expecting to be asked to work extra overtime, such was the continuing demand for orders. Instead, Hilary was told there were about to be imminent lay-offs. Reeling from the shock announcement, she sought out her pal Bridget Marlow and the pair shared a cigarette outside, before the entire workforce was summoned into the top-floor canteen.

"'We're closing – you, you and you have got to go now,'" Bridget relives the moment all of their lives changed forever. The three women had survived the initial cull and were kept on to finish off the remaining orders, but it was a stay of execution. When Corah's "went," Bridget told me, everything else toppled and caused a domino effect across the entire industry. After eventually leaving Admiral, she told me she was made redundant a further four times.

"Happy days, loved it. Wanted to go to work. It was like a family, went through everything together. Got paid good money, socialised out of work." Jill tells me of her years working for Cook & Hurst and then Admiral Sports, wishing to reminisce about some of the happier moments of the group's lives together. "Remember when receivers came in?" she asks her former workmates, "and [they were] taking machines when people were still working on them?"

"But you pinched the chair, didn't you?" Bridget reminds her friend, "right past the security guard."

The laughter of the group dissolves into an expression of sorrow, at what I imagine is the unfairness of how their livelihoods were snatched away from them. In the intervening years, Jill tells me, she believes the standard of living for working-class people like herself has gone backwards. "We struggled after leaving Admiral," she admits, before adding defiantly that "Bridget and I bought our machines." She details how the two women "set up in rented rooms and garages – some terrible places – making jogging suits and sweatshirts," which were sold on local markets.

Bert says he'd often run into old employees at local supermarkets, with some having traded sewing machine for checkout till. Others, like Hilary, became care workers while many more ended up in low-paid service-industry jobs.

It was as if "the factories were allowed to die steadily from the 1970s, and seemed even to be helped on their way in the 1980s by a Conservative government which thought the old industrial cities were too much trouble," writes Andy Beckett.

A year into her premiership, Margaret Thatcher's oft-repeated promise to restore Britain's greatness felt increasingly hollow. ITV reported that business closures had doubled from ten years previously and, 'This year it's the worst figure of all. On present form, more than 6,000 companies may close.'

When it was announced that Admiral's name was among the casualties, Bert told ITV, "The government should be taking more time and paying more attention to the problems of industry, to the companies who have a good track record. Companies that don't have strikes and don't have industrial unrest, companies that do a damn good job, day in day out, and Admiral's one of them."

Thirty-five years on, Bert told me the government of the day didn't "owe him a

Soccer kit firm in crisis

By FRANK PALMER

THE controversial firm that kits out England's soccer stars has run into money trouble.

The company, Admiral Sportswear, has called in a receiver.

But it plans to carry on trading in the hope that someone will make a takeover bid.

Admiral, which also supplies playing strips for Manchester United, Spurs, Coventry, Leeds and Crystal Palace, has been accused in the past of exploiting the schoolboy market.

Its prices have shocked the parents of youngsters who want to wear the same gear as their heroes.

But managing director Bert Patrick has always been quick to point out: "We make a quality product.

"We brought design into kit. This is built into the price."

Last night Mr. Patrick could not be contacted at his home or at the firm's HQ in Leicester, where 250 workers are employed.

163

living," but said he'd felt badly let down at the time.

In the midst of the turbulence Admiral had often been lauded as British business at its best, and a shining example of what could be achieved during straitened times. This was something the ITV documentary team picked up on. As Bert fitted Thatcher's concept of the 'galvanised entrepreneur' so perfectly, they asked, 'Shouldn't he now be flourishing in the free-enterprise climate the government promised'?

"I'd have thought we were absolute copybook stuff for Sir Keith Joseph," Bert acknowledges, referring to the Secretary of State for Industry's pronouncement that 'it was entrepreneurs who created the wealth for society'. It made the 'Mad Monk's' lack of support for companies like Admiral appear even more puzzling.

As Bert said at the time, "There seems to be some sort of preconceived plan, although it's not been publicly owned up to, to let a certain element of industry go to the wall – and then see what comes off the wall in the way of a new company or a slimmed-downed company. I must say, that disappoints me. I'm just hoping that, even though I've gone, that they'll begin to get the thing right before there's many more people go, because that would be a terrible shame."

Such was the company's profile, there was no shortage of interest in Admiral's immediate future, from possible buyers and national media alike. First broadcast on ITV in July 1980, 'Going Bust' was an episode of Thames Television's current-affairs series *TV Eye*, in which reporter Bryan Gould set out to investigate why Admiral had become unviable.

Huddled around my laptop, watching the programme for the first time since it aired, were Bridget, Hilary and Jill, all of whom made a significant contribution to the documentary. The three former employees sat mesmerised as they watched their younger selves.

The company and its premises were of course up for sale, and I suspect the programme makers had been invited along by Bert, keen to use the documentary as a vehicle to attract a purchaser. Mandy Hutchins told me there weren't very many people on the factory floor on the day of filming due to the redundancies. So herself and a few others were placed strategically at machines within view of the camera to make the place appear busier than it actually was. With a shake of the head, she recalls how she would "keep running from one machine to another," and act out the role of an overlocker. We "had to sit there and just go up and down and pretend you were doing it," she adds, feeding an imaginary piece of fabric along the length of the table in front of her.

As the film nears its end, the four women visibly stiffen in their seats, or more accurately bristle, mirroring their on-screen body language. Jill closes her eyes and shakes her head when Professor Patrick Minford appears on screen.

"I don't think he liked taking you on, did he?" says Mandy, nodding towards Jill, who they all affectionately call 'the Leicester Lip'.

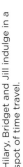

Hilary, Bridget and Jill indulge in a spot of time travel.

Jill is quick to reassure her pal that, "I didn't like him, either." Not that any of the other women need reminding.

Minford was a "free-marketeer" and one of the Prime Minister's economic advisors, which is how he came to find himself in Wigston, having been invited along by the television crew. He set out not only to justify the government's "tough policies," but also to explain to a dwindling workforce about to lose their jobs why high unemployment levels were "natural" and necessary. At the time of the filming, Minford and the women sat across the table were all about the same age, but that's where any similarities ended, as it was clear the two parties inhabited entirely different worlds. As far as the monetarist was concerned, a rising pound was pushing up British prices so workers, including those facing him, needed to accept lower wages in order to compete in a global market.

Jill says she remembers the visit vividly, and describes Minford as "patronising." When she told him she "just couldn't afford to live without a job," he retorted: "Everybody thinks they're on the breadline. I could take you to Central Africa and show you people on the breadline. That's the breadline." The economist told the soon-to-be-redundant machinists that they "should all move abroad if they wanted their old jobs back so badly."

Accounts of this period often caricature workers as overly militant or guilty of making unreasonable demands, but the women sitting opposite Minford that day appear more like collateral damage. Breadwinners coming to terms with a loss of security and the realisation that they no longer have control over their own livelihoods.

Taking on a group of employees whose friends had just been laid off, only too aware that they were facing the same fate, Minford's pep-talk didn't go quite as well as he was probably expecting it to. The 'Leicester Lip' and her pals stood up

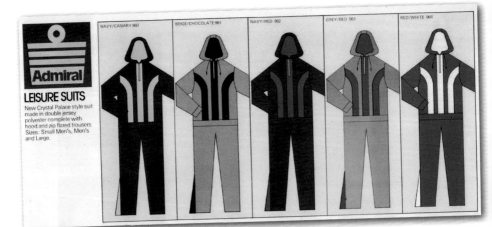

and challenged the policies that were adversely affecting their futures.

"You told him the truth and he didn't like it," Mandy reminds her friend, who's still visibly riled after all this time, and understandably so.

"Sometimes it feels not that long ago," laments Jill, looking down at the exchange between herself and Minford. On screen, she reminds him: "You're telling us to work for lower wages, and you've turned up in that flash car."

The intervening years have done little to diminish Jill's ire. "He talked down to us," and "we weren't going to let him talk to us like that. I don't let my own husband talk to me like that."

After filming, the women told me they received an "appearance fee" from the documentary's producers, that they split between themselves in the toilets. Each walked away with £5, which they intended to spend that lunchtime at the nearby Nautical William pub. Despite being told not to talk to any of the waiting press outside, Jill agreed to another interview with a US reporter, and pocketed another £20 that was also shared among her friends.

Watching the programme 40 years on, Jill's words sound chillingly prophetic in light of recent revelations. Particularly when she tells Minford, "The way you're saying things, it's like going back to workhouse days, in't it? You're going to open a workhouse and work for peanuts again, aren't you?"

Fast-forward to 2020, and a manufacturing scandal in Leicester revealed that some sectors of its garments industry were no better than 'sweatshops', one inspector describing working conditions in a local factory as worse than anything he had seen in the developing world.

Once the dust had settled in Wigston, shock was replaced by anger, followed by an inevitable inquest and finger pointing. Why had Admiral gone bust? Perhaps it had become a victim of its own success, and was swallowed up by the industry it helped create. Or had it fallen prey to the Darwinian rules of the market in an unforgiving environment? 'Foreign competition' is another stock answer, always easy to blame. But none of these theories satisfactorily answers the question. A lack of private investment also played a part, as did a myopic government. High interest rates and a strong pound abroad, as well as the general economic malaise, were other reasons put forward.

"It's been said that Admiral failed because of foreign competition," says John Griffin. "No, it didn't, because the replica business at that time, it was quick response, a lot of it, which you couldn't buy in China or anywhere else. So, as regards the football replica business, it was good. It was good for at least another five years before there could be any dramatic changes."

The spotlight also fell on the capabilities and decision making of the company's board. "The working capital was never there," says John, when pressed about why it all came tumbling down. "We were borrowing too much money. I'd known it for about three or four years. The accountant actually knew." He adds that the banks had put the company owners "on notice" two years before, but nothing changed. "We didn't do anything to help ourselves in the way of financial stability."

It's a mistake Bert acknowledged himself: "It all happened in a few years, really. And I don't suppose we had the financial resources to fuel the growth, give it the rocket fuel it needed."

To some looking in from the outside, it appeared obvious where the problems lay. "In my opinion, Admiral went bust because they stretched themselves over too wide a market and didn't, to use a phrase, stick to their knitting." Designer Paul Oakley touches on a company dilemma. Wanting to become less reliant on a single product, and so expanding the business into other areas. But this saw the company moving ever further from its core business, and what it did best. Another mistake, according to Paul, was to chase after lower-division teams on good cup runs, fearing that a potentially successful club would sign with a rival manufacturer. "I think that they hoped it would go on forever. Whether they actually believed it was another matter. I'm sure on a good day they probably thought that they were infallible, and that this was the start of something big, and there was no reason why they just shouldn't continue."

Perhaps Bert's biggest failing was not calling in the family cavalry until it was too late. Possibly pride got in the way of asking for help earlier, or maybe he genuinely believed he could turn the company's fortunes around again.

Either way, once "Bert had woken up, he was on a hiding to nothing," believes his nephew. Simon Flude had a ringside seat during Admiral's final few rounds in the ring, and as one of those that rode to its rescue, is ideally placed to appraise the firm's financial health at this time. His analysis chimes with John Griffin's earlier evisceration, Simon explaining that, "a private company with limited funds was never going to survive in the international market the business became."

Even the best privately run business would struggle in that climate, let alone one as inefficient as Admiral. The company's only possible chance was to raise significant funds by 'going public' and offering shares; but that option was never on the cards.

"The mentality of family business owners in those days was quite naïve as a whole, really," Simon proposes, "and this outside outsourcing of management and the importing of high-intellect, high-experience management isn't something that we used to do. We used to employ family and experienced in-house operators who would get promoted through the system."

The policy had paid off handsomely with John Griffin's appointment 20-odd years earlier, but by the beginning of the '80s the firm was operating in a very different landscape. Put simply, Admiral hadn't kept up with the global sportswear market it now found itself operating in. And it didn't have anyone at the helm with the relevant experience or nous to navigate a way through it.

These failings were thrown into sharp relief towards the end, believes Shaun, by which time the firm was sourcing some of its clothing lines from suppliers in Asia, for a fraction of the cost of making them in Wigston. It was obvious to all what needed to happen, he says; but his father chose not to relocate abroad.

Yes, it was a decision that ultimately shortened the firm's lifespan. However, as Simon notes: "When the textiles industry moved wholesale offshore, it was the weakest companies that failed first. But they all failed."

"A seduction, a naïve seduction," says Peter Hockenhull with a rueful smile. His decision to buy into the "rag trade" was seemingly as much of a surprise to the entrepreneur as it was to everyone else. The sharp-suited 70-something started working in the petrol industry in the early 1960s for Shell-Mex and BP, before he "built up an operation turning over £5 million a year" from garage forecourts. Given Peter's background, his move into sportswear does appear puzzling, and he nods sagely as he recalls how he got into the world of replica football shirts.

"I was playing squash with this gentleman who owned Admiral Sportswear," which, along with buying his house, is how Peter met Bert. "I liked him very much. He was a very, very sociable, nice fellow. And then, all of a sudden, I heard that the company was actually in a bit of trouble. Bert said to me, why don't I consider acquiring the brand in the UK?" Within a few months, Peter told me, "All of a sudden, I'm in showbusiness. And I don't say that lightly because the perception of Admiral was huge."

After acquiring Admiral's UK rights, the Mancunian retained some sales and warehouse staff, but now all manufacturing would be outsourced to other British-based firms. Bert also stayed in place for the first few months to ease the transition and to show Peter the ropes. "Bert was helping me set the company up. To get continuity, to introduce me to various chairmen of clubs, he was indispensable for the early days. I mean, he was 'Mr Admiral.'"

The new incumbent told the trade press he intended to return the brand to its former status: "Yesterday, Admiral was a force to be reckoned with. My prime objective is to get it to be a force to be reckoned with in the future."

But first he needed new premises to work from. "We rented a property the other side of Leicester. It was an empty warehouse. No heating, nothing. All we had was a desk and a phone. It was evident very quickly that we needed proper offices."

The petrol merchant was able to cut a deal with Richard Turton, and relocated back to Wigston. "I bought all the existing stock, and I bought the Admiral office from the receiver. But in actual fact it wasn't quite buying something, because the UK rights were owned by a company called Frisol."

In effect, Peter had bought a licence from Admiral International Marketing that allowed him to sell the Admiral brand in Britain. "So it wasn't just negotiating with the FA. I had to negotiate with Nico de Vries in Holland." Fortunately for Peter, the two men hit it off, and he says he would come to regard the Dutchman as a 'father'-type figure over the coming months, though initially he had to fight incredibly hard for a worthwhile deal.

"In negotiating with him, we retained the 99-year franchise for the UK. It wasn't an easy thing whereby he could say, 'Oh, there you are, you're a lucky fellow'. He wanted his per cent, his franchise fee."

The Manchester United fan was used to moving in football circles, but he admits his purchase of Admiral thrust him into a world he knew very little about, and one he was completely unprepared for. Even so, Peter knew instinctively that it was imperative to keep hold of any existing contracts. "So what it meant was, if I was going to do this, I was going to be very reliant on the retention of these particular clubs – first and foremost, England."

The task would involve Peter subjecting himself to an FA inquisition. "You've got 20 minutes to sell yourself." Ted Croker's opening words to Peter were hardly welcoming, let along encouraging. The FA secretary had deigned to grant him an audience in a Heathrow Airport lounge before flying off to a UEFA meeting.

Still then in his 30s, Peter says he was desperate to make an impression, and only too aware of his own inexperience. "Since the demise of Admiral, there'd been no real communication" with Lancaster Gate, he admits. So no wonder he felt under an enormous amount of pressure. "I'd met an awful lot of very senior people; but not like this. So I was in a bit of awe. But I knew that I had to do this within the 20 minutes, I had to convince him. If you were to ask me, 'What did I do to convince him?' I couldn't do that now. I can't say 'cos, to be absolutely honest, I can't even remember."

Whatever ambitions Peter managed to impart within his time limit, they ultimately did the trick. "I introduced myself, and remember Admiral was in receivership, which no major operation like England wants to be associated with. So there was a big selling job to convince him that we were the right people to retain the England contract, because that was the flagship."

In a further round of lengthier meetings and "extremely tough" telephone conversations, he did enough to convince the International Committee to give him a chance. "I was honest about my background. I was honest about my plans, what I wanted to do with Admiral. They saw a young fellow who was English, and he was trying to do something, and there was sympathy there."

Still, Peter's UK franchise wasn't yet out of the woods, even if 1980 was very much 'new' Admiral's Year Zero as far as he was concerned. "The next big issue was to go around to all of the clubs, to try to retain them."

By now, Crystal Palace, Manchester United, Orient, Southampton, Spurs and West Ham had all defected to other kit manufacturers. "They saw the demise of Admiral and they just wanted to get out the door head first." All of which added even more pressure to keep hold of the remaining teams. "And one must remember that knocking on the door was Umbro and Adidas, Le Coq Sportif and Patrick, so we were vulnerable at all of these clubs."

"One of the hardest experiences I had was going to Leeds," the Lancastrian admits. "There was an awful lot of questions... Manny Cousins, the board was there, and they were all good Yorkshiremen, and Leeds of course was the original Admiral team, so it was very important." Fortunately for Peter, he was introduced to Elland Road's hierarchy by the man who'd brokered the first Leeds deal seven years earlier. "It was a huge selling to do. But there was loyalty to the brand, there was loyalty because Bert was with me. There was loyalty to Bert."

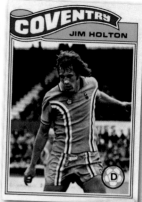

Besides Leeds United, fellow First Division outfits Coventry City and Norwich City also stuck with Peter. Lower down the league, Bradford City, Carlisle United, Grimsby Town, Hereford United, Scarborough and a handful of Scottish clubs also retained Admiral's services.

"So it's a new world, and it was an exciting world" at the beginning. But "I suppose to some extent I was carried along with this. It was very, very hard work. In that particular year, I did 40,000 miles."

Despite the previous year's fall from grace, the nautical trademark still enjoyed a high profile. And "who wouldn't want to be involved in Admiral Sportswear, and be involved directly with kitting out the England football team?" Like her boss, Debbie Jackson (nee Whitmore) also found herself thrown into the deep end, and embarking on what would prove to be a steep learning curve for both.

Twenty-one-year-old Debbie was just starting out in a career in textiles when she joined the reincarnated company as a junior designer. The Leicester Polytechnic student had completed a postgraduate degree in sportswear design and was desperate to impress. "There was massive optimism about Admiral, and again about how Admiral might diversify into other markets, and that was why I was really keen to get on board."

According to Peter, "New Admiral" needed to "broaden its base," and become less reliant on making football kits alone, in what was now a much busier market. The firm drew on its heritage, and started kitting out some of Britain's leading professional tennis players, including Anne Hobbs. "It was very, very evident to me at that particular time that we could never survive on replica strips alone. And therefore we had to diversify, we had to diversify into sports-leisure. And I would like to say that we were more ahead of the Adidas and the Umbro and Le Coq [Sportif] and all of them, in the diversification into sports-leisure. But they had huge financial backing."

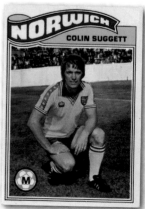

The company's change of direction was clearly signposted

JOHAN CRUYFF

JOCK'S CRUYFF SWOOP

JOHAN CRUYFF is today set for a sensational move to First Division strugglers Leicester City..

The Dutch Master has lined up a deal worth £4,000 a game for 11 matches—and if everything works out, he will make his debut against reigning European champions Nottingham Forest on Saturday.

Last night jubilant Leicester boss Jock Wallace insisted: "Johan and I have already agreed terms. He has one or two problems to sort out but I am very hopeful he will join us on Thursday."

WALLACE . . . I have my man

JOHAN CRUYFF . . . could pick up £4,000 a game

in its advertising, in which its clothing was declared 'great to wear, anywhere', with jogging suits and sweatshirts enjoying equal billing alongside club replicas. Sportswear was morphing into leisurewear, and there was clearly an opportunity to create a hybrid collection of tracksuits. This was, after all, the era of headbands, leggings and step aerobics, recalls Debbie. "We're going back now to the early 1980s, and the dance craze. We all remember Olivia Newton-John with her dance videos." Underpinning Debbie's designs was a range of new stretch fibres being developed in the city, because "Leicester was a real centre of fabric construction and new technology" – including a new kind of wonder spandex called Lycra.

Timing and zeitgeist with any new venture is often everything. "This was the beginning of the London Marathon, so tracksuits and that kind of clothing had become suddenly big business, running gear and so on, the whole thing was kind of starting off." Admiral's '26.2' collection of tracksuits was aimed at a growing market that was attracting lots of publicity.

Under Bert's regime, it wasn't uncommon to spot celebrities in the company's foyer. By now, the visits had largely dropped off, though the Wigston offices did host one of world football's greatest stars in the early months of 1981. Not that anybody noticed at the time, as Johan Cruyff slipped into the premises under cover of darkness for a rendezvous with Leicester City boss Jock Wallace.

All parties were keen to keep their clandestine meeting a secret during efforts to sign the Dutchman, who also happened to be one of Nico de Vries's business partners – hence the choice of Long Street being used for negotiations.

Wallace believed he'd got a deal over the line, and I remember my own YK, if not JFK moment, was seeing a newsstand headline outside Leicester Town Hall, announcing the player's imminent arrival. But sadly the 'Flying Dutchman', or whatever else the *Mercury*'s byline writers would have dubbed him, never made his bow in City's colours.

When Cruyff returned to Spain and joined Levante, some observers concluded that the ageing talisman probably didn't have the appetite for a relegation struggle. Yet, according to Admiral insiders, Cruyff really had wanted to come to Leicester City. Almost incredibly, it was only Britain's strict quarantine rules that ultimately scuppered the deal, as the ex-Ajax and Barcelona superstar couldn't bear the thought of being parted from his beloved pet pooch.

At least, in this rare coming together of football legends, Johan Cruyff had got to see the inside of the iconic Admiral HQ. Even if it was in the dead of night.

The turbulence of the past year had inevitably seen the brand slide further down the kit sponsors' pecking order, but Peter was rightly pleased with his initial efforts to "steady the ship." Particularly as he'd managed to keep hold of the prestigious and lucrative England contract.

"An unbelievable pride as to what I achieved in a period of time, that my team was running out in my strip. For England to be running out in my strip, my shorts, my socks, out there – England? It was the most humbling experience I could ever, ever have."

Peter's pride was shared by Debbie, who described the FA contract not only as the "jewel" in the company's crown, but the main reason the firm was still afloat. "There was massive kudos in having the England contract, being able to make the kit, and of course the huge potential from the replica kit in terms of income from replica sales, where the margins were incredibly good." It was also clear early on that Peter's discussions with Lancaster Gate didn't always run smoothly. "It was a huge challenge for him, and it was a very exciting time. But looking back, perhaps he underestimated the Football Association was quite a political place to be involved in. And I also remember with the licensing fee, the amount the FA took from the turnover was quite considerable, so it was always a struggle to be looking to make a reasonable profit from the replica kit business."

Once the initial euphoria had died down, England seemed to be making very heavy weather of qualification for the '82 World Cup finals in Spain, and reality was once again biting. Not only was Peter getting to grips with an unfamiliar industry, he was effectively a hostage to the whims of the FA, such was his dependency on a very demanding customer.

The situation was making her boss increasingly tense, recalls Debbie. "I think he's a very business-savvy gentlemen. He certainly knew what he wanted. But sometimes things would get heated because of the political tightrope that Admiral needed to go along with the Football Association, what they wanted. I remember certain situations where, 'Debbie, can you get a train this afternoon from Leicester and can you go over to the Football Association and talk to them about something or other?' And there I was, sort of 23, 24, probably without the business experience to take on something like the Football Association, which of course was a very male-dominated environment. I can remember wanting to make sure I said the right thing, and not to upset the FA."

One of Lancaster Gate's biggest gripes was a concern over quality control in the production of England's replica jerseys. Correctly lining up the shirt's V-neck collar with the horizontal stripes across its chest was tricky, and it wasn't uncommon for faulty tops to slip through the net. There was also a problem in matching up the shade of red on these panels to the colour of the material used for the second strip. Other knitwear issues included some of the children's jumpers being prone to shrinkage.

"We had to make sure all the kits, the fabrics were hard-wearing," says Debbie, "so they would go through the twin tub 65 times, or whatever it is, so that little Johnny could wear his kit day in, day out." At the time, she was bearing the brunt of production headaches that, unbeknown to Debbie and everybody else in Wigston, were about to get a whole lot worse.

Peter appeared to be experiencing his own existential crisis, retaining deep misgivings about the business he'd entered into. "No real experience. I've not been to university or whatever, or college with regard to textiles or design or anything else – and so I then eventually started to get worried that people agreed with me because I owned the company, and I was forceful."

Lucky young Matt Lightfoot proudly models his new England jumper.

Despite Peter's efforts, the company was still struggling financially, and was described as 'a risky venture' by the BBC's *Money Programme*, reporting on his takeover and a potential windfall that could alleviate some of the firm's problems: 'In the backstreets of Wigston, Leicester, the management team of Admiral, the sportswear people, plan how to cash in on an England World Cup trip...'

The report went on to outline how much money the company could rake in from replicas and merchandising sales over the coming months. There was just one problem: England hadn't yet qualified for the forthcoming tournament.

Worse, it now appeared highly unlikely that Ron Greenwood's team would do so either, following defeats to Romania, Switzerland and Norway. But then a minor miracle occurred a week before their final group game, which saw Our Boys handed an unexpected lifeline. Romania dropped points against the Swiss, meaning England's fate was back in the team's own hands. Or maybe that should be feet? Either way, a single point against group leaders Hungary at Wembley would be enough to sneak through.

It wasn't just England's prospects that had been looking rocky, given how dependent Admiral was on its FA contract. But the firm's existence, and the livelihoods of its workers, was still in the balance – and now very much dependent on a single football match. "This was a situation where a lot of people's jobs were at stake," says Debbie gravely. "Everything was riding on the result of this one game. There was a huge amount at stake." She reflexively bites her lip when I ask her what the atmosphere was like in Wigston during the build-up to the Hungary match. "Everything was very tense. We knew that our futures depended on this game, in order to go forward for the World Cup. And Admiral's future, really."

On the eve of the game, local television crews descended on Wigston, reporting that the right result was worth an estimated £4 million in orders. ATV's Malcolm Munro optimistically declared that "the recession will fade into oblivion if England qualify." More soberly, he told viewers, "For the staff here, it's not just another game of football, it's hard cash and jobs at stake."

Despite this being an incredibly stressful time, Peter and his team appeared reassuringly calm on camera; but Munro was back into overdrive, announcing, "The sales team are just waiting for the result, and the massive sales plan goes into action. Tens of thousands of authentic England strips will be sent to the shops." All this by way of introducing sales director Gil Hyatt.

"If we win tonight, this will double our sales," Gil joined in excitedly, "and we have the plans all ready. We start straight away. The salesmen start to write orders, and the girls in the office will be starting to write orders for our customers who phone in – because everyone will be wanting England merchandising."

Perhaps unsurprisingly, Hyatt played down the prospect of redundancies should the result go against England, and Admiral. He told Munro that jobs didn't "actually rest on the game, because naturally we have alternative plans, but an awful lot of extra business will be created."

The reality, of course, was somewhat different, as summed up perfectly by Munro as he signed off on his report: "If England go through, Admiral are gambling that every youngster will want to be a World Cup player and be dressed accordingly; but it all hangs in a painful balance."

On a chilly November evening, England emerged from the Wembley tunnel in front of a raucous, packed crowd, with one gathering of spectators from the East Midlands feeling more apprehensive than most. "If you can watch a match with your eyes closed, then I'll be watching the match," Gil announced beforehand.

Peter was also in the stands, watching 'his team' warm up in their pale blue and black Admiral track tops, and admitting to feeling "very nervous" himself.

"We had to win it to go," he confirms, of the crucial evening that would decide whether or not his business had a financial future. "We were paying £200,000 a year. A lot of money to us as a company."

Whether Admiral would recoup any their investment in the England setup was now dependent on its squad and manager. "I always remember saying to myself, "I want to pick the team. It was just so frightening that your success or failure depended on the World Cup. It depended on those eleven players out there."

Even Leicester old boy Peter Shilton was aware of what was at stake when he lined up pitchside for the national anthems. "It wasn't only just very tense for me then, it was obviously very tense for Admiral at the time. That's quite unique in itself, isn't it, when you're sponsoring a national team and your business is [resting] on the result of getting to the World Cup?"

"When you're in a business situation, it takes an awful lot of the fun out of it," Peter Hockenhull told ATV. "There will be 95,000 [sic] people at Wembley enjoying the game an awful lot more than I will be doing."

Not that anybody was having a particularly good time, given the magnitude of the occasion and what was at stake. England had failed to qualify for the last two World Cup finals, and BBC commentator John Motson talked about "no half measures" before kick-off. He reminded viewers that everybody watching, either at home or in the stadium, would be perched on the edge of their seats. Under the Wembley floodlights, Motson implored his audience to "hold tight everybody, because here we go," as the match finally got underway.

Some columnists and doomsayers had been quick to point out that England had been here before, 12 years earlier, when a draw against Poland stopped Alf Ramsey's team from reaching the finals in West Germany. Nobody was praying harder than Peter Hockenhull for the football gods to be kinder this time around.

After a quarter of hour, Paul Mariner put the hosts ahead when Trevor Brooking's wayward shot struck the striker and cannoned off his shins into the Magyars' net. It was a goal he appeared to know precious little about, but that didn't matter. England were ahead. Despite the slender lead, the atmosphere remained taut. When Mariner, Terry McDermott and Kevin Keegan all spurned good chances to double England's lead, it simply cranked up the tension further. Up in the stands, Peter watched on helplessly. He told me how he was "kicking every ball, winning every header and tackle" throughout the entire game.

Shilton was another anxious bystander, as more opportunities went begging at the opposite end of the pitch. "I think the pressure got to us. What made it worse was that we didn't really play," adds the record England caps holder. "If we could've got the second goal, it could've been a real relaxing evening. But when you're 1-0, although they didn't come near our goal, you think in the last two minutes anything could happen. A corner, a free kick. So consequently, until that final whistle it was very nerve-racking."

With seconds left to play, Motson reassured nervous viewers, "We're nearly there," going on to describe the relief at the end as Wembley's greatest opportunity to celebrate since the 1966 World Cup triumph. It certainly was in Wigston.

"I always remember it was rather funny that we were pouring the champagne, it wasn't making a noise and Gil Hyatt was actually doing [a glugging sound] to give the effect because of the radio." Peter Hockenhull's post-match BBC interview, and accompanying improvised sound effects, were followed by an appearance on breakfast television the next day.

Still high on a heady mix of relief and euphoria, he says, "We got shunted all over London, being interviewed all over the place." I asked him what would have happened if England had failed to qualify. "You have to budget for those kinds of things," but "it would have been painful." Reflecting further, he tells me, "It was extremely evident that we had to diversify, because of things like that. I think it's like any business, if you have all your eggs in one basket, and all our eggs were in replica shirts, it's a formula for suicide."

CHAPTER 10
This Time
(We'll Get It Right)

M69 Motorway, April 1982

Leicestershire bookmakers were offering odds on a potentially remarkable county treble: Rutland horse Grittar to win the Grand National, Leicester Tigers to beat Moseley in the semis of the John Player Cup, and Leicester City to get through their own last-four FA Cup tie against Tottenham Hotspur.

Rather than talking about the improbable accumulator, or even City's chances of causing an upset at Villa Park, the chat inside our car is subdued on the short drive to Birmingham. Along with my dad and a mate, we're absorbing the news that Britain is seemingly on the verge of war. A continuous stream of radio reports is confirming news of an Argentine military invasion of the Falkland Islands. Instead of talking about this afternoon's line-up, my friend, who's just turned 17, is wondering aloud whether he's about to be called up.

Guided by a distant set of 'A' and 'V' floodlight pylons, we find a piece of wasteground being used for match-day parking about a mile from the ground. It's the same venue where City made their last semi-final appearance, on a night when Admiral trailblazer Peter Shilton was dressed head to toe in an all-white strip. The luminescent keeper was beaten by Kevin Keegan from outside the box that evening, so it's not the best of omens.

By the time we take up our standing positions, halfway up the massive Holte End terrace, Grittar has already romped home in first place. We'd heard Tigers were trailing, but there was still time for the favourites to mount a comeback. But City faced a much tougher challenge against the FA Cup holders, and sadly Jock Wallace's side didn't really turn up. On a deflating afternoon, Ian Wilson managed to emulate Keegan, in that he also lobbed the ball over a City keeper at the same end; but his long-range own-goal only sealed Spurs' 2-0 victory.

An even quieter journey home was spent listening to updated news reports, which this time also included condemnation of Leicester's travelling support, after some fans booed Tottenham's Argentine playmaker Ossie Ardiles' every touch. Just a few short weeks later, some of the country's tabloids would be peddling jingoistic rhetoric and celebrating the loss of Argentine lives on a daily basis.

The England squad's World Cup double A-side single, 'This Time (We'll Get It Right)' and 'England, We'll Fly The Flag', was released as scheduled by K-Tel later that month. It peaked at number two in the charts, hanging around the Top 10 for three weeks, during which time the players' *Top of the Pops* appearance managed to somehow eclipse their own video cameos for toe-curling awkwardness. The squad proceeded to mime their way through 'England, We'll Fly The Flag', a retooled British Airways jingle, while

swaying from side to side accompanied by cabin-crew members waving plastic flags. It looked like a cross between the Last Night of the Proms and a terrible business conference held in a community centre with no drinks licence.

The entire group was dressed in sets of red, white and royal blue sweaters, featuring an Admiral logo on one side of the chest, and a Spain '82 'Bulldog Bobby' mascot on the other. Ah, Bulldog Bobby. Where to even begin with FA's official tournament emblem? World Cup qualification was a golden opportunity for Admiral to recoup a chunk of its FA sponsorship fee, and it wasn't unreasonable to expect to shift lots of branded merchandising. The run-up was described by *The Guardian* as an 'employment boom' for workers in Wigston and at the other 14 factories that supplied the firm with England kits and T-shirts, as well as sweatshirts, pyjamas, tracksuits, socks, vests, underpants, hats and jeans.

Worryingly though, even before the Falklands crisis or talk of England pulling out of the tournament began, the firm had struggled to move much of its stock. Garments that had been rushed through production at the end of 1981 in time for Christmas remained unsold, and by the following spring an expected cash bonanza appeared to have stalled before it even began. Chief among the unwanted gifts were those bearing an image of a bulldog dressed in an England shirt. Not great news for Admiral, who had bought exclusive rights to market merchandising and souvenirs promoting the patriotic canine.

"We came out with a motif, which was Bulldog Bobby, I remember," says Peter Hockenhull. "The press went into it, saying, 'Oh, it's aggressive,' and so on; but the British bulldog is the symbol," he adds by way of explanation. Presumably the FA's anti-hero was meant to represent the 'Churchillian Spirit of the Blitz', but it was a puzzling choice given England's unenviable reputation for hooliganism. It was also hard to escape the fact that the barrel-chested mutt, dressed head to toe in England colours, looked suspiciously like some of the country's more volatile supporters who were regularly filmed running amok across Europe, throwing bottles and plastic chairs, wherever the national team pitched up. The FA was desperate to shake off such negative associations, which only made the adoption of Bulldog Bobby even more inexplicable.

Bert Patrick, who was still working for the reincarnated company as consultant, always maintained that "there's no such thing as bad publicity". But on this occasion even Bert had his reservations before the press launch at the Grosvenor Hotel.

Even so, both old and new Admiral bosses managed a smile when photographed together with Bobby Charlton, alongside a five-foot-tall cardboard cut-out of the former international's mascot namesake. Bert announced he was hoping to raise £750,000 from commercial spin-offs, but it turned out to be Admiral and not the public that bought the pup, sales falling far short of projected targets.

To paraphrase a well-worn saying, 'no matter how bad things seem', they can always get worse. With four weeks to go until the start of the World Cup, the ongoing Falklands war had cast serious doubt on England, Scotland and Northern Ireland's participation in the tournament. Kevin Keegan is reported to have said, "I would be disappointed if we didn't go but I would support the decision." Perhaps unsurprisingly, sales of World Cup merchandising ground to a virtual halt.

Reporting from Wigston, *Central News* announced that the "Falklands crisis has led to a loss of orders worth hundreds of thousands of pounds." They included a segment in which reporter Bharat Patel sparred verbally with Gil Hyatt in Admiral's foyer, the pair bickering about whether it was the conflict in the South Atlantic or Bulldog Bobby most to blame for the lack of interest in Admiral's wares.

Another Central report, from VVR Clothing in Witney, informed viewers of the firm's decision to ditch Bulldog Bobby altogether, and its return to making jeans without any World Cup-themed patches. A company spokesperson told reporter Geoff Meade, he "had very high hopes at the beginning, initial reaction from the trade was quite positive. We had hoped that things might pick up as the run-in gathers momentum, as the squad's selected, etc. But I think the Falklands is probably the final nail in the coffin."

Disappointing sales were perhaps to be expected in a recessionary market, with retailers becoming more cautious and risk averse – particularly for products with a short lifecycle, which in England's case could be less than a fortnight. But the 'Battle for the Falklands' and the FA's pet dog certainly didn't help matters.

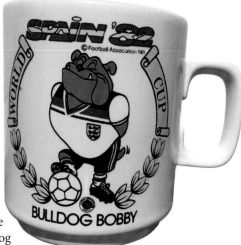

As a footnote to the mascot saga, there was also a promotional single released, called 'We Love Bulldog Bobby'. The accompanying video, filmed inside a factory, featured a troupe of girls singing in unison with a real-life, barking bulldog. And all the while, rows of machinists continued making World Cup vests – even when a line of dancers came oompah-pah-pahing over their shoulders – as if it were the most natural thing in the world.

With fewer club contracts to rely on, the Wigston operation was now almost entirely dependent on its tie-in with Lancaster Gate, says Debbie. "It was synonymous with the Football Association, it was synonymous with England, the England team, so that was a huge connection for Admiral and one which carried the brand, really."

To help maximise the label's exposure, Peter made sure he was on hand whenever possible to ensure the players always appeared in Admiral apparel. He tells me there's nothing quite so disheartening for a sponsor as seeing the individuals you're backing wearing your rivals' clothes. That said, pinning all of your business hopes on a team that had struggled to finish second in its qualifying group wasn't ideal, either. But that was the uneasy position Peter and his staff now found themselves in.

"At the time, I did get the feeling that things weren't right at Admiral for a number of reasons," Debbie says. "The ability to sell enough kit, particularly to the independent sports stores. Whether Admiral was actually able to pay their bills to the FA, because the amount of money they wanted for the agreement was crippling Admiral, really. It was a whole lot of things coming together."

Another major issue facing the company was getting sufficient stock to retailers. Most of the outlets Admiral was selling to were small independent sports shops spread across the UK. Most preferred to order small quantities, selling what they had before reordering. This required the company to maintain a large national sales team, Debbie recalls. "They all drove Cortinas, I remember, a 1.6 Cortina, and they were expensive to keep on the road. And that kind of impacted on the profit. Some of it was about not being able to sell enough kit in the quantities that Admiral required."

By today's marketing standards, the brand's response to slow sales seems quaint, even amateurish: 'In the run-up to the tournament Admiral ran a competition for the best-dressed window in the British Isles. Winners included Davies of Coventry, Harry Parkes of Birmingham and Howard Giles of South Wales.'

Adding further to Admiral's woes, the move into adult replicas had seen an increasing number of cheap fakes and knock-offs seeping into the market. "It wasn't something perhaps that Admiral had thought about to any great degree," Debbie now admits, "about how they would protect the brand."

Defending his company's interests proved a costly experience, says Peter. He told one anecdote about visiting his QC's London chambers, and being charged £500 an hour for the privilege. To add insult to injury, his learned friend was also taking lengthy phone calls to deal with other cases, whilst on Peter's meter. Despite winning several legal actions against various offenders, including Coffer

Sports, Peter says he was still lumbered with a huge legal bill at the end of the process.

Admiral could ill afford to haemorrhage yet more money, which resulted in cost-cutting measures being introduced "out in the field," most noticeably to the publicity budget. "We'd photographed the bulldog mascot for the World Cup, done all that," Neville Chadwick told me, and it appeared to be business as usual in the run-up to Spain. "I'd spent probably three or four months preparing to go to the World Cup, because it was always difficult to get tickets for every match and accommodation. I'd got it all sorted out, everything ready to go." But a fortnight before the tournament's opening match, Nev was told his services were no longer required. "Which was a complete and utter shock to me. So, that was the end of me working for Admiral; but I still went on to the World Cup, and I did freelancing for the national newspapers while I was out there."

Despite the disappointments, company employees were still putting on a brave face with every new setback. Hoping that a run by England to the final would turn the company's fortunes around. Since qualification, Ron Greenwood's side had conceded just one goal and were unbeaten in their warm-up games, lifting the mood in Wigston considerably.

"There was a huge optimism that England could do very well," Debbie told me. Perhaps thinking anything otherwise was just too awful to contemplate. Much of the anticipation was tinged with nervousness, if not trepidation. "It was frantic, everything was geared up for the '82 World Cup, and we all worked very hard. It was a little bit chaotic but it was all about logistics, really. Getting the right kit at the right place at the right time, making sure everything was geared up with fabrics and trims, making sure everything was gonna go smoothly. Which it didn't."

There were misgivings among some young supporters heading out to Spain as well. Not that they let it show. My mates and I listened, mesmerised by older brothers' stories of previous trips abroad, and the possible scrapes they'd get into over in Bilbao. What they lacked in finances, they certainly more than made up for in bravado, as they shared plans to camp in city-centre parks and 'doss down'

COURAGE and England – together a great team.

John Smith's and England – together a great team.

in railway stations to save as much money as possible for beer.

At 16, myself and my mates considered ourselves too young to go. Too skint, in any case. Not to mention daunted by the prospect of a potentially dangerous trip. The Falklands conflict had escalated tensions to a point where confrontations between groups of fans and a paramilitary police force seemed inevitable. Nevertheless, the mood among friends staying behind was positively upbeat about England's tournament prospects. One or two were now regularly parading around town in the white Admiral tops they'd bought with their first pay packets – with shirts costing £9.15 for a 38/40-inch size chest, at a time when most of my mates were taking home around £50 a week.

I must confess, when I'd first glimpsed the new strips two years earlier, I wasn't convinced. But seeing the jersey close up in an adult's size, I appreciated just how stunningly bold and stylish a design it was, exactly like the jerseys the players wore. And soon we'd find out just how similar.

The tournament's opening game saw holders Argentina, including 21-year-old Diego Maradona, take on Euros finalists Belgium at Barcelona's Camp Nou. It was also Adidas subsidiary Le Coq Sportif vs Admiral in the kit stakes. Having signed up with Nico de Vries's parent company, the Belgians turned up in the most Admiral-centric strip imaginable. An all-red 'tramlines' outfit with yellow and white piping – only this time with more Admiral. Much more Admiral. The stripes running down the length of the kit were decorated with scores of tiny nautical badges, and there were larger logos around the sock tops for good measure. It was as if somebody had been given a professional challenge: how many manufacturer's badges can you fit on to a football strip?

As a result, Guy Thys's team ran out looking like the Pearly Kings of the Lowlands; but it was a style that obviously suited Belgium as they also ran out 1-0 winners. One of the tournament's most iconic photographs was taken during this match by Steve Powell, showing Argentina's mercurial number ten with the ball at his feet, looking for a way past a line of six Belgium defenders.

Sadly for Peter and for Admiral, any benefits from the opening day's exposure was lost in the UK after ITV decided to pull the game due to sensitivities around the Falklands war, despite the imminent surrender of Argentine forces.

The FA party settled into its base in the Basque country, and the players made an attempt to ingratiate themselves with their hosts by cheerily donning berets during a photocall. Not that there weren't grumblings about other costumes.

Having previously been sidelined by manager Don Revie in favour of Ray Clemence, and forced to suffer a job-share under England's current manager, Greenwood finally settled on Shilton alone as his first-choice keeper. Yet despite getting the nod, Shilton's mood soured once the team strips were unveiled. "The worst thing for me was that someone came up with the great idea of putting the numbers in alphabetical order, so I wait to become number one for England for quite a few years, and I get number 22. So, it didn't look quite right on the jersey, but it was an Admiral jersey and I remember that very well." Unfortunately, not entirely for the happiest reasons.

It's not clear whether Belgium's logo-festooned outfit influenced what happened next, or if an official or political clampdown took place. But three days later when England faced France in their opening Group Four game in Bilbao, their teamwear appeared without Admiral badges. Peter Hockenhull told me he'd received a call the night before the game from FA secretary Ted Croker, informing him that FIFA was insisting all manufacturers' logos be removed to comply with global TV rights.

But clearly French officials hadn't received the same memo, as captain Michel Platini led his team out the next day in an Adidas strip with its trefoil logos and distinctive three stripes all very much intact. It seems no explanation was ever forthcoming, but the episode had shades of the previous year's European Cup final when UEFA informed both Liverpool and Real Madrid of the need to remove manufacturers' logos from their playing kits before the match. On that occasion, Umbro's exposure in the form of a single diamond on each Reds shirt was literally taped over. Los Blancos' shirt had never carried an Adidas logo; but the three stripes on their shirts, shorts and socks ensured the brand maintained its own powerful presence.

Just as strangely, both England and France would ordinarily have expected to play in their favoured home colours, white and blue respectively, as in their

Logo overload: guess which manufacturer designed Belgium's kit for Spain 82...

previous meetings. Instead, both teams now switched to their second-choice colours of red for England and white for France. It has been suggested the change was triggered by the partial colour clash due to the broad blue band running across the shoulders of England's white jersey. Fortunately, there was a set of unbranded red jerseys among the outfits sent over to Spain, which 'les Rosbifs' would wear in Bilbao against 'les Bleus' – or 'les Blancs', as was now the case.

Whether FIFA's last-minute instructions in Bilbao were born of a genuine desire to avoid a colour clash or as the result of mind games, we may never know. But Mick Mills duly led his England side out into a swelteringly hot Estadio San Mamés, in a set of ill-starred, unbranded red jerseys, just as the late-afternoon temperatures hit 90 degrees Fahrenheit.

It's at this point that Admiral's credibility as much as its teamwear starts to unravel. "The away kit wasn't as good a quality as the home kit," says Debbie, pulling what can only be described as an 'oh dear' expression. It seems no one had considered the possibility of England having to wear a change of colours during the tournament. The inferior-quality red shirts were thought of as "a 'just-in-case' sort of kit," she adds in mitigation.

At the time of 'Kit-gate', Greg Cross was running Quartet Fashion in Leicester, a small manufacturing firm that acted as one of Admiral's suppliers. Recalling the incident, he confirms what people at Admiral and the FA were thinking – or not, as it turned out. "It made sense that they'd got to have something lighter. But nobody had said to us prior, 'We ought to have something a bit lighter because it's going to be hot.' So we just made the same stuff, like your typical polyester shirts."

Peter Hockenhull still insists the away jerseys were made by Robert H. Lowe in Cheshire, though their sorry unsuitability remains unquestioned. And neither firm was exactly tripping over themselves to take credit after the fallout from England's opening game.

"It was probably the hottest I've ever been in a stadium," Peter Shilton recalls earning his 38th cap. "There was not a breath of wind. It was like a bowl. There wasn't a cloud in the sky, and it was roasting." The keeper says the heat didn't even let up in the evening. "It was so hot, it was difficult to concentrate. And obviously we'd only been over there for a week or so before."

And it wasn't only the players struggling with the temperature. "There wasn't any numbers on the shorts the night before the game," Shilton harks back to the nocturnal rush to iron them in place. "And after about ten minutes of the match, because of the heat, the numbers just kept falling off the shorts. Everybody thought it was confetti or paper on the pitch, but it was actually the players' numbers dropping off. I mean, not very professional for a World Cup game; but it's the sort of thing that comic books are made out of really, isn't it?"

England's kit problems didn't stop there. Admiral's red back-up jerseys also proved unfit for purpose, making the players sweat even more, the moisture clinging to the shirts and refusing to dry. According to post-match reports, the players lost a combined six stone in weight, Paul Mariner alone shedding eleven pounds.

Explaining what had gone so terribly wrong, Debbie told me that both of the lightweight fabrics used to make England's home jerseys, Aertex and Dunova, were "only available in white. It wasn't actually manufactured in any other colour, which of course was a huge issue for the new shirts."

Fortunately, the England team performed much better than its kit, and ran out 3-1 winners. Not that the result softened the FA's reaction.

"The first phone call, it was panic. What were we going to do?" says Debbie of her instructions from Bilbao.

"It was an impossible task," is how Peter describes Admiral's sudden predicament as the FA demanded the manufacturing and delivery of new sets of lightweight jerseys before England's next game in three days' time.

Thirty-odd years later, simply listening to Debbie recount her story is stressful, as she confirms "it was rather a mad weekend" for her 22-year-old self. Her first task was to get hold of a batch of Dunova, a breathable material only available in white, from a firm called Robert H. Lowe based in the East Cheshire town of Congleton. Not that it was as straightforward as dropping off a few rolls of fabric, Debbie reminds me. "What we needed to do was to batch dye some white fabric, and there were huge issues around that in terms of making sure it was the right colour, making sure that it could be dyed properly, making sure of course then the stripes could be printed over the red fabric. And we only had, literally, 24 hours. Two days to get the fabric right, so we could make up these shirts."

Making up two new sets of lightweight jerseys – one in red and the other in white – was the easy part, according to the beleaguered design manager. "It was enormous pressure to get everything together, and think – could we actually get the kit out there? But there wasn't a 'Plan B', we just had to get the kit out there as quickly as possible and by any means. And it was quite a scary, scary time." Fortunately, Admiral only needed to produce a relatively small number of shirts, so "we could practically hand cut and make them up. And the excellent machinists put the shirts together. We had to make sure that the quality was there, that the V-neck was quite central to the stripes going across. We wanted to make them as high quality as possible, but of course it was a massive rush."

Then there was the issue of how to get the shirts out to the players for their next match, the following day. "Yes, it was interesting times," says Debbie with great understatement. Having completed stage one of Mission Impossible, she outlined the next phase of the task ahead of her.

"Because I was so young at the time, I perhaps didn't realise the responsibility that had been heaped on me, really. I just knew I had to get from Leicester to Manchester Airport." Fortunately, Debbie had a company car, albeit one that burnt oil. And, having only just passed her test, she admits she wasn't the most confident of drivers. "It was a white Polo T reg, and it was rather unreliable; but anyway, never mind, it was decided by Peter Hockenhull that I would take the shirts in the back of the Polo in a cardboard box, and I would drive all the way to Manchester Airport from Leicester across the Pennines. I'd never actually driven that far before. In those days, of course, no SatNav, no mobile phones. I had a map book and a piece of paper directing me as to where I needed to go." What could possibly go wrong?

The 100-plus-mile journey took the novice driver along Snake Pass, a road still considered to be one of the country's worst accident blackspots. "It was desolate, really. So that was quite a scary journey. And I think I might have gotten a little bit lost." Debbie admits to a few nerves before setting off on her own, "but at the same time it was a bit of an adventure as well, and I suppose at that age you don't really think about what could go wrong. You just think you have to do it. And I know I had in the front seat my needle and cotton."

TWENTY FOUR HOURS LATER
ON THE A57 SNAKE PASS...

Ah yes, the sewing kit. Successfully negotiating her way to Manchester Airport didn't signal the end of Debbie's pentathlon. Next, she needed to locate the Excelsior Hotel where a room had been booked for her to finish off the tops. "When the shirts were made up, there wasn't time to sew on the badges, which would have been the Admiral logo and the all-important England badge. And so I had a stock of England badges that were carefully counted out for me, and Admiral badges. The idea was, I would sit in this hotel room until I'd sewed all these badges on by hand, and that's exactly what I did." But the clock was ticking... "And I was being hurried up by two gentlemen who were going to take the cardboard box and put it on the plane to get the shirts over to Spain."

When I congratulate Debbie on a job well done, she looks somewhat sheepish. "It was the last flight out of Manchester Airport, and they just had to go on," she tells me, palms upturned. "Unfortunately, in my hurry to get the job completed, I wasn't quite able to get the badges in quite the right places every time."

Ultimately, Debbie's precious cargo safely arrived in Bilbao, and England turned out in their breathable new white jerseys for the following day's match against Czechoslovakia. "I was horrified really, because I looked at all the players lined up and I thought, 'Nope, that one's too near to the left; that one's too near to the right; that one's too low; that one's too high.' But the badges were on the shirts, so that was actually the main task; but it was such a rush job."

It was only when Bryan Robson and the rest of the team lined up for the national anthems, before a global TV audience of millions, that it became apparent just how rushed Debbie's needlework had been. Several badges appear uneven or crooked and one even disappears underneath Paul Mariner's armpit.

"But I managed to get it done," exclaims Debbie cringing slightly at the memory. "I do remember actually watching the line-up the following day and scolding myself because one of the badges was slightly lower, slightly that way, that way, because as time was running out it was becoming more and more of a panic

LATE AFTERNOON IN A HOTEL BY MANCHESTER AIRPORT...

to sew all these badges on. I think now maybe I did get a little bit lost, because clearly I ran out of time."

Delving into her bag, she fishes out a small cloth badge, which she proudly holds aloft for inspection. "I did manage to keep an Admiral logo and I've kept it all this time, so that goes back to 1982, and I've kept it as a little memento of my time at Admiral." Breaking into laughter, Debbie tells me she's still not sure whose England shirt was missing a badge for the Czech game.

Peter Hockenhull says he too carried out the same mission, and remembers flying out to northern Spain himself with a bag of new lightweight jerseys made from triacetate fabric. He recalls how he had driven to Heathrow Airport, and was then met at the other end by Terry Butcher. "I was on the coach with them, and travelling from hotel to hotel with guards and guns. I was allowed to stay with the England team and play tennis with Kevin Keegan."

Personally, I believe both trips took place, and that over time the chronology of who travelled out to Spain first has become clouded. But it probably explains why two different versions of England's red away jerseys ended up on the pitch at the same time – including an 'imperfect' set of shirts that had turned up without a single white band across the top of the chests.

In turning around the new, breathable kits so quickly, Peter and his team had pulled off a Herculean feat; but it still wasn't impressive enough to save them from criticism. *Central News* reporter Bharat Patel, not unreasonably, asked whether it wasn't all a bit too late, and wanted to know why a set of lightweight away shirts hadn't been supplied in the first place?

Displaying the dexterity of a seasoned politician, the sportswear boss neatly sidestepped the question. "Well, I think it's a very good point. But the kit that's been provided to England, which they've played all of the world in, has been adequate. But because of the conditions and the humidity in that particular stadium, nobody expected 95 degrees as happened on that particular Monday [*sic*] when the players lost, as you know, up to eleven pounds per man. It is very possible they could have carried on with the kit they've got, but our job is to come up with the best fabric for the best team in the world."

By the tournament's second week, Ron Greenwood's side had safely negotiated its way to the next phase and a round-robin mini-group of games against West Germany and hosts Spain. "Not that they played any better in the Aertex stuff," offers Greg dryly, "because we didn't get far, did we, in that World Cup?"

Late into the evening inside the Bernabeu Stadium, England and West Germany emerged before 75,000 fans. And, just as in Paris seven years earlier, this wasn't just England vs West Germany. It was also a battle between Admiral and Adidas. But this time around, rather than the beginning of a rivalry, it felt very much like the end of one. Once again, Peter was watching on nervously from the stands, while his workforce back in Wigston considered their futures as much as the result, knowing that an appearance in the semi-finals, let alone the final, would give sales an enormous boost – along with their job prospects.

Sadly for England and for Admiral, the game ended in a cagey 0-0 draw. But Greenwood's men still knew that a win by two clear goals in their next match against Spain would guarantee them a spot in the last four. A glorious opportunity, given their disinterested hosts were in effect already knocked out after losing to the West Germans. But despite the carrot of a World Cup semi-final, it wasn't to be, and England lacked the creative spark to break down their Iberian opponents

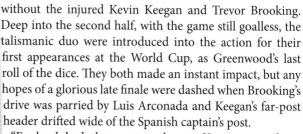

TREVOR BROOKING
ENGLAND

KEVIN KEEGAN
ENGLAND

ERIC GERETS
BELGIQUE-BELGIË

without the injured Kevin Keegan and Trevor Brooking. Deep into the second half, with the game still goalless, the talismanic duo were introduced into the action for their first appearances at the World Cup, as Greenwood's last roll of the dice. They both made an instant impact, but any hopes of a glorious late finale were dashed when Brooking's drive was parried by Luis Arconada and Keegan's far-post header drifted wide of the Spanish captain's post.

"England had these great players. Keegan was there, Brooking was there. They were undefeated," remembers John Devlin. "The nation held its breath, Admiral held its breath. How was this gonna end? And that was it, England were out."

For Brooking and Keegan, as well as for Greenwood, it proved their England swansong. "It was devastating, really," says Shilton. "We just struggled a bit up front to put the ball in a net, and then we drew the second game against Spain, and we came home from the tournament unbeaten. Let one goal in, but we were out on goal difference."

Sadly, it was West Germany and not England who progressed to the semi-finals, and so to an eventual final against Italy. Summing up what we had just witnessed, Devlin says, "England were out. Not only was it the country, the football team's hopes dashed, it was Admiral's hopes dashed, too. That was the end of the journey."

"The last hurrah?" says Debbie, when I ask her about the fallout in Wigston following England's elimination. "I do remember, post World Cup, there were a lot of negotiations between Peter Hockenhull and the FA, and he was locked in lots of meetings, and of course there was word around the office that things weren't looking too good."

Without any extra funding, it would have been impossible for the company to continue in its current guise, says Peter, aware that some people's perception of his British operation was very different to the truth. "What was becoming more and more evident was that you needed millions behind you to take Admiral to where it needed to go. Because it was all about money, [and] I'm not used to just throwing money about."

It wasn't just Peter weighing up all options, and an air of uncertainly hung over the company for months, according to those still working for the firm. "We didn't know, we just sort of carried on as normal, really," says Debbie. "But then there was this realisation that the England contract may be pulled from Admiral. That was a shock for all of us, that Umbro was very much in the running to grab the contract from us. So where is Admiral going to go then? Not a good sign, and yes, our jobs were all at stake."

Perhaps unsurprisingly, Debbie says she began to think about her own future before the inevitable happened. "I got a sense that things weren't right. Peter was quite tense and some of the sales team were made redundant, and at that time I'd got sufficient experience myself to feel that I could actually move on myself with my career and look elsewhere for a new job."

Bobby Robson was also about to take up a new position following Ron Greenwood's planned departure from the FA. The former Ipswich boss swiftly began the overhaul of an ageing England squad, which led to some nervousness in Wigston, where it was wondered whether the 'progressive' head coach would want to modernise the way his team looked in other ways.

There was no immediate cause for panic, but now there was an almost universal sense that the writing was on the wall for the future of the FA's England contract, and indeed for Admiral itself.

By this time, young supporters who'd grown up with the nautical logo during the previous decade were actively looking to change the way they dressed. As Peris Hatton says, "I think it's hard for any manufacturer to maintain popularity and to keep reinventing themselves, and shocking people. I think every company, every brand has got its lifespan."

The firm was still producing replica shirts in adult sizes, but by now many of its first generation of customers were more interested in sportswear labels from Italy and France. "Football at the time had a pretty torrid reputation, hooliganism had almost taken over the game and, yes, the game was darker," Peris reflects. "And maybe with the rivalries between the sets of supporters, maybe being seen in the shirts wasn't the right thing. There were other designer brands that came in, and maybe it was cooler to wear those. And the big, fancy collars; the bright, colourful designs, maybe they'd had their day. And maybe it was time for something different."

CHAPTER 11
I Know It's Over

The 1982 World Cup finals in Spain proved to be Admiral's last shot at the big time. The *Carry On* nature of all the kit capers was as good an indicator as any that perhaps its time was up on the global stage. There was also the issue of finance, or rather the lack of it. Peter Hockenhull still enjoyed the support of the brand's parent company in the Netherlands, but even with owner Nico de Vries's backing, Admiral's UK operation still lacked the financial muscle to compete against the likes of Adidas and Umbro. Despite this drawback, the two entrepreneurs still envisaged a future in which their trademark could prosper, if not dominate, in the sportswear market.

Sadly, it was a business plan that never came to fruition. Just days after Peter had been invited to join de Vries on a skiing holiday in Switzerland, the 48-year-old Dutchman died suddenly of a pulmonary embolism. "So, the dreams that we had for growth, and where Admiral should go, went unfortunately with his death." De Vries's premature passing also marked the beginning of the end of Peter's own involvement with the brand. "It was extremely evident that we could never take it where it needed to go."

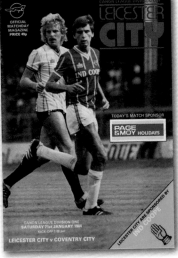

For now, the Leicester outfit was still clinging on to the FA contract, but it was clear to all concerned that its partnership with Lancaster Gate was drawing to a close. Apart from England, all the other star names had long gone. The firm still made kits for local First Division sides Leicester City and Notts County, but most other sponsorship deals were with lower-tier clubs – an unsustainable business model according to Greg Cross, who was still one of Admiral's suppliers. "Having the bigger clubs, you're going to get your revenue back, because there's going to be the shirts being sold. But when you start pouring money out on small clubs, you're never going to get your money back. Hopeless. And it's a shame, because what they had going for a while was excellent."

It wasn't just the profile of its teams that felt a little underwhelming by the early 1980s. The brand's styling also lacked some of its old lustre. "It had lost its appeal," says Rob O'Donnell. "I think I still appreciated it myself because I'm from Leicester, that was what I was brought up on, so I didn't bin it and go over to the other manufacturers." Despite Rob's loyalty, he admits he'd resigned himself to Admiral's fate. "I'd have liked to have seen it as big as it was in its day, but the other manufacturers had taken over. They'd got their bigger market shares, their advertising campaigns were fantastic, and you could see that people were preferring the new Umbro or the new Adidas. I just thought it was quite sad that it had declined in the way it had."

The company also had to deal with another well-documented kit drama around this time, on this occasion not of its own making. The template used for Leicester City's blue and white home strip was without doubt one of Admiral's better creations from that period. A double pinstripe design that's still a firm favourite, if the number of retro reissues worn on matchdays is any indicator. Ironically, the away version is also popular nowadays, which was far from the case 40 years ago, particularly among the club's own players. City's 'unlucky' green and gold kit, reflecting the corporate colours of its shirt sponsors, Ind Coope, was unveiled at the start of the new season in 1983, and then hastily abandoned just over a year later. At the time, Gary Lineker was chief among the players rejecting the

Penalty miss and away strip leave City with red faces

GREEN FOR STOP!

Green definitely does not mean "go" for City. They have yet to be successful in the green and gold colours of their sponsors and the players never want to play in it again.

Its last airing before this absurd reverse was in the FA Cup at Millwall where, again, a 2-0 scoreline went against City.

All superstition is, of course, illogical but it is no less effective for that. City's collective heart sinks when they see the dreaded colours laid out in the dressing room on their arrival — with a full hour to gnaw away at the psyche.

Even I have fallen into step with the general feeling as, on my way to the match, I remarked that if City ran out in green then they had no chance of winning.

Striker Alan Smith, who played quite well at the Hawthorns, admitted: "We are trying to get rid of it. We had already said after Millwall that we didn't want to use it again.

"It might sound daft but you are bound to get superstitions after such a long run without winning in all green but, with Albion in blue and white, there was no alternative."

brewery's cursed livery. A poor run of away results saw City lose 13 League and FA Cup games in their emerald attire. The only win came in a League Cup second-leg game at Chelsea, and even then City lost the tie on penalties.

"Well, it weren't that they were unlucky, it was just that they were crap at the time," chuckles Greg. And, as someone who witnessed many of those abject capitulations first hand, I can confirm City were continually battling against relegation. Not for the first time, Greg received a panicky phone call asking for help to fix an Admiral teamwear crisis. "We needed to do something fairly sharpish, because they'd got a game at the weekend, and we've got these kits. Invariably, we've got shirts all round the factory in boxes, that'd been made for X, Y and Z; but these were like a plain red shirt so it was perfect, really, just to bang a badge on it, and go, 'There you go, just the jobbie.'"

The batch of red jerseys Greg unearthed were unadorned England away shirts of the type used between 1974 and 1979. Sets of plain white shorts and blue socks were also dug out of storage, and that's what City would now wear on their travels whenever there was a colour clash. The result of their next away match in the appropriated England shirts? A 3-0 loss at Goodison Park to champions Everton. "The next week we were inundated with green and gold kit from shop owners saying, 'If they aren't playing in it, you can keep it,'" adds Greg. Not that the change saw a massive upturn in City's fortunes, as the club eventually dropped into the Second Division not long afterwards.

It wasn't only the country's top teams that had turned their backs on Admiral. Many of the young fans who'd once worn their flamboyant strips were now older and less interested in wearing club colours. A generation of terrace fashionistas instead favoured expensive sportswear made by the likes of Ellesse, Fila and Lacoste. The look was adopted by public figures, including some indie bands. A teenage Roddy Frame and Aztec Camera performed live on Channel 4's *The Switch*, dressed head to toe in Sergio Tacchini. It's no surprise that the latest youth tribe to emerge from the street consisted of kids who'd grown up wearing branded replica jerseys, evolving into wearers of designer tracksuits. In many ways, football's 'casual' culture could be seen as an embodiment of Margaret

Thatcher's Britain. Young, smartly dressed, working-class men, many of whom were goal driven, well organised and seemingly upwardly mobile, were pulling themselves up not so much by their bootstraps as by their expensive Diadora trainer laces. As with the original 1960s mods before them, dressing expensively in defiance of socio-economic expectations was a way of standing apart from the proletariat, and became intrinsic to the casual dress code.

To most outsiders, such groups of young men appeared to have just emerged *en masse* from a golf-course pro's shop. But Dr John Cooper Clarke, himself a natty dresser, proffered his own unique take on the subculture, riffing about a once-popular brand of slacks in his poem, 'Smooth Operetta'. Along the way he squeezed in mentions for 'Pringle', as well as 'Airforce blue' and 'Farahs', and dear reader, I must confess that I once owned just such a pair of those slate-coloured trousers.

Writing for *The Face* magazine in 1983, Kevin Sampson noted, "The metamorphosis was very swift and very widespread." He described "everyone at the match" with "bowl-type mushroom wedge" haircuts, adding that "the clothing was much more sports-image conscious, rather than club orientated."

The first time I saw a small group of youths sashaying through town in brightly coloured Fila Setanta tops, I knew immediately how I wanted to dress from now on. Soon my own wardrobe consisted of all of the aforementioned labels, though fortunately I drew the line at wearing the fleetingly popular deerstalker hat.

"I think when casual culture came in, in the mid '80s, the replica market I feel did die a little a bit," John Devlin told me. "I remember going on a school trip once, for a week, and taking along my Umbro Liverpool and Umbro Scotland shirts, and they remained in the drawer the whole time. I didn't feel right wearing them, so something had changed then amongst teenagers in terms of how they supported their teams."

In 1984 Peter told *Central News* his Admiral franchise was in financial difficulties, and explained how the accumulative effect of counterfeiting had taken its toll. He revealed that his company had "lost hundreds of thousands of pounds worth of business" as a consequence.

"The business became unsustainable," confirms Debbie. The company simply couldn't generate enough orders to cover its losses as well as its England

sponsorship payments. A new contract was being renegotiated with the FA but, "it just blew Admiral out of the water." Instead, Lancaster Gate awarded the business to Umbro and agreed a five-year deal worth a reported £1 million per annum – a sum far beyond Wigston's means, acknowledges Debbie. "It was quite clear that the amount the FA were expecting from a relatively small company was really too much for Admiral. I think Peter had decided that he'd given it his best shot, and that it was time for him to move on to pastures new, which he did."

The distraction of running a sportswear brand had taken Peter away from his core business, and the following year it was announced that Admiral Sportswear UK had been placed into receivership. "I needed to go back to my garages, because five years was more than enough," he told me. The Mancunian now freely admits he had been too autocratic, and says he should have joined forces with someone else to help run things, or else taken on a partner. "Did I want to sell 50 per cent of the shares there, or 50 per cent of the shares there? No, I didn't. But should I have done? Yes, I should've done, because they had the nous. They had what I didn't have, their experience and their knowledge and their professionalism in certain aspects. So, do I have regrets? Yes, major regret there. Maybe it was egotistical. I didn't need them... but I did."

With brutal candour, Peter told me had been too naïve, entering into a business he had no prior experience of. "I apologise for saying this to the industry; but I've found it's full of liars, cheats and thieves. I'm not talking about everybody in the industry, I'm talking about some of the experiences I had, which I found dismaying and, yes, I battled against it. An awful lot of retailers wouldn't pay until they [got] more product. You know, they dragged it out. So that affected your cash flow greatly."

Put simply, Peter was the wrong person to head up Admiral's UK operation, at the wrong time. "I suppose I felt I had the Midas touch, because I was very successful in the petrol industry at that particular time. And I think everybody can have their head turned." Such was the pulling power of the Admiral name. The prospect of taking over the reins was clearly too exciting to walk away from. It was a "world of showbiz," as Peter puts it. "I've no regrets with regard to the experience, no regrets with regard to the people I met. It was a great ride. A great seduction. But a naïve seduction."

Peter wasn't alone in walking away from football in 1985. 'A slum sport played in slum stadiums increasingly watched by slum people,' is how the *Sunday Times* described the less than beautiful game. Mass pitch invasions and running battles at Luton was followed by disasters at Bradford, where 56 spectators died in a fire, and rioting at Heysel that led to the loss of a further 39 lives when a wall collapsed. An horrific end to the season included harrowing images of those being crushed to death beamed live around a world in shock. English football and its supporters became European pariahs, while domestic attendances dwindled yet further. Only hardcore fans remained, but by now all groups of young working-class men were viewed suspiciously as 'the enemy within', whether attending football matches or an industrial picket line. The political landscape had been shifted by the hand of government as it waged war against trades unions and privatised state-owned industries, signalling a change in the country that would last forever.

I wasn't exempt from the disenchantment, and the despondency in and around Filbert Street was palpable. City's struggles were often played out in front of sparse crowds, in which the players' echoed shouts rattled around dilapidated stadiums, while supporters looked cautiously over their shoulders.

"Replica shirts weren't worn as much, and there was a different kind of football fan about," observes John Devlin. It's true. Such were the times we were living through, scarves and club colours were to be avoided or worn judiciously, particularly to away games or matches where violence was expected. "Obviously, in the UK and England especially, it wasn't a particularly good time for football. There was the hooligan element, and I think the replica shirt market just quietened down," laments John.

Not that the replica business ground to a halt entirely. There were still people willing to invest their money, particularly in a household brand name like Admiral. The sales and marketing rights covering the UK were picked up by Rodney Germinder and his family from Watford, who had other clothing and footwear interests. Greg Cross continued to supply garments to the latest rights holders but his connection to the sportswear brand was dwindling. "One or two people had a little attempt to resurrect the name of Admiral because it had built up a substantial name, but it never really amounted to much. And certainly, by that time, my business was down the tubes."

Greg's own company became another casualty in a local textile industry that had been decimated. By the time he eventually called it a day, he says Admiral's standing and the quality of its strips had declined markedly. By the end, he was still making kits for Bradford City, Cardiff City and Hull City, as well as for scores of amateur clubs, but any whiff of glamour had evaporated long ago. "Admiral were being put forward as the poor man's business side of it. Your Adidases and people like that were the top end, and Admiral were considered the cheap and nasty end." Production costs were squeezed further still, and the quality of the work was compromised. Describing a business that was literally coming apart at the seams, Greg told me players would "be running around and the badge'd be half hanging off because it hadn't stuck on properly, or it'd come off altogether."

There was also a more delicate kit malfunction at a game I attended in 1987. When I ask Greg about this potential urban myth, he picks up the story from when he was tasked with carrying out a personal fitting for Leicester City's new giant Finnish striker, Jari Rantanen: "He's got a great big arse," Greg reminds me, stretching out his arms. "The guy's enormous. So we got some stuff made up."

I have a vague recollection of 'The Mighty Finn' scoring against Plymouth Argyle under the Filbert Street lights – a game Greg remembers for other reasons.

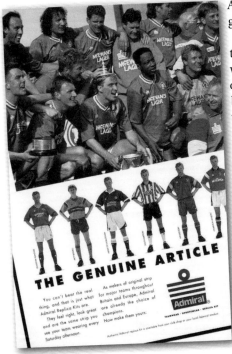

The following morning, he was summoned to the office of manager Bryan Hamilton, who told him, "'We had to play the whole of the second half with Rantanen, with his bollocks hanging out of his shorts. He'd split them underneath the gusset.'" Appropriately enough, the incident occurred after the hefty striker stretched into a sliding tackle, in full view of the East Stand. The Finn was apparently, "one of them that wore nothing underneath his bloody shorts, so when they split, his meat and two veg were there for everyone to see, hanging out. Yeah, that was a memorable night.."

Admiral's worldwide marketing rights continued to be held by Frisol Oil up until the end of the decade, when the baton was passed to Warwick Sport & Leisure. A return to the Midlands, though by now

the brand's umbilical cord to Wigston had long been severed. The new owners signed up the country's two leading rugby union sides, Bath and Leicester Tigers, seeking to move into other markets as well as to grow the football business again post Italia '90. The company sponsored Glasgow Rangers for a couple of years in a deal described by the firm's marketing assistant Daniel Gidney as one of the biggest replica club kit contracts in world football at that time.

But it was the label's return to prodigal sons Leeds United that felt most apt – especially for a campaign they entered into as reigning First Division champions. Admiral became both the club's kit supplier and shirt sponsor, lining up alongside the similarly nautical-clad Middlesbrough and Wimbledon, at the start of the inaugural Premier League season in 1992.

However, this time around there would be no rekindling of the alchemy or success enjoyed by Bert Patrick and John Griffin 20 years earlier. The brand's owners were unable to capitalise on football's renaissance, or the arrival of big money at the beginning of the Sky era, struggling instead to maintain a presence in 170 countries, and ultimately to compete against Adidas and Nike's duopoly. Warwick eventually called it day towards the end of the '90s, and the trademark was acquired

Derby County's 1984 Centenary kit was a late Admiral gem.

by International Brand Licensing, a business demerged from clothing retailer Hay & Robertson. This fresh undertaking to turn Admiral's fortunes around also foundered, and the nautical insignia all but slipped out of the footballing public's consciousness.

Admiral did still have its moments though, including bizarrely sponsoring 'Madchester' band Happy Mondays, and its logo also popped up on the teamwear in the 2001 feature film *Mike Bassett: England Manager*, in which Ricky Tomlinson's eponymous character oversees a series of hapless events, reminiscent of the brand's own 'real-life' World Cup kit crisis. But Admiral's finest latter-day moment in the sun was surely its appearance on England's cricket whites during the wonderful Ashes defeat of Australia in 2005.

By the following decade, Genesis Sports secured Admiral's marketing rights for Europe, Middle East and Africa. The Manchester-based company now supplied branded teamwear to several professional teams, mostly in the Americas but also closer to home, including the strips of AFC Wimbledon, Shrewsbury Town and Queen's Park in recent years.

The firm also reissued a range of replica jerseys for English and NASL teams from Admiral's 1970s heyday, alongside a heritage-inspired line of casualwear called Admiral Gold, sold in Sainsbury's supermarkets.

"People have this love for old shirts," acknowledges John Devlin. "There's always been a huge interest in retro shirts, and Admiral have embraced that and really produced some wonderful versions of their old kits. There's definitely a massive fondness for Admiral designs, even now."

When I mention this to former designer Lindsay Jelley, she's incredulous. "You can buy the replica Admiral kits? No. Well, that does amaze me." After a brief pause she announces, "I'll have to go and have a look. Perhaps I could do that thing now where you go, 'Oh, that was mine, that was mine.' How funny."

During my chats with John, he raises a point that resonates immediately. "It's ironic that we're selling to the same people that bought the replica shirts back in the day. People criticise people in their 40s and 50s for wearing football shirts – they say, 'Aren't they too old to be wearing them?' But these people were the original replica shirt wearers in the '70s, and I think that nullifies any criticism. It's just their way of supporting their team. It doesn't matter if you're fat and 50."

"I can still hear the knitting machines and the swishing noises they used to make but, sadly, it's gone now," Debbie Jackson tells me. "What I remember fondly about Admiral was the fact that it was very much about the local community in Wigston. It was very much about Leicester." Standing in front of the derelict factory on Long Street, surveying the yard its 200-odd workers crossed each day to clock in and out, the company's remarkable rise appears even more impressive. The replica kits business has become a global behemoth, and it was all birthed and nurtured within the walls of such a modest site. Of course, Admiral didn't do it all on its own, but this is where it all started: the cradle of replica-isation.

Within the industry, there was a certain sense of inevitability that Wigston's empire would eventually come crashing down following such a meteoric rise. More than one ex-employee likened the firm to *The Mouse that Roared*. Paul Oakley told me, he "did feel that there was a weakening of Admiral's offering over the years, and that the big boys were circling and would take over eventually, and they became 'the brand'. Admiral's legacy is starting the ball rolling in the first place. After Admiral, it gradually developed, so that now you look at any football match and you'll see the spectators divided pretty equally into their team's colours. And Admiral started that. It was definitely for kids when we started, and it gradually started moving up to adults. But the core concept lay with Admiral, yes, of branding items, that's where it all started."

Similarly, John Devlin is in no doubt as to the Wigston firm's importance to the replica kits market today. "Essentially, it's one of the leading income generators for the big clubs around the world. So whenever you see a replica shirt, nine times out of ten you're thinking, 'that's come from an Admiral initiative way back 40 years ago'. The popularity of replica shirts today among supporters isn't waning, it's still there. They're still sold in the hundreds of thousands, and it's because of that Admiral legacy."

Ultimately, neither incarnation of the original company was able to fully capitalise on its success or its groundbreaking ideas. Bert Patrick and Peter Hockenhull were both acutely aware of leisurewear's potential but neither owner was able to grow with it.

"If they'd managed to hang on to their contracts, then they could have been massive. Certainly, challenging Adidas in that market," believes Paul.

Bert admits, "It would've taken much more money than I could've possibly,

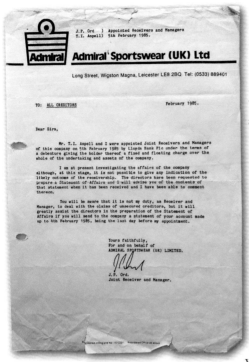

sensibly, arranged to have invested in the company or borrowed from the bank." But "who knows?" he adds. With the right partner, Admiral could still have been a "major player" and ended up as big as Nike are today.

It wasn't just Bert and Peter's loss, of course – an entire workforce and community suffered as a result of Admiral's demise. The collapse of manufacturing has had a corrosive impact on towns and cities throughout the country, as thousands of jobs have been laid to waste. "It does seem a shame," notes Lindsay Jelley. "Those women were incredibly skilled, the speed at which they worked and the dexterity of just handling the fabric. And all the different machines – your overlockers, your machinists, your trimmers. Every one is a different skill. It's a big loss."

A company that was often described to me as a 'gem' failed for a myriad of reasons, with a lack of working capital and financial clout high up on most observers' lists. But there's also a real sense of a government abandoning a viable business and effectively handing over the replicas industry on a plate to Adidas and Nike. Even the profitable Umbro was eventually swallowed up by Oregon's billion-dollar business machine. Conversely, the first Fred Perry polos, which were made in Leicester in the early 1950s, continue to be manufactured in the city today, though I accept that it's not a straight, like-for-like comparison – rather an example of a 'heritage' brand still flourishing in the UK. Sadly, that's a description that can no longer be applied to the naval insignia that was once instantly recognisable to football fans everywhere.

"The absolute magic of that company cannot be overstated," Simon Flude told me, recounting an anecdote that goes a long way toward summing up Admiral. "I'll never forget sitting in reception, waiting for Bert to finish a meeting. I was sat opposite this wizened old man, huddled in the corner, keeping himself very much to himself, and I wondered who the hell he was. And Bert came bounding out and shook hands with Sir Stanley Matthews! To sit in a textiles manufacturer's office in Wigston and have Stanley Matthews sat opposite you was pretty special."

The prominence of branded leisurewear and the ubiquity of replica jerseys hasn't come as a surprise to Bert. "It moved into the adult market, which inevitably it would do from kids and women, and of course it's moved across to other sports."

His one-time right-hand man, John Griffin, says, "It is remarkable. It's almost a regulation for most of the men to buy a shirt."

The latest club top has almost become a mandatory accessory to watching football, whether at a game, in the pub or at home. Paying out for a newly released replica at the start of each campaign is now as routine as renewing a season ticket – not that wearing it is confined solely to match days. On any high street or holiday beach you'll see men, women and children displaying their football allegiances, in an easily identifiable fashion. Whichever way you measure its success, the replica-kit industry appears to bigger and more popular than ever, and there are no indicators to suggest this will change any time soon.

The last word on the matter must go to Bert. When I asked him about Admiral's legacy, he told me, "We were responsible for starting a multi-billion-pound industry. It wasn't there before, really, but that's what it grew to be. Admiral was the vehicle that moved off into the unknown, and it just developed from there. Because we had the vision, we were a team, and the world was our oyster."

CHAPTER 12
World In Motion

In *Richer Than God*, David Conn has written about the transformation of English football through the prism of supporting Manchester City, going on to describe how clubs have manipulated the sale of nostalgia to supporters: "City's retail minds have refined, over the years, the art of locating the emotional g-spots in supporters always close to bursting with sentiment. When I once found myself upstairs in the shop, lingering too long, and actually welling up, over a limited-edition box set devoted to Colin Bell memory worship, for which the City store wanted £125, I realised they knew exactly which buttons to press."

If club megastores don't sate your appetite for nostalgia, there's an entire cultural industry to fall back on, including an infinite number of articles, podcasts, Twitter accounts and Facebook groups, alongside documentaries and reruns of old TV shows, as well as hundreds of books. Of which this is yet another. There's also any number of niche chat forums and a never-ending warren of YouTube memories into which you can disappear for hours on end. I can't even pick up a set of keys or open the fridge door without seeing one my childhood heroes smiling back at me.

But nowhere is football supporters' demand for the past better served than in the reissuing of club shirts from previous 'golden' eras. Score Draw and Toffs, as well as clubs themselves, have all released retro lines of 'classic' shirts, enabling fans to identify with a favourite starting XI, or a particular period in their club's history. Or so the theory goes. From my own unscientific matchday studies, some 'iconic' shirts aren't necessarily from particularly successful seasons, but are perhaps a reflection of when their wearers first started going to games.

I too jumped on the bandwagon in 2012 when I first began developing an idea to make a short film about Admiral Sport's early days. The project evolved into a documentary I produced and directed for ITV called *Get Shirty: how a small Midlands underwear firm changed football forever.* An unexpected benefit of making the film was the perfect excuse for buying as much vintage memorabilia as my compulsions desired. Shooting involved recreating a 1970s family home, a living room and kitchen being dressed accordingly with period props, while another space was turned into a football-mad youngster's bedroom. Lots of *Shoot!* magazines were bought off eBay, I had a few lucky charity-shop finds, and some of my own 'treasures' were liberated from the loft.

The effect of walking into the finished set was both familiar and unnerving. I was immediately transported back to the bedroom I occupied as a young teen. Staring back at me were the same posters that had adorned my own Anaglypta walls. A pensive Steve Whitworth was still guarding the post at Loftus Road, while a smiling Keith Weller continued to ooze '70s chic. Both, of course, were

wearing the Admiral strips that my mates and I coveted so badly. *Get Shirty* attracted a sizeable audience and received favourable reviews when it first aired in 2016, a couple of days after which I received a phone call from Bert telling me his old factory had been burnt down. Having stood derelict for over 20 years, the Long Street building had been attacked by arsonists, with one tabloid speculating on whether the fire

Ashes to ashes: Admiral's Long Street HQ after the fire.

was linked to the programme that had just aired. Bert joked that it was an act of revenge by Coventry City supporters who had never forgiven Admiral for their chocolate-brown kit.

When I visited the smouldering site the following week, it was still emanating fumes that could be smelt a block away, and the charcoaled husk appeared destined for demolition. Thankfully, the shell of the old factory survived, and by 2020 photographs appeared on social media suggesting that the site was being converted into apartments. No announcement has been made on what the new block will be called but one would hope the developers make a nod to the past. Or at the very least make sure the exterior is decorated in an array of brightly coloured stripes, chevrons and diagonal lines.

Some of Admiral's original shirts from the 1970s and '80s are still available today; not necessarily matchworn kits but replicas that were once owned by young fans. This hasn't gone unnoticed by designer Paul Oakley, who told me, "I did look at one, I think it was from a specialist supplier, and they were asking £300 for a men's 1980 England kit. And it actually said 'slight bobbling' on it, so it had clearly been used, and they wanted £300, which I find incredible."

Other Admiral offerings have since achieved design classic status, and the National Football Museum displayed a small collection of original Admiral shirts in 2015. Four years later, this was followed by a larger exhibition about the history of kits entitled: Strip! How Football Got Shirty.

Vintage apparel remains much sought after by dealers and collectors alike, including Peris Hatton, who turned his hobby into a part-time business after buying up a lockup load of 'dead-stock'. "There's a lot of people in my sort of age group, trying to just get that memory back. Yeah, you can buy modern, remade copies. You pay £40 maybe for one of those down at your local sports shop or online. But for me, okay, it might be a bit too small to wear, but it's the original, and if you can get the original for the same sort of price or a little bit more, if it's in perfect and bagged condition, why not pay a little bit more?" Smiling broadly, Peris proudly holds aloft a much-prized, original 1970s 'tramlines' Wales jersey. "Still in its original packaging, never been out of the bag. We're looking at £125. But they are incredibly rare, to find them bagged in this sort of condition. It's almost a once-in-a-lifetime these days. Very few have survived."

It's easy to understand the appeal, and I only come away from Peris's empty handed because he didn't have an original Leicester City top in his possession.

"That's easy," he answers, when I ask him what's the rarest or most expensive original Admiral shirt he's ever owned. "Without any doubt, it's the [Coventry City] chocolate-brown away shirt. We've seen pictures of players like Ian Wallace wearing them back in the late '70s, and you'll be lucky if you see one of those turning up for sale every two or three years, it's that rare a shirt. As of the summer of 2022, Peris told me the last children's replica "choccy-brown shirt" he saw for sale sold for around £800, while the current market value is around £1000. "They weren't popular at the time, they're not overly loved now; but because everyone wants one, you just can't find them. And that's the Holy Grail."

It's not just middle-aged supporters getting dewy eyed over original replicas. More recent shirts, including many from the '90s, are often worn as style pieces by Millennials. Certain replicas are also now eminently collectable, so garments that were once bought new for £65 and were destined for a charity shop after a couple of years, can now swap hands for hundreds of pounds, often via specialist online dealers selling to customers around the world. Writing in *The Face* magazine, Alex Christian notes, "A bog-standard Sports Direct replica has the potential to capture the imagination of fans. That crumpled England top in the bottom of your wardrobe? Yup, it's probably worth something. Because woven in with the polyester is a priceless thread of nostalgia."

As for the current state of designs and styles, John Devlin is left sartorially unimpressed for the most part, believing much of the fare to be fairly homogenous and anodyne. Outside of the superclubs and their 'exclusive' designs, most other teams are served by similar templates, resulting in lots of identical kits in different colourways across the world's leagues. There were of course template kits in the '70s and '80s but the pace of change today means a never-ending cycle of regurgitation and much, much more of the same. Clubs routinely launch third strips and sometimes also 'special editions' to boost sales even further.

In 2021 Brentford bucked the consumption trend by announcing they were sticking with the same strip for consecutive seasons, citing environmental concerns and the financial impact of Covid-19 on its supporters; but whether this move catches on remains to be seen.

Marmite brown: love it or hate it, Cov's 'chocolate' kit is a classic.

How big is the replica shirt industry today? Europe's elite clubs are each believed to shift around three million official jerseys every season, Manchester United leading the way with an estimated 3.25 million sales. As for the financial worth of the industry, you can take your pick of barometer. Some claim the global sector, dominated by sportswear's world superpowers Adidas and Nike, to be worth around £2.5 billion, while even fairly modest top-flight clubs are believed to pocket over £1 million a year from kit sponsorship.

The first kit contract Bert Patrick and John Griffin brokered with the Old Trafford club was worth £15,000 per annum, the same amount it took to sign up the England team in 1974. At the time of writing, it was reported that the Football Association had signed a contract with Nike up to 2030 that could be worth in excess of £400 million.

"The Admiral model is still around, except on a much, much larger scale," says John Devlin, who describes an industry in which firms are under huge pressure to fund deals with the world's biggest clubs. "They have to sell a lot of shirts, which is why the marketing of replica shirts now is very aggressive. New kits have to come out every year to keep this momentum, to keep the shirt sales up." John highlights how some of today's sportswear brands are bigger than the clubs they supply. "You can look at an Adidas shirt and say, 'That's Adidas,' more than perhaps say, 'That's Chelsea.' Definitely, brand power is very important, and I think sportswear firms are very clear, very cunning, very careful about how they manufacture and promote their brand on the shirts that they supply. Arguably, that comes from Admiral."

It's a point not lost on Peris, who notes, "Today, we've got a world full of these huge companies, soulless companies as I'd almost call them, really. You go back 40 years to this small company in the middle of the country, coming up with these fantastic ideas – could

somebody do like that again today? Probably not. They went out there and ripped up the page and said, 'This is how it's going to be from now.' And it's a fabulous story that will probably not be repeated."

Arguably of greater significance to suppliers and retailers is the continuous fusion of sportswear and fashion. Style bible *GQ* magazine recently labelled Serie A side Venezia FC 'the world's most fashionable football club,' in recognition of their chic replica range that sold internationally. Walk around most towns in the world and you'll see people wearing heavily branded casual clothing. An influence that dates back to the early days of the Wigston's firm's first Leeds United deal, believes John Devlin. "Not only have Admiral revolutionised the replica kit world, you could argue that there's actually been a huge impression on fashion generally."

Couture is no stranger to this heritage. During the summer of 2022 Admiral announced a collaboration with The Jam and released a rather natty limited-edition sky-blue jersey based on Paul Oakley's iconic early '80s England design. It was accompanied by a similarly splendid black and orange effort honouring The Style Council – an inversion of Zambia's strip from the same era. "I love what Admiral have done with these shirts. Very cool," purred the bands' equally stylish former frontman, Paul Weller.

Explaining the joint venture, Admiral's marketing and sales manager Theo Hamburger told me the launch coincides with the 40th anniversary of The Jam's last gig in 1982 – the same year Admiral made its bow at the World Cup finals in Spain.

Meanwhile, on the modern-day football field, Coventry City this year delved back into their own annals and launched a pastiche of the 'tramlines' shirt their team first sported over 40 years earlier. Fortunately, both the Sky Blues and manufacturer Hummel resisted the urge to resurrect the club's much-derided chocolate-brown away colours.

Author

Much to his frustration, Andy Wells hasn't managed to find a photo of himself wearing his first Admiral-made replica football shirt. Typically, the curled image that has surfaced is of him dressed in the detested red tracksuit he first refused to wear. Such compromises over archive use have stood him in good stead for a career as a documentary film maker. Having worked in the independent sector for over 25 years, the producer-director's last few offerings have seen one or two 'passion projects' make it on to the small screen, including ITV's *Get Shirty*.

Andy lives in South-East London with his partner Antonia and their cat Muzzy, but a life on the South coast is beckoning, even though this will make journeys to watch Leicester City even harder. Also found among the family albums was the

yellowing Kodak Instamatic snap above, taken in Skegness in the mid '70s. Over 50 years later, Andy's dress sense and frown are uncannily similar.

Picture Credits

Special thanks to Neville Chadwick Photography for access to their wonderful archive, these selected images serving as a reminder of Neville's great work over the years: cover, 11, 27, 28, 30, 48, 50, 60, 67, 68, 77, 83, 84, 98, 102, 113, 122, 129, 134, 139, 146, 150, 176, 178, 186. Simon Kimber: 6, 94, 107, 174, 205. Barrie Farrell: 17. John Varley, WellOffside.com: 21. Clinton at Chunkywestham ebay shop: 37. Neil Jeffries: 43. Paul Gough: 47, 210. Rob O'Donnell: 58. Gavin Haigh: 61, 211. Nathan Fereday: 75. Rob Stokes: 82, 184. Lindsay Jelley: 86. Malky@thedonspool: Scotland 125. Mike Roberts: 147. Sue Williamson: 152. Bert Patrick: 154. Peris Hatton: 161. Matt Lightfoot: 174. Stuart Page: 181. Dave Morcom Photography: 194. Sean Simpson:

197. Adam Jenkins: Cardiff 199. OldFootball Shirts.com: Pompey 199. Phil Lowe: Derby 201. Dave Price: Leeds x 2, Plymouth, Birmingham, Southampton, Boro 201. Shane Jackson at historicfootballshirts.co.uk: 209. Football Shirt Cottage @FootballShirtCg: 214. Dave Riley: Stoke City 215. Carhandle @carhandle: Fraserburgh Gala, 1978 champions 215.

Grateful thanks to David Sque for allowing the use of his original illustrations from the *Get Shirty* documentary. Also to the following for letting us photograph their vintage shirts and collectables: Peris Hatton, toy-toys @toy_toys_shirts: 4, 60, 62, 80, Wrexham 125, 142, 143, 167. Jonathon Wheatley: 70, 71, 95, 104, 111, 148, 158, 185, 187, 191, 203. Neville Evans, thenationalfoot ballshirtcollection.co.uk 151. Martin Bennett: Courage 183.

212

Acknowledgements

Firstly, I am indebted to my partner Antonia for her support whilst I was writing this book, without which such undertakings are not possible. I'm grateful to my sister Sue for digging out family photos and for filling in some of the blanks in our shared history. Jim Nally's advice and direction gave me both the rationale and confidence to start and then finish this project. Thanks also to the following cheerleaders for their unstinting encouragement; Liz Convey, Jackie Kibble, Freddie Martin, Diana McGreachan, Dave Squires and Aidan Woodward. I will be forever grateful to Frank Kibble for his initial research all those years ago. Thanks also to Ken Edgar, who told me a horse called Get Shirty was running at Haydock the day after I finished the final draft. It romped home at 10/1, and here's hoping that's a portent for its namesake's own success.

I'm grateful to Derek Hammond and Gary Silke from Conker Editions. There really was only one publisher for this story. It was important that whoever took on *Get Shirty* wished to honour Admiral Sportswear's legacy as much as I did, and this book has been produced with the same love and attention with which it was written.

A very special mention must go of course to all of the people who were interviewed for the original documentary. Without your contributions, and willingness to share anecdotes and memories, none of this would have been possible. It was a privilege to listen to your experiences during the highs and lows of such an incredible ride, and I am humbled by the trust you've shown in letting me share your stories. To that end, I wish to thank; Jean Bettoney, Neville Chadwick, Mick Channon, Hilary Cottam, Greg Cross, John Devlin, Nick Frost, Dave Glover, John Griffin, Peris Hatton, Peter Hockenhull, Norman Hunter, Mandy Hutchins, Debbie Jackson, Lindsay Jelley, Jill Langton, Bridget Marlow, Paul Oakley, Rob O'Donnell, Bert Patrick, Peter Shilton, Dave Tazzyman and Fiona Thorsby. I am also grateful to all of the people who replied to my appeal in the *Leicester Mercury* way back in 2013. Every single conversation added another piece to the Cook & Hurst jigsaw.

Since embarking on this book all of the following have been invaluable in offering up their opinions and thoughts, and sharing further insights into Admiral and the wider textiles and sportswear industries; Alan Bennett, Bobby Brown, Kerry Brunton, Jane Cross, Tim Edson, Simon Flude, Tim Gardiner, Daniel Gidney, Theo Hamburger, Jon Holmes, Shaun Patrick and David Rudkin.

I'm also indebted to all those who have helped with my research over the years. Generously sharing snippets of information and archive, as well as many of the photos, and pieces of memorabilia featured in these pages. This includes many of the interviewees already mentioned, and I am also forever grateful to Bernadette Griffin, John Hutchinson, Colin Hyde and Leicester University, Rob Stokes, Jonathon Wheatley and the Wigston Historical Society.

Thanks also to Wim Hogeveen for translating articles in the Dutch press covering Frisol Oil's involvement with Admiral. As well as to David Sque for his wonderful illustrations, and for allowing their use in this publication. I would also like to take this opportunity to praise film editor Pawel Slawek for his remarkable work in helping to create the documentary.

I've undoubtedly missed some people off this list, from a project that's been rumbling on for ten years, and I humbly apologise for my oversights. I hope former employees will share this book with their family and friends and trust you all enjoy this latest addition to the Admiral Sportswear narrative.

Sadly, some of those featured in this account are no longer with us, including Neville Chadwick, John Griffin, Bridget Marlow and Bert Patrick. I dedicate and trust this book is a fitting tribute to you all.

Andy Wells, August 2022

Teamwork

Grateful thanks to everyone who subscribed to 'Get Shirty'.

Gavin Haigh | Alan Thompsett | Paul Price | Keith Welch
Phillip Bell | Barry Dempsey | Rob Stokes | Paul Town
Stephen J Halliwell | Andrew Kehoe | Gary Barnes | Bob Wells
Callum Cherry | Alan Whybrow | Paul Crompton | Ed Wells
Reidar Weltzin | Shaun Patrick | James & Arthur King
Chris Wigginton | Alwyn Lindsey | Paul G Flude | Robbie Flude
Philip Bird | Derek Hirst | John Shaw | Peter Belton
Henryk Cynkar | John Harrison | Simon Sheldon | Peris Hatton
Edward Singleton | Mike & Barnaby Albiston | Mike Roberts
John Pietralski | David Badura | Sean Wenlock | Rob O'Donnell
Alex Ireland | Björn Melin | Mark Pritchard | David Riley
Rod Maher | John Fyfe | Bernie Connor | Alessandro Bacci
Adrian Vanstone | Malc Brown | Rik Anstee | Kevin Worboys
Tony Tomlinson | Howard Tomlinson | Graham Weaver
Andrew Bartlett | Tony Sealey | Russell Osborne | Philip Lowe
Matthew Whiting | Stephen Payne | Sam Hollingsworth
Stephen Hodgson | Will Gamble | James Hanley | David Miles
Rob & Clair Lapper | Richard Sandford | Jennifer Clayton
Chris Marsh | Eddie Garvey
Stephen Quinn | Nick Mernock
Steve Lawrence | Roberto Gotta
Kevin Goodings | Brian Leitch
Phil Darwin | David Hucker
John Walker | Kenny Christie
Jon Hebblethwaite | Peter Lown
Balbi Murrell | Glenn Murrell
Pete Nunwa | Anthony Holder
Ryan & Kiera Nunwa

Gary Smithurst | Dave Squires
Andrew Griffin | Gary Oliver
Jonathan Ridley | Philip Lowe
Menzies Clark | Matt Holden
Dave Gwilliam | Grant Nuttall
Steve Haynes - Lesta Imp
Simon Rowe | Paul Burns
Paul Kittel | Gavin Woodrow
Mark Bradley | Steve White
Roman Rataj | Roy Mason

Prof Lee Bosher | Norman Kincaid | Justin Temple | Ian Ray
Roy & Melanie Sanderson | Kate, Tom, Matthew & Christopher
Diana McGreachan | David Tazzyman | Richard Tazzyman
Frank Kibble | Isabella Kibble | Jackie & Steve Kibble
Paul Stacey | Emily Burditt | Jay Short | Luke Champion
Alfie Jackson | Shaffe Khan | James Nally | Richard Robinson
Aidan Woodward | Mark Barker | Martin Bolton | Neil Kirke
Glen Middleton | Richard Neal | Dave de Man Lapidoth
Gareth Hart | Jimmy Barrie | Phillip Bell | David Holmes
Andrew Collon | Geert Pielage | Chris Harding | Alex Banks
Stewart Henry | Max Henry | Noah Henry | David Langthorne
Martin Langthorne | Ashley Gray | Matthew Harvey | James Scott
Lee Piddington | John Hague | Dave Phillips | Gareth Price
Phil Duffy | Peter Johansson
Tony Dwyer | Martin Skinns
Mark Newman
Wayne Tomlinson
Jonathan Brown
Donna Langton
Luke Langton | Linda Cross
Robert Johnson

Admiral

Bert Patrick

OWNER

John Griffin

Managing Director

Peter Hockenhull

New Owner

The Workers

1972 - 1980

Neville Chadwick

Photographer

Debbie Jackson

Design Manager

Lindsay Jelley

Designer

Paul Oakley

Designer

Peris Hatton

Shirt Collector

John Devlin

Football Writer

Peter Shilton

Goalkeeper

Greg Cross

Manufacturer

Norman Hunter

Defender

Rob O'Donnell

Shirt Collector

Jill Langton

Overlocker

Mick Channon

Striker

Mandy Hutchins

Machinist

Ryan Murrant

Tony@fleet29

laurensteve

Alan Thompsett

Kevin - Boyne Newtonhill Primary School

Roger Watling

Gareth Wilson

Tim Justice

Matthew Jones

Genevieve Justice

Rob O'Donnell